DIRTY WORK

Melia was waiting for me in the lobby of the Stamford Marriott.

"The girl will be back tonight," he said. "Kill her tomorrow after ten in the morning."

"Why do you want her hit?" I asked.

"She's caused trouble, a lot of trouble, and the guy she's going with is messing up," he answered.

He said nothing more but motioned for me to follow him out to the parking lot. We stood by Melia's car waiting for Russo to show up with the $5,000 and the gun.

"You know if you want to come back down here," Melia said, "I got other work for you to do—places to burn. I got lots of work here."

"Well, I'll have to think about that... When do I get the other ten thousand dollars?"

"What other ten thousand dollars?" he said with a look of surprise. "You're supposed to get another five thousand."

"Hell, no," I snapped. "Cosimo said the job was worth fifteen to twenty thousand. Now you're telling me ten thousand!"

"It's ten thousand. If you make sure she disappears and isn't found, I give you a bonus—an extra one thousand dollars. That's it!"

Out of the corner of my eye I could see Agent Schimen in a telephone booth maybe twenty-five feet away. There were agents hidden all over the place, snapping pictures of everything that was happening.

With the gun he handed me a picture of a blond woman. "That's the one I want killed," he said. "Remember, if she disappears, there's a bonus."

MAFIA ENFORCER

Cecil Kirby
and
Thomas C. Renner

BANTAM BOOKS
TORONTO · NEW YORK · LONDON · SYDNEY · AUCKLAND

MAFIA ENFORCER

*A Bantam Book / published by arrangement with
Villard Books*

PRINTING HISTORY
Villard edition published March 1987

Bantam edition / July 1988

*Bantam Books are published by Bantam Books, a division of
Bantam Doubleday Dell Publishing Group, Inc. Its trademark,
consisting of the words "Bantam Books" and the portrayal of a
rooster, is Registered in U.S. Patent and Trademark Office and
in other countries. Marca Registrada. Bantam Books, 666 Fifth
Avenue, New York, New York 10103.*

To my wife, Nancy, who makes all things possible, and to my daughters, Dawn, Elaine, Jacqueline, and Sandy, for their patience and love.

—T.C.R.

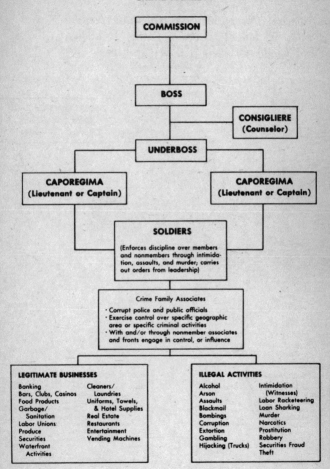

TYPICAL ORGANIZED CRIME FAMILY

COMMISSION

BOSS

CONSIGLIERE (Counselor)

UNDERBOSS

CAPOREGIMA (Lieutenant or Captain)

CAPOREGIMA (Lieutenant or Captain)

SOLDIERS

(Enforces discipline over members and nonmembers through intimidation, assaults, and murder; carries out orders from leadership)

Crime Family Associates
· Corrupt police and public officials
· Exercise control over specific geographic area or specific criminal activities
· With and/or through nonmember associates and fronts engage in control, or influence

LEGITIMATE BUSINESSES

Banking	Cleaners/
Bars, Clubs, Casinos	Laundries
Food Products	Uniforms, Towels,
Garbage/	& Hotel Supplies
Sanitation	Real Estate
Labor Unions	Restaurants
Produce	Entertainment
Securities	Vending Machines
Waterfront	
Activities	

ILLEGAL ACTIVITIES

Alcohol	Intimidation
Arson	(Witnesses)
Assaults	Labor Racketeering
Blackmail	Loan Sharking
Bombings	Murder
Corruption	Narcotics
Extortion	Prostitution
Gambling	Robbery
Hijacking (Trucks)	Securities Fraud
	Theft

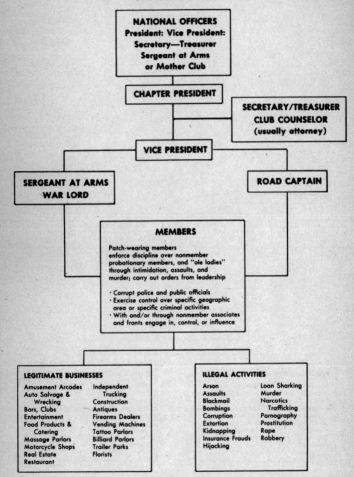

**TYPICAL MAJOR MOTORCYCLE
GANG CHAPTER**

**NATIONAL OFFICERS
President: Vice President:
Secretary—Treasurer
Sergeant at Arms
or Mother Club**

CHAPTER PRESIDENT

**SECRETARY/TREASURER
CLUB COUNSELOR
(usually attorney)**

VICE PRESIDENT

**SERGEANT AT ARMS
WAR LORD**

ROAD CAPTAIN

MEMBERS

Patch-wearing members
enforce discipline over nonmember
probationary members, and "ole ladies"
through intimidation, assaults, and
murder; carry out orders from leadership

· Corrupt police and public officials
· Exercise control over specific geographic
  area or specific criminal activities
· With and/or through nonmember associates
  and fronts engage in, control, or influence

LEGITIMATE BUSINESSES

Amusement Arcades
Auto Salvage &
  Wrecking
Bars, Clubs
Entertainment
Food Products &
  Catering
Massage Parlors
Motorcycle Shops
Real Estate
Restaurant

Independent
  Trucking
Construction
Antiques
Firearms Dealers
Vending Machines
Tattoo Parlors
Billiard Parlors
Trailer Parks
Florists

ILLEGAL ACTIVITIES

Arson
Assaults
Blackmail
Bombings
Corruption
Extortion
Kidnapping
Insurance Frauds
Hijacking

Loan Sharking
Murder
Narcotics
  Trafficking
Pornography
Prostitution
Rape
Robbery

Contents

PART FOUR—Government Witness

Foreword

Cecil Kirby may well be the most disarming professional criminal I have ever met—and I have met hundreds during my thirty-three years as a journalist-author, twenty-six of those years as an organized crime investigative reporter.

Kirby is many things to many people. Charming, soft-spoken, deceptively polite, he does not fit the public mold of the outlaw biker or the perceived characterization of an underworld enforcer. Yet he is both—the first and only outlaw motorcycle gang member and leader to become the chief enforcer for a Mafia-type crime family.

To the former attorney general of Ontario, Roy McMurtry, he is Canada's Joe Valachi, the "first real breakthrough in penetrating the conspiracy of silence" that shrouds the Honoured Society or Calabrian Mafia and other Canadian organized crime groups, including outlaw bikers.

John Schiman, a veteran FBI agent who worked with Kirby in Connecticut to save a woman's life, describes Kirby as a "suave, self-assured [criminal who] knows how to handle underworld figures . . . the best double agent I have met in my ten years as an FBI agent."

And the leadership of the Honoured Society and outlaw motorcycle gangs in the United States and Canada consider Kirby so dangerous that a price of $100,000 or more has been promised to killers who can find and assassinate him.

MAFIA ENFORCER

Since becoming a Canadian informer and witness, Kirby has saved the life of the mistress of a Connecticut Calabrian Mafia leader; at least temporarily prevented the murder of a Toronto Mafia chieftain; solved more than seventy bombings, arsons, and attempted murders; and provided authorities with information, evidence, or testimony that resulted in the conviction of at least thirty-six criminals, including three high-ranking Calabrian Mafia leaders.

At age thirty-five, Cecil Kirby has lived a life of crime that spans the highs and lows of the organized underworld. More than sixty arrests fill his criminal file. There are multiple convictions for break and entry, assault, extortion, crimes for which he has spent a total of less than four years in jail. And there is a controversial immunity agreement, necessary to obtain his testimony and the recorded conversations of criminals, that exonerates his participation in more than seventy crimes ranging from extortion, bombings, and arson to assault, attempted murder, and homicide as a result of a bombing.

Kirby's curly, reddish-blond hair frames an impish, almost boyish face that often breaks into an infectious smile. Sky-blue eyes twinkle with a devilish delight as he engages interviewers in word duels, smiling broadly when he knows he has disarmed or shocked them. Yet the infectious smile and musical laugh can change suddenly to a deadly scowl while eyes harden to steely coolness in unexpected moments of anger. In those moments the taut, muscular chest and arms of an avid weight lifter flex, the mouth hardens, and language that only moments before reflected what appeared to be a mild-mannered young businessman suddenly mirrors the gutter vocabulary of a vicious enforcer and assassin and the criminal underworld Kirby lived in and often dominated for nearly fifteen years in Toronto.

I first met Kirby on September 13, 1983, in an office provided by Canadian journalist James DuBro, who was trying to convince Kirby to appear on a television show with him. Kirby wanted to have a book written about his exploits. My concern, at that time, centered on the threat of organized crime that was proliferating to an awesome extent and with growing sophistication in Canada and the United States.

Kirby and I decided to meet again before I left Toronto. As a sign of good faith, Kirby provided me with a stack of documents and news clips that he had brought with him in a brown leather briefcase. He agreed to permit me to use them and whatever information we taped in subsequent meetings for news articles I hoped to write about the new criminal groups I had been investigating.

Of particular interest to me then and now were the growth of the Calabrian Mafia and the apparent lack of intelligence about it by American law enforcement. More important was the public's ignorance of its existence. As early as 1975, I had written about the operation of a Calabrian Mafia group that had come from Siderno, Italy, and were known as the Sidernese. They were then active in counterfeiting, extortion, murder, business infiltration, and the pizza industry, but little was known about them except what was being compiled by Canadian authorities, particularly the Ontario Provincial Police, the Royal Canadian Mounted Police, and Canadian Immigration.

It has been my primary objective in writing books—first on Vincent Teresa, later on Michael Hellerman, and more recently on Antoinette Giancana—to provide the public with hitherto unpublished views of organized crime from people who have either been a part of it or have lived with it. Cecil Kirby provides a unique point of view on this world.

When Kirby and I met for the second time, there was no advance notice, only a ring of a telephone, Kirby's voice on the other end, and, within what seemed like seconds, a pounding on the door of my room at the Royal York Hotel. As I peered out from behind the door, I could see two burly plainclothesmen, members of a three-man team from the Special Enforcement Unit (Canada's equivalent of the U.S. Marshals' witness protection section), standing in front of my door.

"You Tom Renner?" one of them asked.

I nodded affirmatively, noticing a walkie-talkie he held in one hand and the high-powered pistol he had under his coat. "That's right," I said. "Who are you?"

The plainclothesman flashed a police identity card for the Toronto Metropolitan Police and asked me for some identification, but said nothing more.

I ushered the detectives into my room. While I showed my New York driver's license and police press pass to the plainclothesman, his partner checked every nook and cranny of my room, including the door to an adjoining room, closets, and under the bed.

Once the room, the hallway, and stairway exits of the floor on which I was staying had been thoroughly searched, the detective I had first talked to spoke into the walkie-talkie and told Kirby it was safe for him to come up. Within a minute, he and two other men appeared. Making sure the door was locked, they left Kirby in my room, with two men stationed at either end of the hallway. Kirby sat down, a walkie-talkie at his side, to begin the first of what was to be a series of interview sessions that were to span two years and take place in less desirable locations throughout Canada.

During that first, four-hour interview, I fully realized Kirby's importance in showing the links that had been forged between outlaw motorcycle gangs and so-called Mafia groups. Law enforcement had for some time suspected that there were criminal links and business ties between cycle gangs and Mafia groups. Until Kirby surfaced, however, no member of a cycle gang had stepped forward as an informer-witness to make his role with both criminal groups public. Formerly a club vice president, Kirby, in fact, is still the only high-ranking member of an outlaw motorcycle gang to become the chief enforcer for a Mafia-type crime family.

Disclosures of business ties between motorcycle gangs and Mafia groups were beginning to surface in 1983. In Philadelphia, members of the Pagan motorcycle gang were engaged in drug trafficking with members of the

Foreword

Angelo Bruno crime family. Rebellious members of the Bruno family recruited bikers for hits on others within the family. A special report prepared by the office of U.S. Attorney Dan K. Webb in Chicago found that there was a "sinister criminal association" and a "loose alliance" between gangster flunkies of Chicago mob boss Anthony (Big Tuna) Accardo and the Outlaws, a motorcycle club that resorted to extortion, kidnapping, and murder to supply for profit nude dancers and prostitutes for Chicago mob clubs and massage parlors. There were other investigations in Detroit, Arizona, California. None provided the graphic documentation that Kirby did.

By 1985 both the Federal Bureau of Investigation in the United States and the Criminal Intelligence Service of Canada agreed on one thing: Outlaw motorcycle gangs represented significant organized crime threats to both countries. Their hypothesis was supported by a growing body of evidence from U.S. Senate committees and federal trials from Philadelphia to Chicago, which details extortions, kidnappings, murder, narcotics trafficking, counterfeiting, white slavery, and brutality at a level that is difficult for even the most hardened observer to comprehend.

A new sophistication has emerged among outlaw bikers. The image of the apelike, "dirt-bag" bikers who took over towns to rape and pillage has evolved into that of a computer-age mobile criminal who uses electronics, computers, and high finance to thwart law enforcement and the courts. Outlaw bikers now invest in real estate, bars, restaurants, motorcycle shops, and other business ventures. Their reputation for brawn and unbridled violence has enabled them to obtain contracts to act as strikebreakers for an international oil company; to provide drugs and bodyguards for an internationally famous country singer; to muscle in on rock concerts and rock groups; and to engage in multi-million-dollar narcotics-smuggling enterprises.

An internal FBI report entitled "Outlaw Motorcycle Gangs," dated June 1985, placed the total membership of the four major U.S. gangs—the Bandidos, Hell's Angels, Outlaws, and Pagans—at more than 3,800, and that figure did not include the 800 smaller gangs, whose membership may exceed 2,000. A CISC annual report released to the media in Canada in 1985 put total Canadian outlaw motorcycle gang membership at more than 725.

A frightening add-on increases those membership figures. Police and federal agencies on both sides of the border say that for every known member of an outlaw biker gang there are ten associates. That means there are 65,000 bikers and associates dealing in crime in Canada and the United States.

Those associates have been described by the Ontario Provincial Police as the "support group—businessmen, prostitutes, lawyers, fellow travelers, recruits, hustlers, and con men who cooperate with outlaw bikers in crimes ranging from robbery and theft to murder and mayhem."

Cecil Kirby was an upper-echelon member of Satan's Choice, once the most vicious and powerful motorcycle gang in Canada. As a chapter vice president, he knew and traveled with members of other outlaw cycle gangs, including the stateside Outlaws. He possessed accurate, documented information about outlaw biker crimes ranging from murder and extortion to white slavery and narcotics trafficking.

In Chicago, Philadelphia, Arizona, and California other witnesses have testified about outlaw biker gangs, but they could testify only about their gangs, and the scope of their knowledge was generally regional. Their gangs—the Hell's Angels, the Outlaws—were international, with branches in Australia, Austria, Brazil, Denmark, England, France, Holland, Switzerland, and West Germany as well as Canada and the United States.

The scope of Kirby's experience goes far beyond painting a portrait of the international outlaw biker. Kirby became the only non-Italian to be accepted by the inner circles of the Honoured Society, to become their trusted chief enforcer and hired assassin of a "locale's" (crime family branch's) boss.

* * *

Foreword

The Honoured Society is an emerging crime organization in both the United States and Canada. Its existence in Canada has been documented since the late 1950s, when large numbers of Italian immigrants, mainly from Siderno Marina in the southern Italian province of Reggio di Calabria began arriving in Canada, and later in the northeastern United States, primarily New York, New Jersey, and Connecticut.

In August 1971, Toronto Metro Police uncovered a twenty-seven-page, handwritten document while searching the home of a Toronto man for unregistered guns and counterfeit money. Translated from Italian, the document disclosed the rituals, responsibilities, and penalties for members of the Honoured Society, a secret organization that had flourished for hundreds of years in southern Italy. Similar documents were uncovered that same year in Australia, where another branch of the organization operates. The society was strikingly similar to the Sicilian Mafia, with its code of *omertà* (silence), blood rituals for membership, close blood-family ties, and a ruling council similar in structure and responsibilities to the Mafia's and Cosa Nostra's separate boards of directors known as the *commissions*.

Though the Sicilian Mafia was the dominant criminal secret society, the Honoured Society was *the power* in southern Italy, corrupting every level of government, controlling the construction industry, and forcing local police and the judiciary to dance to its tarantellas.

Police in Italy and Canada found that the Honoured Society often worked closely with the Sicilian Mafia where mutual concerns coincided in major crimes. In recent years, Italian police are known to have warned Canadian authorities that the Canadian branch of the Sidernese Honoured Society may be the most insidious and dangerous criminal organization to emigrate to North America in decades.

By 1973 New York and Canadian police documents indicated that the Honoured Society's members were operating in Indiana, Ohio, Massachusetts, and Pennsylvania as well. In all there were an estimated 1,000 members in the United States, 400 in Ontario, at least several hundred in Australia, and approximately 2,000 in Calabria. They were heavily engaged in counterfeiting, the construction industry, pizza parlors, the smuggling and sale of illegal weapons, and narcotics trafficking. Police discovered there was even a hit-man exchange.

While Canadian law enforcement, in particular, had credible evidence of the existence and operation of the Calabrian crime organization, and had made some arrests, they had been unable to penetrate the inner structure of the organization during nearly a decade of investigation. American authorities had had far less success, depending almost entirely on the tidbits of intelligence provided by their Canadian counterparts.

That set the stage for Kirby, the outlaw biker who had become the trusted Calabrian enforcer and wanted immunity for past crimes in return for his testimony and an eventual agreement to carry a body mike. With that body mike he would record Honoured Society bosses and others ordering him to commit crimes including extortion, arson, assault, and murder.

Kirby, with a flair for derring-do, recorded the conversations of Honoured Society crime bosses and helped police at least delay the planned murder of Toronto mob boss Paul Volpe. He is also responsible for saving the life of a Connecticut woman by convincing mob bosses he'd carried out a contract to kill her while FBI agents kept her in hiding.

On the witness stand Kirby was equally poised. At least seventeen criminals, many of the major Honoured Society mafiosi, are now serving long prison terms, at least one for life, for murder, arson, assaults, extortion, and a host of other crimes. Scores of other major crimes have been solved through Kirby, resulting in perhaps as many as one hundred arrests on charges of murder, arson, narcotics trafficking, and robbery. His information tipped off a plot to take over the small Caribbean nation of Dominica and foiled plans to blow up nightclubs.

Kirby will always live in danger, with a bounty on his head that has been estimated at between $100,000 and $250,000—a bounty that will more than likely never be paid to the outlaw bikers and Honoured Society mafiosi sworn to hunt him down and kill him.

Because of this bounty and attempts on his life and those of some members of his family, Kirby has had a deep reluctance even to mention the fact that he was married and divorced and that he had a daughter by that union. Both the ex-wife and daughter are currently living somewhere in Canada under secret identities. Kirby is honestly and deeply concerned about their safety. He is also concerned about the safety of his immediate family— his father, mother, and brother—and about his ability ever to see any of those in his present and past families without endangering their lives. As a consequence, Kirby feels that the less known about them and his relationship with them, the less likelihood that a crazy biker or wild Calabrian hit man trying to make a name for himself will target them in an attempt to flush him out. It has been tried, unsuccessfully, largely because of protective measures taken by law enforcement agencies in Canada.

Today Kirby lives by his wits, the sixth sense of a streetwise criminal. He is a fox who has often gone to the protected henhouse to gather information about those hunting him. His mobility and the chances he takes to keep his intelligence alive worry many who have protected him. He, and those who may be with him, is at risk every moment of every day.

There is nothing heroic about Cecil Kirby. He has lived a violent, often brutal life and has hurt a great many people. He has killed, he has lived off the proceeds of prostitution, he has blown up restaurants, intimidated contractors, plotted murders, and stalked his victims like a hunter tracks animals in a jungle. When he faced the likelihood that his own life might be terminated by the very bosses with whom he had plotted the deaths of others, he took the route of the informer to survive.

The deal he cut with the Ontario attorney general is very controversial. In return for his testimony, Kirby was given immunity from prosecution for past crimes. He was also guaranteed subsistence and protection for five years or until he concluded his testimony.

Without Kirby, there would have been no penetration of the Honoured Society and no conviction of its bosses. Calabrian-ordered murders, extortions, arsons, and other crimes would have been carried out. At least one defense attorney has grudgingly admitted in private to media representatives that he advised at least one of his clients to plead guilty to charges rather than face Kirby as an avenging witness because "he is so devastating" on the witness stand.

Because of his life of violent crime, Kirby has been reviled for eluding jail, for receiving subsistence for himself and his family from Canadian authorities, and for being allowed to work on a book with me for his own profit. In 1984 and 1985, public pressure led to attempts to introduce legislation in Canada to prohibit Kirby or any other criminal from profiting from any book or media production based on their criminal lives. Crown prosecutors who had extolled Kirby's worth as a witness and arranged for his immunity and subsistence waffled under media heat, claiming that they didn't know he was writing a book, that he shouldn't profit from past crimes.

Kirby, through it all, has kept his word. He has been brutally frank about his criminal life and has made no apology for being what he is. He has fought openly and publicly with prosecutors over subsistence agreements, with the support of his attorney. He has broken free of the protection once provided by Canadian law enforcement to survive on his own, moving from area to area while assassins still hunt him. It has not been easy.

Since I have known him, Kirby has moved at least a half dozen times, at least twice in the belief that outlaw biker assassins knew his location and were on their way to kill him. He has had to work for minimum wages, seldom enough to pay his way, because subsistence checks were as much as two months late. He has tried to obtain work under his new identity only to be turned away because some of his so-called protectors provided prospective employers with his criminal record without specifically identifying him as Cecil Kirby. Many of the government's promises of job training, relocation, family protection, funds to move to safe harbors, and help with a new life have not been fulfilled.

I have worked with scores of witnesses over the last decade or more. All have had problems with witness protection programs, some valid, some not. In my judgment, it would be nothing short of a miracle if any other witnesses made a deal with Canadian prosecutors unless they had public guarantees that they would not have to face the indignities and broken promises that Kirby has had to live with.

I have written from the personal accounts of scores of criminals. Each has added to the public knowledge of the world of crime. Kirby provides something extra—a rare inside view of two different organized crime groups and how they prey on the public.

THOMAS C. RENNER

PART ONE

Outlaw Bikers

1

No Honor Among Thieves

The Honored Society [L' Onorata Societa] is a
secret organization of criminal parasites, like an
insect that attaches itself to a flower and bleeds
it. It infiltrates all the economic fields in Calabria.

Dr. Alberto Sabatino, Chief Commissioner
Criminal Intelligence Branch
Central National Criminalpol of Rome, Italy

It was May 1979 when I first began to suspect that my
safety as the personal enforcer–hit man for Honoured
Society crime boss Cosimo Commisso might be in jeopardy.
My suspicions were aroused as we sat together eating
at the Casa Commisso, his banquet hall and the Calabrian
Mafia's meeting center, which he and his brothers, Remo
and Michele, owned and operated not far from Toronto's
Little Italy. There were no threats, no special incidents,
nothing unusual said, just a sort of eerie feeling that I got
in my gut as I listened to Cosimo talk about murders and
vendettas and the traditions of Calabria.

I knew he was talking about the Calabrian Mafia, or
the Honoured Society as it's generally called, but the
actual names were never mentioned. In all honesty, I can't
remember hearing him or his brothers use either name.

3

MAFIA ENFORCER

When they said anything it was usually in terms of "our people" or "our family," not the "Mafia." I've also heard police call his group the Sidernese Mob or Mafia.

Cosimo and his brothers were born in a small southern Italian town called Marina di Gioiosa. It was a town of about 25,000, on the water, and very close to Siderno Marina. Siderno is the birthplace of the Calabrian Mafia or Sidernese Mob of Canada and the United States.

Cosimo was just fifteen when he came to Canada with his mother, Emilia, in 1961. He didn't grow up on the streets as a fighter and hustler like me, but he did grow up with a tradition that had its roots in Calabria and in the family.

He told me his father, Girolamo, was killed in some sort of Mafia shoot-out in 1949 in Siderno. And his family knew Michele (Mike) Racco, the old Siderno mafioso who was sort of the godfather of all the Calabrian hoods in Ontario and even New York before he died of cancer in 1980.

From the time Cosimo and Remo were kids in this country all they, particularly Remo, could think about was avenging their dad's murder. Remo was always calling people in Italy mafiosi and relatives, and sometimes traveling to handle contracts or what Cosimo would call "affairs of honor." It was, I suppose, from this tradition and because of Racco that Cosimo and his brothers became big shots in Toronto and eventually headed their own crime family.

By the time I met Cosimo through a trucker friend in 1976, he was what they call the capo bastone, or crime boss of one of several Calabrian crime families. A lot of coppers think Remo is the brains behind Cosimo and may really be the boss, but they don't know.

I know, because I worked for them both. Cosimo is the boss, and Remo pays him the respect due a boss and an older brother. Remo is like a lightning rod. He draws a lot of the heat because he's out front on a lot of deals, like going to Italy all the time and meeting with other bosses.

But it's Cosimo who's calling the shots, running an outfit that's become known and feared as Canada's Murder Inc.

Cosimo was only thirty-four at the time I was sitting with him in the Casa Commisso, but he was a Mafia boss in every sense of the word. He weighed about 180 pounds, which is 60 pounds more than he weighed when he was in jail a year or so ago. He had an Italian accent so thick that at times I could hardly understand what the hell he was saying. He was married and had two kids. His wife was Jewish, strange enough when you think about his Calabrian traditions, but she was quiet, you never heard from her, and he treated her with respect whenever I saw them together at home. But when he stepped out of his home to meet me or some of his Mafia friends at the Casa Commisso or at pool halls or even in cars and restaurants, he was a different man.

Cosimo pushed himself back from the kitchen table at the Casa Commisso. He belched with satisfaction as he wiped tomato sauce from his mouth and brushlike mustache and picked at the last remnants of meat stuck in a lobster-tail shell on the plate in front of him.

He gulped down some red wine, belched again, rubbing his belly. A peculiar smile crossed his face as he watched me toy with the small plate of spaghetti and lobster in front of me, eating slowly, savoring the flavors that his cook, a soft-spoken Italian woman in her fifties, managed to brew into the dishes she created. She was a great cook, a real nice lady who was always whipping something delicious together for me whenever I showed up at the Casa Commisso. With all her cooking talents and her kindnesses to me I could never remember her name. I still can't.

"It's good, no?" Cosimo asked.

I nodded. "It's good, yes," I answered and continued eating. Cosimo kept talking, but the conversation wasn't about food.

"You know, it's not too long ago when one of my uncles, he's involved in a war between our family and

5

another family back in Italy..." Cosimo said softly, glancing around the kitchen to make certain we were alone and no one was listening.

"We went after that other fuckin' family," he said. "They had this big fuckin' house in this village near Siderno. It took awhile, but we got into this house when the whole family was there and we shot and killed everybody in the place—even the little *bambino* in the crib."

For a split second I thought he was bullshitting me until I looked up from my food at that round, moonlike face and that unbrushed, scraggly hair of his. His sleepy, dark brown eyes danced with a hidden deadliness I'd come to know over the years. I knew this was no tall Mafia tale. It was a matter-of-fact, you-kill-everyone-opposed-to-you true story, told without emotion but with obvious satisfaction.

He was giving me a little historical lesson in the ways of the Calabrian Mafia in Italy, particularly Siderno. But there was more to it than just a little tale of vengeance. "But why kill the kid in his crib?" I asked.

Cosimo sort of smirked as he answered. "If you don't kill the kid as a *bambino*, he will grow up and kill you, kill your family later. It's the way of Vendetta."

Cosimo was working his way up to something that he wanted me to handle, and there was something about the way he was doing it—about the story of the murdered family, about the tales of his father's murder—that was bothering me. I wasn't squeamish about the murders. What the hell, I'd been around murder and violence for a long time as a biker and as Cosimo's enforcer. But I got antennae that sense things that are wrong for me, and those antennae were vibrating and warning lights were going off mentally.

I had worked for Cosimo and his brothers for about three years. While I never really questioned what they wanted to do, I always had an uneasiness about some of their assignments.

Maybe it was because they had short arms when it came to paying for the work I did. They were always shortchanging me or pleading poverty or claiming they hadn't been paid for the jobs they'd hired me to do.

Maybe it was because I wasn't Italian. I knew that I could never be a real member of their organization and that Irish-Canadians are expendable to Calabrians. They talked in Italian a lot when I was around—like they didn't want me to know about something.

Anyway, I always had the feeling that they didn't really trust me any more than I trusted them. But they needed me, and I knew a helluva lot about their operations and the crimes they were involved in. Because of that I figured that I would either disappear or I'd be killed at some meeting, like my predecessor.

So I took precautions. I usually picked the places where we'd meet, places I knew, places where I could control things around me. I'd pick the time, usually on short notice, and I'd never tell them where they could find me. In fact, I carried a telephone pager around on my belt so that they could reach me without ever knowing exactly where I was.

I was also careful about the assignments I took from them. Whether I was handling a bombing, setting up an arson, or plotting a hit, I did things my way, without giving them any details of when or how I would strike.

Cosimo, like his brother Remo, still had close ties with mafiosi in the old country. Remo, for example, had gone back to Calabria to handle a hit in the early 1970s. That trip was a revenge hit—a hit that involved some of those behind the killing of his father. It also had something to do with "family honor" in the village where the brothers had strong family ties.

Remo never forgets. Neither does Cosimo. Because of that I'll always be looking over my shoulder for them or their relatives and family members. They want to kill me more than they want to eat, and maybe one day they will.

Cosimo told me that Remo was in a car in Italy with some other Siderno Mafia members looking for some of those responsible for the slaying of his father. His enemies must have known about it, because they ambushed the car and machine-gunned it. Two of the men he was with were killed. Remo escaped, but his trench coat was riddled with holes.

Remo brought the coat back to Canada to show his family how close he'd been to death. It was like a medal, a badge of honor. He even showed it to me one day and laughed about the bullet holes and the scar he got on his face in the shoot-out.

On June 7, 1976, the body of an eighteen-year-old kid named Salvatore Palermiti was found shot to death in a place in Toronto called the Bayview Ghost, an old, ruined apartment building that was left half finished by a builder who ran out of money.

I never knew exactly how the kid's murder and Remo's shot-up trench coat and trip to Italy fit together, but there were two stories told by the cops and friends of the Commissos. At first, the cops' story rested on this Palermiti kid's shooting out the windows of a Calabrian shop owned by the relative of a Mafia friend of Remo's. Remo's friends had another version. They claimed the Palermiti kid was involved in the Siderno shoot-out.

The coppers, in later years, questioned me about this murder and about the kid's relationship to Remo, who they said was one of the last people to be seen with him. They said the kid was sent to Toronto by his father. Among the people the kid went to see while his father tried to cool things down with the mafiosi in Calabria were the Commisso brothers. It didn't work. They weren't about to forgive and forget. The cops also were told, but could never confirm, that the Palermiti kid was one of those who shot up Remo's car in Calabria.

The bottom line to Cosimo's stories at the Casa Commisso was a rather wild murder plot he wanted me to carry out—not in Canada or the United States, but in Calabria. And his target wasn't just any Italian or Canadian hood, it was Girolamo (Momo) Piromalli, the most powerful Calabrian boss in southern Italy.

"Cec," he said, "we got this job for you and it's important, very important!"

Now when Cosimo said a job was important, it was *important*. Usually jobs were just jobs. I'd handled extortions, bombings, beatings, card game rip-offs, plotted murders—you name it. For me the bottom line was always money. For Cosimo, the bottom line was always results. Up to this point, he had never said that anything was as important as this was supposed to be.

"What's the job," I asked, "and how much are we talking about?"

"It's gonna pay good," he answered. "It's worth ten thousand dollars, and we pay all your expenses. We arrange everything for you."

"What's the job?" I pressed.

"We want you to do this person," he said. "We get you to Italy. We arrange for all your travel there and back. We set things up—*booma boom*—it's over. You got the money in your hand and we get rid of this pig."

Piromalli lived on "a big estate" in Gioia Tauro, a steel-making town in southern Italy. The area is also supposed to be one of the best for growing olives, oranges, and mandarins. Cosimo said the estate had guards all around it, but they had a way of taking them out. "If you do this job for us," he said, "it's gonna help all of us—it's a big thing for me and my friends."

"Why not use someone over there to kill this guy?" I asked.

"No, no, no," he said. "It must be kept a big secret. We can't use anybody from there to do this job. It'll leak out. We need you."

My father didn't raise a stupid son. Curly-haired, blondish, blue-eyed Canadians who don't speak Italian don't exactly blend into the scenery of the mountain country of Reggio di Calabria. It's a place where the mob runs everything from shops and hotels to politicians and cops.

"Hey, Cosimo, I'll stand out like an Arab sheik in a Dublin pub," I said. "They'll spot me in a second, and even if I could do the job, I'd have less chance of surviving than a snowball in hell."

Cosimo waved his hands excitedly in the air, shaking his head vigorously. "Don't you worry," he said. "We got this plan—we get you in and we get you out and you get your money, no problem."

Cosimo emphasized over and over the importance of maintaining secrecy—that absolutely no one must know about the plot, that I couldn't talk to anybody about it, not even his brothers.

Cosimo told me that Piromalli was the mafioso who bossed a big kidnapping ring in Calabria, one that in July 1973 had kidnapped J. Paul Getty III, the then sixteen-year-old grandson of the oil billionaire J. Paul Getty. For his safe return, Cosimo said, Piromalli's people had demanded a $2.9 million ransom. The kid was finally released after being held for five months, but not before Piromalli's men cut off one of his ears and sent it to the Getty family to force them to pay the ransom. Piromalli was arrested with six others and then acquitted because the cops couldn't come up with enough evidence.

Cosimo said that there were fifteen or twenty in the kidnapping group, who collected nearly $200 million in ransoms in less than five years. The racket was booming until 1978, when Italian police arrested fifteen more Calabrians, including Piromalli's brother Giuseppe.

Before those arrests, Piromalli and his Honoured Society had kidnapped more than a hundred people, including industrialists and heirs to big fortunes, and collected some really big ransoms. A year before Cosimo talked to me about Piromalli, I remember having seen stories about their collecting a $600,000 ransom for the release of an Italian businessman named Giovanni Fagioli.

I knew that this couldn't be a scheme that Cosimo'd hatched all by himself. Remo and others in Calabria had to be involved, and in my gut I just knew that I wasn't supposed to come out alive—that maybe this was their way of getting rid of a non-Italian hit man who knew too much about their affairs.

"I don't know, Cosimo," I said, rubbing my chin and looking as deep into his eyes as I could to see if there was something he was hiding from me, something else I should know. "I'll have to think about it and let you know."

"Okay, Cec," he said. "You think. Guaranteed—it's ten thousand dollars and it's safe."

Cecil Kirby in Calabria—it didn't make sense. I had a nagging feeling that it was a setup, that I was going to be taken there to hit this Piromalli fella and then they were going to do me on one of those back roads of theirs or leave me by the body of Piromalli or something like that. My sixth sense told me no, but the money made it interesting. I liked the intrigue and excitement. It was something to think about—carefully.

The Piromalli murder scheme, I learned later, was all part of a Mafia struggle for leadership in Calabria that had gone on since the 1949 murder of the Commisso brothers' father. But their father, police told me later, was never higher than what they call a *Sgarrista E. Cammista,* the same thing as a soldier in the Cosa Nostra. He was the kind of guy who approached businesses to extort money, and he could give orders to members of his group, associates that are called *Picciotti,* people like me, who place the bombs, beat up the victims, apply the muscle, and collect loan-shark debts or other fees.

Cosimo said that Mafia power in Calabria was so absolute that even international companies knuckled under to their demands. He said that in the early 1970s a hotel chain came to Siderno to build a big hotel. About halfway through construction it was bombed. The Mafia didn't want outsiders in their town. If there were going to be any hotels, they'd own them and build them.

The big Honoured Society boss before Piromalli was Antonio Macri. He controlled all the Calabrian families like a boss of bosses, but he didn't like change. Most Calabrians don't. They stick to the old ways of making money. New ways, like narcotics trafficking, were not allowed. But the money was too big, and Piromalli was too ambitious. In 1975, Macri was gunned down when his chauffeur-driven car stopped at a main intersection in Siderno. Cosimo said that five or six men jumped from nowhere and shot everyone in the car except Macri's right-hand man, a guy named Frank Commisso, who was a distant cousin of Cosimo's.

Piromalli tried, but couldn't get the power that Macri'd had. He remained a local boss, not a boss of bosses, and rivals hated him for killing Macri. The Commisso brothers had sided with factions that opposed Piromalli. That's why Remo had gone to Calabria and gotten involved in some firefights. That's why, I supposed, they had turned to me to handle Piromalli's killing.

I had bought a pass on the plan to kill Piromalli only because Cosimo kept putting it off and he died from natural causes.

Finding a way out of a Calabrian organization that sometimes kills just because they're insulted isn't the easiest thing. I knew that there was only one way it would end—I'd be lured someplace by Cosimo or his brother to collect some money or plot some job and I'd be killed.

In October 1980 I was facing trial for break and entry as well as extortion and assault. They were the latest in a series of criminal charges, acquired since my youth, that now numbered more than sixty. I was certain I would be convicted on one, probably the B&E, and, if I was, I'd do big time.

My choice was doing a long stretch in jail and probably being killed there by one of the Commissos' people or be done by the Commissos outside prison walls. The trouble was, I didn't know who the hell to talk to. I had never found a cop I could trust.

I had tried trusting a cop named Terry Hall of the Ontario Provincial Police (OPP). Hall was a particularly tough cop who had become a thorn in the ass of the Vagabonds, one of Toronto's worst motorcycle gangs. He had become their shadow—turn around in a bar and he was there. Step out of the house, and there he was on the street. Always hounding them, breaking their balls, making their lives miserable. He had put the fear of God into them. He was a tough cop and an honest cop, and they were afraid of him. I couldn't understand why all these big, rough bikers were so afraid of just one cop.

One night in 1978 I heard from a biker friend of mine, Armand Sanguigni, that the Vagabonds had put out a contract to kill Hall. Hall, he said, had hounded them too much and charged too many of them with crimes. He said they were busy collecting money to pay for a hit man to do him in. "They're desperate to get rid of this copper," he said.

I figured I'd do myself and Hall a favor by tipping him to what was happening. I called him, met him, and told him about the murder plot. I figured I'd get some consideration down the road from him if I was charged with something. Well, I was charged later on, but I got no consideration from him at all—not even a thank you for saving his fuckin' life. I should've let them do him. Anyhow, I knew I couldn't turn to him to get any help on this case. He'd already told me to go to hell.

On October 11, 1980, I took a chance and called the Toronto Royal Canadian Mounted Police (RCMP) National Crime Intelligence Section and asked to talk to someone. I got a break that day—I got to talk to Corporal Mark Murphy.

I didn't identify myself to him that first day. I simply told him that I was a former member of the Satan's Choice motorcycle gang and that I could provide him with a lot of good information if he could help me with some charges I had pending. He didn't promise me anything, but we talked some more and I gave him some information that he found was accurate.

At first he wasn't impressed. He still didn't know my name and referred to me only as "Joe." Still no promises. Then I began feeding him information on narcotics dealers, on prison beatings and murders, on robberies and other crimes, and I dangled promises that I could deliver much,

much more, including information on everything from arsons and murder to the Commissos and their organization.

Up to that time I had no intentions of becoming a witness or doing anything but providing tips to Murphy. All I wanted in return was a light sentence. Murphy was willing to talk to Crown prosecutors for me, but he was opposed by biker cops from the Toronto Metropolitan Police and the OPP, including Hall.

That really jammed me. If I didn't keep cooperating, one of those cops could put the word out on the street that I was an informer, and I'd have bikers and rounders [independent street hoodlums] out to kill me along with the Commissos. If I did keep talking, I'd still go to jail for a long term because the cops wouldn't listen to Murphy.

It was the Commissos who gave me the bargaining chip I needed. They handed me a $20,000 contract to kill a good-looking broad in Stamford, Connecticut, Helen Nafpliotis, the girlfriend of Nick Melia, a convicted receiver of stolen goods and the brother of a ranking member of the Calabrian Mafia in Canada and Connecticut.

I was certain that this hit contract was really part of a plan to take me out. They wanted this Nafpliotis woman killed, all right, because she was costing them money—money they were losing because Melia wasn't paying attention to business. But I knew that if I took the contract, the chances were they'd do me after I'd done her. If I didn't handle it, they'd have her killed anyhow, their suspicions about me would be raised another notch, and I'd probably be hit anyhow.

It was February now, the Commissos were pressing, and I hadn't told Murphy. As I tried to make up my mind about what to do, I found myself wondering where it had all begun. How the hell had I gotten myself into a mess where my future, my life, rested on the whims of some cops and some crazy Calabrians?

2

Born to Violence

I was born in 1950 in Weston, a suburb of Toronto, and from the time I was in kindergarten I was fighting with kids around me, fighting to survive. My parents weren't rich—they had to work like hell to make enough money to support the family—but we weren't poor either. I mean I never wanted for food or clothes. I may have had to use an outhouse at the cottages we lived in or I might have had to walk a mile or more to get water for the house, but there was always good, wholesome food on the table and plenty of it, and there were always enough decent clothes for everyone.

Where we lived was a tough neighborhood. I guess you'd say there was an ethnic balance. There were Irish and English, Jews and Poles, Italians and Greeks, but there weren't any Latins or blacks, or any Orientals that I can remember. An Irish kid, like myself, had to stand his ground and fight his way through kids of other nationalities who were out to establish their reputations and uphold their origins. So I fought, and I was always getting into trouble for playing hooky or running away. I just didn't like school.

I didn't go look for fights, don't get me wrong, but there were kids who would try to push me around, and I wasn't one to be pushed. Someone would give me a shove and bang! That was it. I'd lose my cool and start fighting. Many a night, I'd come home bruised and bloodied and my dad would give me hell and then ask, "You whip him?" and I'd nod my head and say, "Yeah, I beat him." He'd say, "Good. Go get cleaned up." Sometimes it was a draw and sometimes I got the hell kicked outta me, but as far as I was concerned I was a winner 'cause I didn't knuckle under to anyone. I never told Dad I lost. He wouldn't have wanted to hear that anyhow and I didn't need sympathy.

By the time I was ten, my parents moved to Wasaga Beach, a small resort community about one hundred miles north of Toronto on Georgian Bay off Lake Huron. My mother, Muriel was her name, wanted to change my environment, hoping the fights would stop and I'd do better in school. It didn't do any good. The fights went on, and I missed as many as one hundred days of school in a year.

During the summers I played baseball for a team in Stayner, about four miles from where we lived, and it was there that I began hanging around with other kids who broke into cottages. The break-ins were mainly for excitement. We never got much money or valuables. The idea was to fool the coppers, watch 'em scramble. The satisfaction was in never being caught.

Within three years my parents were divorced. They just stopped getting along. They were always fighting. My dad, Kitchener Kirby, moved back to Weston. He'd never liked Wasaga Beach, and he'd had trouble earning a living there. My mother stayed there, and after a few months I told her I wanted to go live with my dad. There was a helluva argument, but finally she agreed to let me go.

My dad and I were pretty close. I guess I've always admired him. He's got a lot of courage. During the war Dad was a motorcycle dispatch rider in Europe with the Canadian army. When he came back he became a trick bike rider in the circus. He used to ride the barrel and take the bike through hoops of fire and everything. There wasn't much he couldn't do with a bike, and a lot of the bike-riding skills that helped me be a top biker with the outlaw biker gangs, like Satan's Choice, were developed through him.

Dad was also a regular playboy. He'd been married three times, and when he wasn't married he always had all kinds of girlfriends. For twenty to twenty-five years he was a waiter in hotels. He was also a hotel bouncer. He could always handle himself and still can, even though he's in his seventies. Until a short time ago, he could still ride a motorcycle with the best of them.

Dad had remarried when I moved in with him, and at first I resented my stepmother. But I found she really wasn't a bad person after I got to know her. Dad tried his damnedest to reform me, but there was no way. We'd argue a lot, but even with the arguments we got along. My stepmother, Mary, was good to me. She always stuck up for me, and both of them were always bailing me out of jail.

Mary died in 1979. She'd been an invalid for almost a year, but she didn't complain. Neither did my dad. No matter what happened they both always stood behind me.

It wasn't long after I moved in with my dad, maybe two months at most, before I got kicked out of Weston Senior Public School for fighting. It was a helluva fight, the biggest they'd had in the school's history. I took on this big, tough senior who'd been trying to push me around. Within minutes we were battling all over the grounds, with a crowd of more than two hundred students cheering and urging us on.

Both of us were covered with bruises and blood before some teachers came out and stopped it. The next day we were called before the principal and disciplined, but I was warned that if I got into a fight again, I would be bounced from school. Easy to say. There were too many wise guys who wanted to see how tough I was. Within two weeks I was in another fight and bounced.

I moved on to Roseland Public School in the Mount Dennis area of Toronto. In the first month, I must have gotten into ten fights, all of which I won. My reputation as a tough kid was following me, and every so-called tough in the school was trying to take me on. It was sort of like being the fastest gun in the West—there was always some wise guy who thought he was faster and tried to draw on the guy with the reputation. So I beat them up, one at a time, sometimes two. Things got so bad that by the end of the spring semester my desk was in front of the principal's office.

I got thrown out of Roseland by the summer, but not before I had met and either fought or become associated with a number of students who were, like me, to become members of motorcycle gangs. Some of them were to fight with me, others against me as members of rival gangs. Our lives would never be the same.

I can't say there was anything about the environment, or our economic stature, or our ethnic backgrounds that made us that way. It just happened. I think we just drifted into the gangs and got into trouble. The only thing we all had in common was that we played hooky a lot. We all bumped around on the streets and hung out in garages because we wanted to become auto mechanics. It seemed everyone in school wanted to be an auto mechanic then.

The principal, I forget his name, was glad to see me go. A month before the end of the semester, he called me in and said he was tired of seeing me. "Go home, Cec," he said. "Let's figure you've passed everything without taking any tests." He and the teachers just wanted me out. They passed me to a higher grade so I wouldn't return to their school the following year.

I was supposed to go to George Harvey High School as a ninth grader after that, but the summer break came and I never went back. Instead, I went to work driving a truck for a Ford dealership in Toronto.

I had turned sixteen by then, and I'd started buying old cars—1956 Fords and Chevrolets—reconditioning them, and selling them. I enjoyed that. But I was still getting into fights even then, hanging around in parks with youth gangs. That was also the year I got my first conviction and taste of jail.

Born to Violence

* * *

The trouble started when I visited some old friends at Wasaga Beach. We drove to Collingwood, which was about six miles away. We went into this restaurant and got into a fight with three other guys. Two of my friends took off and left me on my own. But I was a tough kid by then, and I beat the hell out of those guys. As soon as I walked outside the restaurant, I was arrested.

Later that week I appeared in court with the three stiffs I'd wound up beating up. They got a $50 fine each for causing a disturbance and fighting. The judge had other plans for me. After giving me hell for being a troublemaker and a street tough, he told me I'd learn more if I spent some time behind bars. I got ten days in jail even though it was my first time in court. It doesn't pay to win a fight sometimes, even when you're outnumbered, a lesson that came back to haunt me again and again.

The ten days were no picnic. The judge sent me to the Barrie County Jail, fifty miles north of Toronto. On my second day there some guard handed me a rag to wash the floors with and I refused. I wound up doing the next nine days in solitary confinement.

Spending nine days in the hole—in solitary—was probably, in the long run, better than spending it with the others in the jail, who were hard core. At least it was quiet, and I didn't have to fight my way out of some lousy creep's attempt at a jail-house rape. They gave me a Bible to read, and I fooled them—I read the whole thing. Those nine days in 1966 prepared me for what I had to face later.

The next time I was in jail I was just seventeen, and it didn't have any impact on me. That time I went to Toronto's Don Jail for a weekend, until I could raise bail. A year later, after I was convicted of a minor assault, the judge sentenced me to thirty days in the same jail.

The Don Jail was like an old castle, but it was the wrong place to put teenagers. All the rabble are in a place like that—the drunks, the homosexuals, the perverts, the sadists, the killers—you name them, they're there. You might as well go to a sewer. The smell there is the same. It might be cleaner, but the smell is the same.

I remember this sixteen-year-old kid was having a terrible time. I don't know what he was in for, but he cried all night that first night. I expected to see him hanging in his cell the next day. You see things like that, young kids being abused by other prisoners. They shouldn't be put in a place like that. They should be in minimum-security jails, away from the hard-core criminals and perverts.

The routine in a place like Don Jail was boredom. All you could do was sit around, read books, or play cards. They'd let you out in the yard for fifteen to twenty minutes every day. You'd walk around about ten times and then you were back in your cell and that's where you sat the rest of the day. There was no weight room, or recreation room, no nothing. They had me in dorms half the time and cells the rest. I must have known a dozen guys in there, a lot of them bikers, who seemed to always be in the can.

When I got out of jail, I was still fighting and changing jobs. Then in late 1968 I started working for a concrete company. It was there that I met "Jimmy G," who was a member of the Toronto chapter of Satan's Choice motorcycle club.

At the time I owned a Triumph motorcycle, and I had a real love for cycling. But you don't do much cycling alone—not if you want to avoid trouble. You've got to belong to a club or an association, something. Other than the hell-raisers I sometimes hung out with, I had no one to ride with. So, after almost a year of associating with Jimmy and his friends, I asked him if he would help me become a member of Satan's Choice.

In August 1969, with Jimmy G's sponsorship, I started "striking." Striking is a probationary period that bikers go through before they are accepted into the club. For the Choice, striking lasted eight weeks. During that time I had to do whatever I was told to do, from cleaning the bikes of other members to proving that I could handle myself in fights. Sometimes those fights were on bikes, sometimes in hotels, other times in the clubhouses.

During the striking period I was asked to do a lot of what would be seen as sensible things. I was asked, not told, to help in fights or to steal motorcycles. And there were some stupid things, like running to the store for hamburgers for the whole club or cleaning the bikes of all the members.

Striking was showing that you were man enough to be a member of the club. Just to get to the striking position you had to prove you were good enough to someone in the organization so that the membership would vote you in as a member.

It was, in a way, something like being initiated into the Mafia. Your sponsor had to be a member, he had to be willing to be responsible for you, and you had to go through a probationary period of proving yourself before you were accepted. If you cheated a member, violated his rights, or became an informer against club members, you could be voted out, beaten to a bloody pulp, or killed, and very often members were. Outlaw bikers like myself have codes of silence that we had to live by.

There were a couple of big differences from the Mafia, of course. You didn't have to be Italian or from one ethnic group to be a member, although blacks were usually banned. Instead of going through a rite of initiation—in which blood was drawn and mixed while the recruit was required to swear eternal fidelity on pain of death—biker recruits or strikers sometimes had to literally eat shit while swearing loyalty to the club.

There was one biker, Howard (Pig Pen) Berry, who loved to make new recruits squirm by dumping buckets of pigshit and urine over their heads and not letting them clean themselves off all day and night. Berry was a tough biker. He had a reputation as a killer in North Carolina, where he rode with the Outlaws for a while. He loved fights, and he was a master biker, but he could be a mean bastard when he was riled. He wore thick glasses, which made a lot of people think he was a patsy—until he hit them. When Berry hit, it was like being hit by Man Mountain Dean. In Florida one time, while hiding out with the Outlaw motorcycle gang to avoid an attempted murder rap in Canada, Berry got into a street brawl and had his nose and jaw broken. He went out and got a gun and shot the guy who had pushed in his face. He did time for that job, and for shooting another guy in the belly with a rifle in Canada.

The public has an image of the biker as a hairy-ape type, with long smelly hair, World War II helmet, iron crosses, full beard and mustache, dirty pants and boots, with a total disregard for people, their feelings or property, or any sense of morality. All those are probably true and then some.

In truth, most members of biker gangs in the States and Canada like scaring the individual so he spreads fear through stories, often exaggerated, of how terrifying bikers are. Fear was and is our principal weapon—it's the bikers' badge of honor, their way of intimidating the common folk and the businessman and making it pay off for them. A biker can spread fear because he has the safety of numbers. If he was one on one with the ordinary guy, he wouldn't be so brave. The thing that stops the ordinary guy from taking him on is the fearsome look and the patches that signify membership in a gang.

When I joined Satan's Choice in 1969, I joined a gang that was very much in that public image. The violence, the smells, the dirty clothes—all those intimidating things the public's come to expect—were part of the Choice. The public feared us. We were the biggest outlaw gang in Canada, and we had close relationships with the Outlaw motorcycle gang, which had chapters in Florida, Illinois, and North Carolina. It was more than friendship.

Satan's Choice supplied the Outlaws with Canadian Blue valium and speed from our labs and with women for their topless joints or for prostitution. Some of the women were sold for $1,500 or more, others were given away. Sometimes the Outlaws supplied us with the same things.

But more often than not we provided each other with cooling-off places—places where members could hide while the cops searched for them on either side of the border. If a Choice biker was wanted for murder or assault or robbery in Canada, Big Jim Nolan, the head of the Outlaws, would make sure he had a good hideaway in Chicago or Fort Lauderdale. And while he was in hiding he was given women and drugs or whatever else he wanted.

Big Jim's doing double life for some murders in the States, but he'd beaten Florida charges of shotgunning three Hell's Angels and dumping them in a rock pit in 1974. There were also stories circulating among biker gangs about his skinning some Hell's Angels bikers alive before he killed them, but he was never convicted of anything like that. The Hell's Angels and Outlaws have been warring for years, killing each other, killing and beating members of other gangs that associate with either one. If they'd ever stop fighting and work together, the cops would have a helluva time trying to tame them.

I knew from the beginning that trouble and violence were part of life in Satan's Choice. I knew there might be a shooting and I'd be there; I knew that I might be in the same room or the same house when someone raped some broad and we'd all be charged with it; I knew there would be other crimes that I'd probably participate in with them. I didn't care. It wasn't that I joined the gang to do something like that. It just came, and I wanted the excitement.

Satan's Choice was, by then, Canada's largest and strongest motorcycle gang. It had fifteen chapters in places like Montreal, Ottawa, Kingston, Toronto, Peterborough, Richmond Hill, Hamilton, Kitchener, Saint Catharines, and Windsor. Each chapter had ten to fifteen members, but people in the community thought a chapter had as many as three or four hundred because they were so loud and violent and because members of other chapters would often join one chapter on a run on a town. But the most that were in the Choice while I was in were about 220 active, full-time members.

Today all that's changed. Now there are only a few chapters left, because the club split up in 1977. There are maybe fifty to sixty Satan's Choice members now in Toronto, Kitchener, and Peterborough. The rest are all part of the stateside Outlaws and Hell's Angels gangs, which set up chapters in Canada and are now fighting and killing each other, mostly in Quebec.

The image of the scraggly bunch of bikers who went around raping girls has also changed. Some bikers have gotten smarter and richer. A lot of them wear three-piece suits. They invest in business and real estate, they run narcotics rings, they testify at public hearings, and they often present an acceptable public appearance. They are still as violent as they ever were, just smarter. They have no intention of blending into the mainstream of society. They are outrageous outcasts and they love it. It's one of the reasons we called ourselves the one-percenters, the worst 1 percent of the population. We wore a patch to show we were outcasts.

In all the years I was a motorcycle gang member, and those were seven long years, I found maybe only 10 percent of all the members—whether they were from Canada or the United States or wherever—could handle themselves and fight one on one. The rest, for the most part, would never get into a fight unless there were ten guys to back them up, because they couldn't bloody well fight. A lot of the members had joined because they needed and wanted the protection of the rest of the members.

Strikers are at the lowest level of the club. It's like being a plebe at West Point—all the upperclassmen can give him orders. It's the same with a striker. It's a chance for the club to see if you have what it takes to be a member or if you're just an idiot who wants to get in on the pack's action.

Sometimes it took a lot of guts to finish the striking period, to pass all the tests members wanted. I remember one striker who was told to hold up pop bottles in his hands while members shot at them with a .22 caliber rifle. He survived with a few cuts and some bleeding, but he could have refused. If he had, though, he probably wouldn't have made the club.

You are told when you start striking that you do not have to break the law if someone asks you to. But you have to be nuts if you think you're going to join a motorcycle club like ours or some of the others around North America and not break the law. I mean, it's part of our life-style.

Jimmy G told me when I joined I would find that I'd always have very close and reliable friends in the chapter, that members helped each other out when they had trouble, and that they always stuck together wherever they were. That was true up to a point.

The Toronto chapter was a diverse group. Jimmy G was a laborer. I was a truck driver. We had a plumber, a stock market office executive, an electrician, three narcotics dealers, an insulation installer, a couple of professional motorcycle thieves, some safecrackers, and an explosives expert. It was with this group that I got my baptism of fire, my skill as a bike thief, a burglar, and an enforcer. And it was here that I saw my first murder.

3

Clubhouse of Assassins I

Some members of Satan's Choice wear a patch on the backs of their jackets that says simply, "In Memory of John Foote." I never wore that patch, but it was Foote and maybe two or three other members of the Choice who trained me in the fine art of crime. Foote is dead now. He was killed in November 1975 by a friend of mine in a fight over a dope deal. Before he died Foote taught me much of what I needed to know to handle explosives and use them for cracking safes, extorting contractors, and blowing up buildings.

Before he became a member of the Choice, Foote was what they call here in Canada a rounder. It's a term that's been used for more than twenty years to describe street criminals who can operate around bars and clubs and hotels and sell drugs, set up gambling operations, negotiate street deals for stolen goods, or run high-stakes, backroom card games. Rounders are tough people who live by their wits and are always around the right places to make the deals. That's why they're called rounders. They're all-around street hoods, who can handle just about any kind of deal.

Foote was one of the toughest of the rounders. He was a vicious street fighter when challenged. He'd killed more than one man in his travels. He was also a brutal enforcer when he had to be for those who paid him enough. He was originally from Scarborough. He weighed only 175 pounds, but he could bench-press 450 pounds.

For years Foote had worked for a well-known Toronto bail bondsman when bail was still used in the Canadian court system. He got to know a lot of the criminals in Toronto because of that association, including outlaw bikers. He often dealt with bikers when they were setting up safecracking jobs or wanted to use explosives to scare the hell out of some businessman who wasn't paying tribute to Choice members, or when they were doing break and entries of businesses and homes. He also collected loan-shark debts from street hoods and businessmen who sought out an ex-bondsman for shylock loans. Those that were delinquent in payments frequently got visits from Foote.

When I first met Foote, he wasn't a member of Satan's Choice, but he was often at the clubhouse and he frequently turned up at field days, when biker clubs and bikers showed off their skills by competing against each other. It was just before one of these events, in the summer of 1973, at a popular resort known as Rice Lake, that Foote introduced me to the first murder victim I'd ever seen.

I'd arrived at the clubhouse early one morning to get ready to leave for the event. Foote came to the house and confessed to another biker and me that he had the body of a Choice club member in the trunk of his car. The victim was a popular biker named James Lyons.

"We were doing this B&E [break and entry] at a farmhouse in Pickering," he said, "when Jim opened the door to the house and was shot in the shoulder by this farmer. I was hiding in the brush when I saw the farmer walk over to where Jim had staggered and fallen and I saw him shoot him in the head. When the farmer went back to the house, I ran over, picked Jim up, and carried his body to the car. When I left I could hear sirens in the distance," he added.

At first we didn't believe him, but we went to his house in Scarborough. He took us to the rear of the driveway, where his car was parked. Three other Choice members were also there. Foote opened the trunk and lifted a blanket, and I saw Lyons lying crumpled with a bad wound in his shoulder and his head distorted and bloodied.

I never really understood why Foote told us or showed us the body. He just did, and then he and one of the Choice members, a burly, bearded character named Jim, took Lyons's body and buried it on a farm in Brighton. The body has never been found. In fact, Lyons's murder has never been reported as a murder. None of us believed Foote's tale. We all thought he'd killed Lyons himself.

Foote had a terrible temper, and he was homicidal when he got mad. Lyons was really killed because he cheated Foote on a drug deal, ripped him off, so Foote blew him away, blew away half his head with a shotgun at close range. Outlaw biker drug deals usually ended up with some sort of violence. Everyone's paranoid—everyone thinks he's being cheated or there's an informer in the group. That's why I never dealt in drugs except as a courier.

As for Jim, he's the only one who knows exactly where Lyons's body is. He's involved in narcotics and he's a police informer. In October 1982 I found out that he was stopped by police at Blind River, Ontario, near Sault Saint Marie. He was carrying a high-powered rifle, a .357 Magnum revolver, and two pictures of me, as well as a quantity of cocaine. He told police he was on his way to see a man both of us knew in Sault Saint Marie, a town where I was supposed to appear two days later, on October 21, to testify in a mob extortion case. The police couldn't prove anything, but I've always been certain that he was there to kill me as part of a contract. There was also another motive. By killing me he would eliminate one of the few remaining people who could identify him as a participant in the Lyons disappearance.

I told the RCMP about Jim and the Lyons murder and where I believe Lyons was buried, but they never did anything about it, probably because Jim was working for them on other cases.

To stop questions about Lyons, Foote and members of the club spread the word that Lyons had taken off for Vancouver. Nobody ever questioned that. His only relatives that I knew about were his mom and dad, and they didn't know he was dead until I talked. He was never close to them, so they didn't ask questions either.

The only real danger to Foote or gang members was Lyons's girlfriend. They sold his big Harley-Davidson motorcycle and some other belongings, gave her the money, and told her to take off and keep her mouth shut. They bought her off cheap. She knew he was dead, but she never talked. She never knew that club member Mike Everet, who is now doing four years for dealing in drugs and having illegal guns, took the diamond and gold rings from Lyons's fingers to wear himself. Any doubts I might have had about honor among thieves were laid to rest right then.

Foote used to keep large quantities of explosives in a warehouse he had in Scarborough. If they'd all gone off at one time, he'd probably have blown half the town up. He didn't just keep dynamite there. He had C-4 plastic explosives and all kinds of timing devices. It was impressive. Most of it was stolen.

By the time I met Foote I knew something about explosives, but not a helluva lot. I'd learned a little from a gang member we called Rupert, who showed me how to handle dynamite and put blasting caps in with fuses. The fuses I'd used with Rupert were crude, made with gunpowder. I learned to figure, by the length of the fuse, how long it would be before the spark reached the percussion blasting cap to explode the dynamite. The trouble was, some fuses burned faster than others, and that could be a real hazard.

I remember my first experience with a bombing device came with the Twelfth Division of the Metropolitan Toronto Police Force. I was with a biker named Jesse, who had a real buzz on for the coppers and wanted to throw some dynamite through the window of the division's headquarters. I talked him out of it. I had visions of a bunch of coppers being blown up and our becoming the object of a continentwide manhunt. It would have been a disaster. The alternative I got him to agree to was to let me throw the bomb he'd made at the rear wall of the division. He waited in his car for me to do the job.

He had a full stick of dynamite, but I cut it in half and used a fuse of less than a foot. I put it in a bag, lit the fuse, and threw it at the cement wall. It never quite made it to the wall, because as I threw it a cop drove up. I just turned and started running. It went off faster than expected—while I was still running across a nearby field about a minute later. The whole incident was hushed up by the cops, who never reported it to the newspapers. They never caught either of us. The bomb only blew a hole in the ground. But before now only a handful of cops and bikers knew that Satan's Choice members had tried to blow up Metro's Twelfth Division.

Foote's instructions eliminated a lot of the risk. I wouldn't have to run like a deer to escape the effects of a bomb because he taught me about different timing devices—how to hook explosives up to alarm clocks, how to use pressure switches to set off bombs, how to set mercury switches. He gave me a lot of on-the-job training with all the different types of switches and bombs. He constantly reminded me, "Remember, Cec. In this business, your first mistake is always your last mistake—you never get a second chance." I found that wasn't necessarily true. I made a number of mistakes in rigging bombs and I survived, but I admit I was damned lucky.

Foote had a lot of sophisticated bombing techniques that he'd used successfully, but I learned some on my own through studying various books. Without Foote's instructions—and he spent three years on and off teaching me the ropes with various devices at the warehouse, in isolated areas outside Toronto, and while doing safecracking jobs—I would never have been equipped to do the kind of extortion bombings I had to do later on. A lot of the techniques he taught me I used later when Cosimo Commisso and his buddies hired me to intimidate rivals and contractors who stood in their way.

The use of explosives was really a sideline of Foote's. Crime in every form was where he was at. It didn't matter if the victim was a friend or a former business associate. One of those associates was a tough bodyguard for a businessman Foote dealt with and sometimes worked for. The bodyguard had been busted for selling hot diamonds without telling the businessman he was supposed to be protecting. So the businessman decided to teach his bodyguard a lesson, and he used Foote as the teacher.

Foote told me that the businessman had told him his bodyguard had a lot of money stashed in his house and that if we broke in at a certain time we could keep all we found. So we cased the house for a few nights and finally broke in. We even waited for the bodyguard to come home. Foote wanted to grab him and beat the hell out of him until he told us where the stash was. So we sat and sat and sat—for six hours we sat and the bodyguard didn't show.

Finally Foote said to hell with it. But he wasn't about to leave empty-handed. He took statues, collectibles, rifles, anything he thought he could peddle for a few bucks. Then, at his direction, we wrecked the house—a really beautiful, expensive place. The final touch was left for the dining room, where the bodyguard had this costly mahogany table that was so polished you could see your face in it. Foote was always calling this bodyguard a "rat," so while I stood with him, he took a knife and carved the word *rat* in the middle of the table. Then he looked up at some antique paintings on the wall and he slashed them to shreds.

There was a weird smirk on his face as he finished slashing. "That'll teach the son-of-a-bitch for not bein' around to show us his stash," he said with a chuckle. "This'll drive him wild." When Foote saw his businessman friend the next day, he told him what had happened, and the businessman gave us each $100 because we didn't get as much as he'd promised us.

Foote was finally killed in 1975 by another close friend of mine and his, biker John Harvey. Harvey's about thirty-two now. He has a long record of convictions for obstructing justice, theft, assault, possession of stolen property, and manslaughter. The manslaughter conviction came in April 1977, and was the result of Foote's shooting.

Both Harvey and Foote, as members of Satan's Choice, were dealing speed [methamphetamines] that had been manufactured in one of the club's secret drug labs. The speed, sometimes called Canadian Blue, was popular with bikers and other street people both in Canada and the States. The Choice labs, for a long while, were among the chief drug suppliers for the stateside Outlaw gang.

An argument over a split on the take in one of their drug deals led to Foote's death. Harvey told me that Foote suddenly went wild as they argued, shouting, "I'm gonna kill you just like I killed Lyons." Harvey said he walked up to his apartment and got his gun, a .38 caliber revolver that I'd sold him about a year before. It was one of several guns I sold bikers and rounders that were later used in homicides. Harvey said he then walked downstairs to an apartment that Satan's Choice was leasing. Foote was there. Harvey shot him once in the chest but it didn't stop Foote. He just kept coming at him. Harvey had to shoot him two more times before he stopped him and killed him.

There were three other members of the Choice in the room at the time. Harvey ran back upstairs and dropped the gun in a hole in the wall near the stairs. The cops investigated the shooting, and three weeks later Harvey was charged with murder. He got two consecutive two-year jail terms for manslaughter instead of a life murder rap because he had a smart lawyer. Besides, in Canada you don't get much for doing a bad guy. Harvey's attorney, Clayton Ruby, had painted a pretty black picture of John Foote the criminal.

* * *

Clubhouse of Assassins I

Murder was almost a way of life for members of motorcycle gangs. The same summer I saw Lyons's body in the trunk of Foote's car, I saw two members of Satan's Choice stuff the body of a young white male into the trunk of a car at the Choice clubhouse in Toronto. The kid—he was in his early twenties—was a victim of club discipline, a discipline that says if you testify about club members being involved in crimes, expect to get killed.

People who want to testify against outlaw bikers—whether they are Outlaws in Florida, Hell's Angels in New York or California, or Pagans in Philadelphia or Long Island—can expect to be the targets of intimidation, beatings, or even murder. This kid had been warned to keep his mouth shut, but instead he told the cops about the two club members who were involved in an armed robbery and a drug rip-off attempt in Collingwood, a small town outside Toronto.

When I arrived at the clubhouse I saw two bikers and club members, Mike Everet and Armand Sanguigni, putting the kid's body into the trunk of a car. Sanguigni told me that they had picked the kid up at a well-known motorcycle shop run by a Choice member. They shoved him into the car and drove away. When I saw him he was gagged, his hands and legs were tied up with rope, and he wasn't moving. He'd had the hell beaten out of him by those involved in the drug rip-off. He'd apparently lived through the beating, so they decided to silence him permanently. One of those involved injected battery acid into his arm. By the time I saw him he was dead.

I found out from Sanguigni, who was killed himself several years later, that he and Everet took the kid to Peterborough. From there Howard Berry and another biker took the body to Rice Lake and dumped it in. They didn't do the job right. They anchored him when they dropped him in the lake, but he still had air in his lungs. A few days later, the body broke loose from the weights and bobbed to the surface. The cops raided the clubhouse in Toronto and the Peterborough clubhouse in hopes of finding evidence. They didn't get what they were looking for, and no one was charged with killing the witness. It's still listed as an unsolved homicide.

Intimidation of witnesses has been a technique that outlaw bikers have used for a long time both in the United States and Canada. Most of the bikers I knew, whether they were in Toronto or Fort Lauderdale, had long criminal records but very few convictions. The reason was simple. They all used threats and bribery and beatings to make witnesses disappear. Sometimes witnesses ended up like that guy in Rice Lake, but more often than not it was the fear of what bikers might do that made witnesses lose their memories or take long vacations.

Back in 1974, I stabbed a guy during a fight in a bar in Toronto's West End. I had been in there drinking with a girl when about ten Indians started mouthing off. They were high on firewater. A couple of them shouted something at the girl, so I calmly got up, walked over to them, and motioned to them, saying, "You, outside. Not just one of you—all of you fuckin' assholes—all of you outside!"

The first guy I said something to followed me, and as I got out the door, I wheeled and stabbed him right in the gut the first time, and in the chest the second time. He stood there, dumbfounded for a minute, then he stumbled back and fell into the arms of some of his buddies, who by then had all started to come storming out the door to take me on. I started fighting like a wild man.

I had a baseball bat in my van in the parking lot. I made a dash for the van, got the bat out, and began dealing with it. Two other guys in the tavern who knew me came out to help me fight the mob of Indians—three of us against ten.

I remember one of the Indians shouted, "Oh, you think you're tough with a bat, eh?"

I said, "Yeah, I'm tough—you take the bat," and I gave it to him. I beat the hell out of him without the bat, and within two minutes I had the bat back and I was working some other Indians over. And the guy I'd stabbed had returned to fight some more.

Two weeks later the cops charged me with assault and wounding. They had four witnesses against me. One of the Indian's girlfriends had gotten the license number of my van before I took off.

It took a little doing, but I found out where the witnesses lived and paid them a visit. "Look," I said, "here's two hundred dollars. Take a vacation around court time." So the guy I stabbed, his girlfriend, and the rest of his family took off just before I had to be in court.

When I did appear to face the charges, the cop that had filed the complaint took the stand and testified that the witnesses had disappeared. The Crown prosecutor explained to the judge, "Your Honor, we're going to have to drop the charges. We can't find the witnesses to subpoena them." Then he added, looking over at me, "And I don't think I will ever find them." He made it sound as if I'd killed them and dumped them somewhere. He thought he was making me look bad by that. But the judge dismissed the charges because there was no evidence, and by intimating I'd killed the witnesses, the prosecutor had added to bikers' mystique among the general public. After hearing or reading that, who in his right mind would testify against Cecil Kirby, outlaw biker—or any outlaw biker?

The more intimidation is used, the more it adds to outlaw bikers' prestige, despite what cops try to do to stop it. A lot of members of outlaw gangs joined to become part of that intimidation, to scare people on the street in a group because they couldn't do it by themselves. They didn't have the guts. They also figured it was a way of getting girls. For some reason broads flocked to outlaw bikers, to become part of that atmosphere of fear and violence.

There were others who used the gangs as a cover for narcotics operations. A lot of independent narcotics operators get ripped off—are robbed of their money and their narcotics stashes—because they aren't members of Mafia gangs or outlaw biker gangs or Colombian mobs, or some other group. So some of these independent drug dealers joined the bikers or teamed up with a biker gang. It was sort of an insurance policy. The premium was splitting some of the profits with the gang. But more often than not, many of these independents wound up getting killed or ripped off by the bikers who were supposed to be giving them protection. The money is big and the greed is bigger.

4

Clubhouse of Assassins II

One of the earliest criminal ventures I got into when I joined Satan's Choice was safecracking. I learned the business after I transferred from the Toronto chapter to the Richmond Hill chapter, where I met two brothers, Duke and Chuck Bernard. Chuck was an expert safecracker who had spent half his life in jails in Dorchester and Kingston.

I didn't know the first thing about cracking a safe when I met them, but it wasn't long before I realized that not only was Chuck an expert but he had someone who was tipping him off about the places to hit. Sometimes it was an employee of the company he hit, who wanted a quick buck. Sometimes it was a girlfriend who worked in the place or knew someone who worked there. Sometimes it was a deliveryman or a salesman who told him what to look for or that the company kept more cash than usual in the safe on certain nights or on weekends. Whatever information he could get he used to his advantage. I learned that technique, as well as others, from him. I also learned safecracking isn't the most risk-free criminal activity to get involved in.

My first job with Chuck was a bearing company in Malton, Ontario. We cased the place for a couple of days first. By that I mean we found a way to gain access either by applying for work, posing as deliverymen or salesmen, or shopping in the area. The idea was to see where the safe was located, to find out what type it was, and to check out the burglar alarm systems. We'd also carefully find out if there were guards or dogs and when they might be around. If a place looked too well protected, we'd pass.

The bearing company wasn't, and we got $1,500. On that job I was "keeping six." That's a safecracker's code name for someone who is assigned to watch at a window for cops or to check out and deactivate any alarm system that might screw up the job. While one man is keeping six, two others are either peeling or blowing the safe.

In the more than dozen jobs I went on with Chuck, we almost always went through the roof to bypass the alarm system. We'd use a fireman's ax and a railway bar to cut through the roof. Most roofs were made of sheet metal that was easy to cut open. The exceptions were wooden roofs, which took a lot longer to break through.

We already knew the whereabouts of any alarms. Once inside, we'd either deactivate or bypass the alarm, then we'd turn the safe over on its front and cut the back open with an ax. That's called peeling the safe. The safes that we picked to work on were generally made of the same material—sheet metal on the outside, three inches of asbestos rock with wire mesh after that, and then one more sheet of metal and you're inside. At least most of the time. A notable exception was a safe we hit at a market named Food City in the town of Oakville.

When we cased the Food City job we noticed that there was a wire going into the safe, but we figured it was just a door wire. Although I didn't have Chuck's experience, I had a funny feeling about the wire. As Chuck started cutting the wood away around the safe, I told him not to hit it.

"Let's use a torch this time," I said. "I got a feeling there might be a sensor inside there, or a bugged line."

Chuck and another member of our B&E Team didn't listen. They hit the safe and suddenly all hell broke loose. Alarms went off at the safe. We grabbed our equipment and ran like hell out the fire door. More alarms went off. They were going off everywhere. We ran to the yard behind the store, jumped into our car, and saw the cops coming. There was no way we could outrun them on the road, so we pulled the car into a nearby driveway and lay down on the seats while the cops came past us from every direction. Then, while the cops searched the area, we drove off quietly—unseen and empty-handed—but at least not heading for the jail house.

None of the safes we hit, including the Food City safe, was solid steel. They were all the cheap sheet metal safes that could be peeled with the ax through either the back or the top. We never went through the front door of the safe. That would have taken too long unless we were using explosives, as I did once at a restaurant with Foote. Peeling a safe took at the most twelve or fifteen minutes.

Weather very often played an important role in planning a job. We did most of the jobs when it was raining or there was a snowstorm. We hit restaurants, supermarkets, catering establishments, and bakeries. In the dozen jobs we did, we got maybe a total of $32,000. It wasn't very profitable, but it gave us pocket money. With all the new technology and alarm systems, safecrackers are a dying breed. It just isn't worth taking the risks.

The job I remember best was the Community Credit Union in Collingwood in early September 1971. I remember it for two reasons. First, it was the first safe job that I was convicted for. Second, Collingwood was a community where I had left a lasting impression as a biker.

I had cased the place pretty well. I'd walked in and, using a phony name, asked an employee about opening an account. He took me to the safe to show me how secure my money would be. The safe he showed me was a Dominion Safe, about five feet high and four feet long. There were obviously no alarm wires going to it, but there was a silent system for tellers to alert police to a holdup. Later in the day I went around back and cut the telephone wires going into the place. My mistake and that of my partners was not noticing that there was someone in the area when I did that.

Chuck and I sat in a grocery store parking lot and watched to see if the police came after I cut the wires. Nothing happened, so we figured it was safe. We came back that night and broke in through a basement window in the rear of the building. Then we went upstairs. There were no wires on the window then, but you can bet there are now—it's really bugged today. Anyhow, we rolled the safe over into the corner and peeled it apart with fire axes and a big crowbar. It was just like opening a can with a big can opener.

We were expecting to find a lot more money than we did. We opened all the cash boxes in the safe, and all that was inside was $5,000. There was a lower part to the safe where I was sure there was a lot more money, but we'd already been in the place fifteen minutes, and we couldn't spend more time breaking that drawer open.

A few days later, I was arrested. My lawyer told me that it was a tough case to beat and that I'd be better off pleading guilty.

"The most you'll get is six months," he said. He was right. I had been charged with break and entry and theft, but my lawyer cut a deal and I pleaded guilty to willful damage of a public improvement—cutting the telephone wires. I got a year's probation. The copper that charged me with the job was furious.

"You get the hell out of this town, Kirby," he shouted, "and don't you ever fuckin' come back. I'm sick of you and all your biker cronies."

He had good reason to be sick of me. A year before I'd partied with some Satan's Choice gang members and gotten a little high. I told them I was going to make Collingwood remember the Choice. So I got a bucket of special paint, went to the top of the town's tallest water tower, and, standing on the railing, painted "Satan's Choice" all over the tower. Next to it I added, "Fuck the World."

I don't know why, but it took about three years before they painted it over. For all that time, every daylight hour the people who lived and worked in that town had to look at "Satan's Choice—Fuck the World." It drove the police chief crazy. He knew I'd done it, but he couldn't prove it. He couldn't even remove it. All he could do was look at it and fume and listen to angry residents.

Between safe jobs and other crimes, I was moving up in the organizational structure of Satan's Choice, first in the Toronto chapter and then in the Richmond Hill branch. In my first year as a member, I was made road captain, a very important post in any outlaw biker gang. It's the road captain who, with the chapter president and other officers, is responsible for mapping out the route that the members are to follow when they go to a function. He also has to ride up and down the line of bikes to keep them in formation, divert traffic, and stop it at intersections if necessary. The road captain always rides up front, at the left side of the chapter president. To do all that, you've really got to know how to handle a bike, and you have to move at speeds of up to eighty to ninety MPH. Later on I also acted as sergeant at arms—a sort of enforcer who walks around with a baseball bat or some other instrument to whack guys in the head when they get out of order at club meetings. And I was vice president of the Richmond Hill chapter. But it was as road captain that I got my spurs in field events.

Field events are competitions where outlaw biker club members who aren't warring get together in the States, Canada, Australia, or Europe to test their skills as cyclists. They are also times when bikers have a helluva party. They get drunk or stoned, they play cards and gamble, and sometimes they tear up the nearest town if they're not properly welcomed. For the most part, though, field events are chances to test your skills as a biker and have a good time.

Field events would be advertised a month or two ahead of time. Flyers would be sent to all the outlaw clubs: the Vagabonds, the Outlaws, Hell's Angels, the Crossbreeds, Satan's Choice, the Paradice Riders, or a half dozen other clubs in the United States and Canada. Tickets would be sold at five bucks each to get in, and the sponsoring club would sell beer and hot dogs through the day. Sometimes there would be a party the night before on the location, sometimes the night after.

On the day of the competition, there'd be ten or twelve events, and trophies for first and second places. The events were in two classes, an A class for Harley-Davidson motorcycles with 1,200-cubic-centimeter motors, and a B class for the smaller bikes, 500 to 750 cc. There were competitions for individuals and for teams. There were drag races for a quarter mile or less; there was the body pickup race, where we had to race to one end of the field, pick up a passenger, and race to the other end.

One of the most popular events was called the balloon race, where each biker had a passenger with a balloon tied around his neck or his back and a paper baseball bat. Bikers would ride around in circles while their passengers tried to destroy the balloons of others with the bats. The last biker and passenger with a balloon were the winners. Very often people got hurt in these events because there'd be twenty, thirty, or more bikes whirling around in a cloud of dust running into each other. If you had a grudge against someone from another club, this event would give you a chance to smack him right in the teeth and just about knock him out. Many a fight between outlaw clubs began this way.

The most controversial event of all, however, was the chicken race. It got the Animal Humane Society all over us—they stopped the race for a while when they found out what we were doing. The event called for a live chicken or turkey at one end of the field and the bikers at the other. Everyone would race up, and the passenger on each bike would jump off and try to grab the chicken or turkey, which was staked out and, of course, alive. Whoever came back with the biggest piece of the bird or the whole bird was declared the winner. Very few chickens or turkeys survived. They were usually torn apart by the bikers' passengers, who'd return to the finish line covered with blood.

Then for laughs there was a shit race. We'd put a golf ball in a bag of manure, usually pig or cow shit. Bikers were to race into the field, and the first one to find the ball and come back with it was the winner. I remember seeing one guy come back with the ball in his mouth. There were some real weirdos in those competitions.

Of course, there were the power turn races, where you lean your bike over and go around in circles, tearing up the ground with your wheels in high-speed turns. I won a couple of those.

As good as some bikers were, they often watched in awe when my father would ride a motorcycle. Dad didn't like the outlaw club, but he accepted the fact that I was a member and that I loved motorcycle riding. He gave me the love of biking. I can't remember when he didn't have at least three or four bikes around the yard.

When I was very young, about ten years old, he used to sit me in front of him on the gas tank of the bike. Then one day, as we were riding like the wind, he shouted in my ear, "Cecil, you want to hold the handlebars?" I nodded excitedly and he added, "We'll go down the street—now hold the handlebars and keep the bike up." I was excited, steering the bike for the first time, sure that the whole of Weston was watching me. They weren't. I looked behind me and there was Dad, standing on his head on the rear of the seat.

He used to tell me that when he was younger he rode his bike down Dundas Street, a main thoroughfare of Toronto, where they had streetcar tracks. He said he'd lock the throttle, get on the side of the bike, put his feet on the steel rail, and slide along with the bike pulling him. He was also a great one for riding his bike along the river in the wintertime. He'd put his ice skates on and ride with his bike beside him. He was young and crazy and he loved daredevil riding.

*   *   *

In Canada or the United States, the theft of motorcycles is a major problem for insurance companies and law enforcement. Almost every biker I knew or met from Fort Lauderdale to Toronto had a stolen Harley-Davidson or was using parts from one to keep his bike running. It's big business for outlaw bikers, who not only steal parts but sell the parts from stolen bikes through motorcycle shops they own in nearly every community where bikers operate. In fact, the theft of motorcycles got so bad in Manitoba that insurance plans there will not include theft coverage for bikes.

The best of the outlaw biker thieves was Bob Gray of the Paradice Riders. He was about six feet four, 250 pounds, and extremely strong. He also had a very loud mouth. At a party he was always the center of attention. As loud as he was, he had the stealth of a fox approaching a henhouse when he was supplying speed to Outlaws and Choice members or stealing motorcycles. I don't think there was anyone in the States or in Canada who had ever successfully heisted as many motorcycles as Gray had.

For a time I helped him steal motorcycles. I was a piker next to him. In my lifetime as a biker, I stole maybe thirty or forty motorcycles. That might be a month's work for him when he was moving around. As good a thief as he was, if you were his partner in a deal, you had to watch him. Greed would go to his head. He'd take the gold out of your tooth if you kept your mouth open too long. I learned to keep my eye on him in any deal after he slid one by me at a pop festival in 1971.

The festival was being held at Rock Hill. By the time I got there, Gray had already stolen one bike. That was no small trick when you consider that police covered every entrance and exit. It seemed like hundreds of coppers from the Ontario Provincial Police were there. When I saw Gray he was looking for a way to get the bike off the festival grounds without having the coppers inspect it and discover it was stolen. He said he wasn't the only one who'd stolen a bike, that a biker called Al from Satan's Choice had also taken one.

"Look, Bob," I said, "wait here awhile while I think of a way to get you and the bike outta here."

"Okay," he said, "you figure a way and we split what I get."

So I checked out the grounds and found a barn near the entrance. When no one was looking, I set the barn on fire and returned to where Gray was. By that time the flames were roaring into the sky, smoke was curling overhead, and people were yelling and screaming while the coppers and firemen raced to put the fire out.

I hopped on my bike and shouted to Gray, "Bob, you follow me with that bike, right now."

He was laughing like hell. "Cec, you're a pisser," he shouted, started the bike, and roared off behind me.

When we got to the gate, the coppers were just waving everybody through. They didn't stop anyone. There was too much confusion. Right behind us was the Choice biker, Al, with his stolen bike, but he decided not to follow us. "I'll take it out later," he said. The next morning he tried to get the bike out and was stopped and charged with bike theft.

Now Gray and I couldn't get far because there wasn't enough gas in the stolen cycle, so Gray had to abandon it at the National Park on Airport Road that night.

"I'll go back and get it later," he said, hopping on the back of my bike.

Two or three days later, when I saw him again, I asked about the bike. He said he'd gone back and found it gone. I shrugged and didn't think much of it until another Paradice Rider, Warren Smith, who had been in a prison reformatory with me, told me about some bikes he'd stolen.

"You know I went with Bob Gray out to this park on Airport Road one day and damned if he didn't come up with a Harley he'd hidden in the bush there that he said he'd stolen at the festival."

So Gray had ripped me off. He'd gotten the bike, sold it, and kept everything for himself.

I remember one day we were in a suburb of Toronto

together when he saw a Harley sitting in a guy's driveway. The poor guy was cleaning the bike, and Gray went over and watched him working for a minute and then he began talking to him. Suddenly the bike owner left to get something. As soon as he entered the house, Gray was on his bike and gone like the wind.

Gray had other techniques, too. He used to read the newspapers like a hawk to see what bikes were on sale. When he found one that interested him, he'd visit the seller and convince him that he should take it for a test drive. That would be the last that seller ever saw of the bike.

Gray would even steal stolen bikes from the guys who sold him bike parts that he'd stolen in the first place. Like Charles (Chuck) Yanover, who in 1970 was just a small-time hood like the rest of us. He owned the City Custom Cycle Co. in Toronto and from there sold stolen bike parts that bikers brought to him. Later he was convicted of theft and possession of fifty stolen motorcycles, charges that resulted in two and a half years in jail. At the time, Gray was selling him hot bikes, I was, dozens of guys were. I remember I stole a brand-new Triumph with only ten miles on it. I took it apart and sold the damn engine to him for only forty dollars. He was making a fortune on the deals, and bikers were getting ripped off when they sold to him.

One day, Gray decided to steal Yanover's personal bike. Yanover went bonkers. He ran screaming to the police, who were laughing so hard they were crying when they took his theft report. I ended up with the bike. A member of the Richmond Hill Satan's Choice sold it to me. Then Gray came to me and said he could make even more money and get back at Yanover for chiseling us on other bike deals. Together we stripped the bike and sold it, piece by piece, back to Yanover. We sold him all but the front end. When we were through Gray told him he'd been buying back pieces of his own bike. Yanover didn't say a word. His face was red as a beet, but he didn't say a word. About five years later, I showed him a bike I was riding and pointed to the front end. "There's your front end, Chuck," I said with a chuckle. He didn't think it was funny but he didn't say anything—just walked away.

Stealing motorcycles, I learned, was one of the easiest rackets around. It was also very profitable. On the average we'd get $800 to $1,000 a bike if we didn't have to take it apart. If we stripped it and sold it for parts we'd get more than double—$2,000 to $3,000, depending on who we were dealing with. Harleys were selling at from $6,000 to $7,000 apiece new then.

To steal a bike, the most important thing to do is case the area—map out the easiest and safest routes of escape, check out neighborhoods to prevent being spotted, and watch the bike owner to see how careless he is.

A lot of bikes were spotted through newspaper classifieds, or at motorcycle shops, or in neighborhoods where we knew bikers hung out. Once we spotted a bike, we'd take a couple of days to case the area and then drive up in our van. We had a big set of bolt cutters in the van that could cut any chain or lock that could be used on a bike. We'd break the lock, usually at night, wheel the bike down the street quietly, and put it in the waiting van.

Sometimes there were close calls. The owner of a bike I'd selected to steal in Richmond Hill came home earlier than expected and I got jammed between his car and the bike. I slid underneath his car to hide. When he walked by I could have grabbed his foot, that's how close he was to me. He went into the house. Within seconds I was out from under that car, on his bike, starting it, and taking off.

When we stripped a bike, we'd usually sell the parts to other outlaw club members. Fenders, gas tanks, windshields—there was always someone in the biker gangs who needed parts for his bike, and we could get those parts faster than a shop could, even one that had the franchises for Harley-Davidsons and Triumphs.

Among the popular items were cylinder heads. Everybody looked for cylinder heads. We sold ours to a motorcycle shop owner named Sissy, who gave us top dollar and would buy all we could lay our hands on. And we kept our own spare parts shop in a garage in Richmond Hill.

I preferred selling the bikes as is, without stripping them. It was a pain in the ass to strip a Harley. It could take eight hours, and my back would be killing me afterward. Some bikes, smaller ones, might take only four hours, but it was still back-breaking work. A lot of the time was consumed pounding the identification numbers away with a ball-peen hammer or drilling the numbers out, then placing an aluminum weld over the hole and stamping the casing with new numbers.

When we did a strip job—and most biker clubs wherever they are do this—we took the bikes apart right down to their nuts and bolts. We'd drill the numbers out of the transmission casings, out of the frame, and sometimes out of the engine casings. Most of the time we'd throw away the engine casings because it was too difficult to get the numbers off them. When it was too much trouble to drill off the numbers of the engine or transmission, we'd take them to a lake or a construction site and dump them. For those we kept we'd weld over the numbers, grind the weld down, and leave it like that, selling it to someone who was making a customized bike, who was willing to put the motor over the frame numbers, and who knew he was getting a hot product but didn't ask questions and paid the price. Or, when possible, we'd restamp the engine casing, which was made of aluminum, and repaint the part.

Sometimes we felt the theft hadn't been reported, so we'd send someone down to the local police department saying they were interested in buying the bike and asking them to check the numbers of the bike on their hot list to make sure it wasn't stolen. If it wasn't listed, we'd get a document from the police to show that the numbers had been checked and therefore the bike couldn't be stolen.

There were also insurance scams. Brothers in one club would report a theft while the other would cannibalize the bike, rebuild it, and sell it as a home-built bike. They'd get the $8,000 insurance claim for theft and the sale price of the home-built, maybe $4,000 to $5,000. Some of the Harleys were valued at as much as $12,000, and the insurance companies paid off. I made thousands that way. I also landed in Guelph Reformatory in 1972 with some other bikers because we'd stolen motorcycles from a cycle shop.

Guelph Reformatory is a medium-security prison about sixty miles west of Toronto. It's not the worst prison in the Canadian system and it's not the best. The food was terrible and they made you work hard on the bush gang. The bush gang is a bastardized version of the southern U.S. prison chain gang, only without the chains. It got the name *bush* because heavily guarded prisoners worked in cedar brush and forests in parks owned by the Ontario provincial government.

The prisoners had to cut down the cedar trees, parts of which were sectioned off into fence post sizes and sent back to the reformatory, where other prisoners stripped them. Other parts of the trees were stripped, finished and formed, and made into picnic tables, which, in turn, were sent back to Ontario's parks.

When I started on the bush gang, I wasn't the strongest guy around, but working with axes and saws, and lifting the trees started to build me up. It also gave me some incentive to work out with weights with another Satan's Choice member, John Murdoch. When I started I couldn't press much more than 120 pounds. By the time I left Guelph less than a year later, I was pressing nearly 330 pounds. I was also ready—through associations I'd made at the prison with other outlaw bikers—to graduate to the higher and more violent levels of crime.

5

Girls for Sale

Girls are as much a part of outlaw biker life as are drugs and violence, and they are probably our weakest link. They often carry our guns, hide our drugs, front for our businesses, gather information for us about cops and other bikers or places we want to rob, and act as our couriers in drug deals and other crimes. That gives them access to a lot of evidence that could put members of biker clubs in jail. So cops do their damnedest to get the girls to talk. Bikers often kill some of the women to protect themselves, because they think they have become or might become informers.

That's one of the reasons many girls—some of them from Canada—disappeared or were tortured and murdered in Florida by members of the Outlaws. The cops would find them in pieces, or crucified, or they'd just never find anything because the bodies were dumped in the Everglades, where the animals finished them off.

Girls disappeared for other reasons, too. Sometimes they had worked as prostitutes and dancers in topless bars too long—became too old and used physically at sixteen and seventeen and eighteen. Others tried to run away from the club members who owned them. Some cheated on the money they were supposed to turn over, and some just weren't making enough money.

Girls for Sale

I can't say if any of them were actually killed by Satan's Choice bikers, or the Paradice Riders or Vagabonds or other Toronto gangs. I didn't see any killed, but I know a lot disappeared across the border and haven't been seen or heard from since. A copper I know once said to me that there was no way of knowing how many women disappeared from Canada in white slavery and were killed. "It's like trying to document missing children," he said. "They're just swallowed up in the traffic and there's no one around to trace them."

He was right. Bikers from the Canadian clubs were selling girls for from $500 to $2,000 apiece across the border. A biker just had to make the right arrangements in the States and deliver the girl to the border, and members from the Outlaws, Satan's Escorts, or some other gang would take over. Some of the girls were as ugly as sin or so spaced out they never knew where they were, but they brought bucks to the bikers, who made them work for still more bucks. "If they got four limbs and a hole they're worth money," a biker friend of mine once said.

The Outlaws are one of the two biggest cycle gangs in the United States, and they're now very big in Canada. In the 1970s they were our allies and they used to come to Canada to buy drugs from members of Satan's Choice. They also bought and sold weapons, bought and sold counterfeit money, and bought some of our women. Sometimes the women were given to the Outlaws to hustle in their body rub shops [massage parlors] and topless bars in Florida and Chicago.

The public thinks we get most of our broads through fear or rape or kidnapping. That's what the media likes to play up—the kidnapping of some girl who's held captive and raped by all the gang members. Well, there is some of that, but for the most part bikers don't need to grab women off the street and rape them—the women flock to them like bees to honey. That's the truth.

Biker women are worse than rock star groupies. Most of them come asking for sex and companionship and to be someone's "old lady." They have no families or they're on drugs, and they need money. So what happens to them happens to them. Their families don't even care enough to tell the cops they're missing.

In 1970 a lot of bikers hung around the Yorkville Village, one of a number of hippie hangouts. The girls hanging around clubs like that always needed money to buy dope. So a lot of the bikers, myself included, would show these girls where to go and hook, peddle their bodies.

We'd send them to special hotels and bars on Front Street or on Charles Street, where there were a lot of men looking for action. They were told that they had to give us a percentage of what they made to guarantee protection from pimps. Some guys took 50 percent, some guys took it all and gave the girls drugs to keep them working. When the girls weren't making enough money for them, or when they said they wanted to go on a trip with their biker pimp-boyfriend, they'd be taken to the border and sold to some other biker gang member. The Outlaws or other gangs would use them for a while and either sell them again or kill them because they'd seen or heard too much.

Satan's Escorts members would come to Canada to socialize a lot with members of Satan's Choice. Some of the Choice members would set them up with girls to take back to the States. They'd just deal them to the Escorts as a favor or sell them for as little as $100 or $200. Some of the broads were sold a bill of goods—promises of a vacation, a trip to sunny Florida, a good time. "Work for them [the Escorts]," the Choice bikers would say, "and come back in six months if you want." They were conned. I never saw one of them come back and dozens of them left.

It worked in reverse, too. There were times when the Escorts and Outlaws sent American girls to Canada to work for Canadian biker clubs. A lot of them disappeared, too.

I wasn't any better than the rest of the bikers who had their own stables of girls working for them. I didn't sell any of the girls that worked for me and I only took 20 percent from them, but I was pretty much doing the same thing as everyone else. I had four girls working for me at one time, but I only did it for six months.

On good weeks the girls were pulling down from $200 to $500 a day each, and I was collecting from $200 to $800 a day. That wasn't every day of the week—maybe three or four, but it was a nice income. Plus there were some fringe benefits, like making love to them.

I was making it with all of them—sure I was. I'd have been a fool if I didn't. I'm human and I don't need to rape some broad to get what I want. But they were a pain in the ass with their jealousy, and after a few months I got tired of it and just had one working for me. The others took off.

I didn't chase them down, beat the hell out of them, and make them go back to work for me like most of the bikers would have. What was the sense? If they don't want to work for you they don't want to work for you and they weren't really working for me. I was their insurance policy.

Now some of the other bikers were hustling the girls, really pimping for them, and I didn't like that. I wasn't about to hustle tricks for some broad. That's why I took a small percentage. I was just giving them protection, not drumming up business for them. I wasn't a pimp. If anybody tried to beat them up or rip them off, I'd catch up with the guy and beat the hell out of him.

I remember one of my girls was a really gorgeous blonde called Cindy. She was about twenty-three. She wasn't a hippie, just a good-looking woman who wanted to hustle for a buck. I met her in Cedar Beach, where she was working at the hotel. Cindy was drinking at this bar when I picked her up. We started talking, and before long she told me she wanted to leave waitressing and get back into being a hooker. I told her I knew some good spots she could work, spots some of my other ladies worked.

Cindy went right to work. I'd drive her downtown and drop her off at the places where she'd pick up the johns and work them. She had trouble only once. One of her johns beat her up. She called me and I found out who he was. I called him at his home. His wife answered the phone.

"I got some business with your husband," I said, "lemme talk to him."

She didn't argue or give any excuse that he wasn't there, just called him to the phone. When he got on, I said, "Friend, you got a choice. I can talk to you or I can talk to your wife about the girl you went out with last night." He didn't answer. So I continued talking. "I'm her boyfriend. You can come out and talk to me privately or I can come to your house and talk—and your wife can hear it all. Either way."

"No, no, no!" he said excitedly. "I'll come."

"Okay," I answered. "Meet me at the North Hill parking lot and bring some money. Come alone if you're smart."

He hung up and met me where I'd told him I'd be. I got into his car, grabbed him by the collar, and put a gun up to the side of his head.

"You beat my girl up when you got through," I said, "and you didn't even pay her, louse. Give me the two hundred dollars."

He was shaking as he handed me the money. Right then I punched him hard in the jaw. You could hear it crack. I left him lying there and drove away. I never heard a word from him. Neither did Cindy. I gave her all but fifty bucks.

The hippies turned hooker were always high, always having problems with some john or pimp who wanted to muscle them, and I'd have to come in at all hours of the day and night to settle the problem. All the bikers did.

There were a number of guys in the biker clubs who would pick up one or two girls hanging around the streets near the Yorkville Village, bring them back to the clubhouse nearby, put some clothes on them, and send them back out on the street. When the girls would come back, the bikers would take some of the money from them, give them some dope, and send them back out on the street again. It was real easy. The bikers just had to give them some dope. To pay for the dope these hippies, some of them were fifteen, sixteen, some older, had to work the streets.

Some professional pimps, mostly black, tried to take the girls over by beating them up and hassling them. We didn't have that kind of trouble too often though. The pimps knew the girls were protected by the bikers, and they would stay away. They didn't want the trouble.

Some of the bikers weren't satisfied with shaking down the hippies and regular prostys for their street money and free lays. They had a thing about taking women off the street or grabbing them in the clubhouse and raping them, getting clubhouse gang bangs going.

When we were hanging around the Villager and the women were all doped up on the street, some gang members would grab them, drag them back to the clubhouse, and start screwing them. Before long everybody in the clubhouse was joining in. Sometimes members cut loose their own women and let them get raped. Very few girls who were raped ever went to the cops.

One was attacked by two brothers and a biker they called Larry. The brothers said that some girls had told them to stop and see them. So we stopped at an apartment and one of the brothers went in and came out about a half hour later. We left without anyone saying a word.

Two days later I was driving around and I got stopped by the police for indecent assault. I said, hey, what the hell is this all about? The cops asked me was I with Larry and these two brothers when they assaulted a woman in a Keele Street apartment. I didn't know what the hell they were talking about, but I found out. The brother that had come out of the apartment like nothing had happened didn't tell any of us he'd raped the woman. We were kept in jail for two weeks without bail. When we went back to court, the case had been withdrawn. I don't know who did it, but somebody got to her—threatened her life, I guess— and she withdrew the charges.

I knew one biker in prison like that. We called him

Nutty. His real name was Gary. If he found a broad in the biker clubhouse alone, he'd rape her—you could count on it. Almost 99 percent of the rapes that took place in the clubhouse in Richmond Hill involved him.

I know there's been a lot of talk about bikers that have forced cars off the road and attacked women and entire families. In all the time I was a biker I can only remember once when it happened and Nutty was involved. He forced a whole carload of girls off the road and grabbed one of them and threw her on his bike. She just thought she was going for a ride, but she ended up being thrown in a biker's car and getting screwed by about twenty guys.

The sale of women and drugs between the Outlaws of the United States and Canada's Satan's Choice really heated up in the 1970s. When I first met and visited with a lot of the top Outlaw members in Florida in 1974 and 1975, they weren't as big as they are today, but they were every bit as tough. They hated the Hell's Angels as much then as they do now. The war between those two gangs— the two biggest in the world—has been going on for more than twenty years, and wherever they rumble across the same turf, bodies drop. I guess more than one hundred on both sides have been killed either in Canada or the United States in various "battles."

I went to Florida to meet some of the Outlaws with "Mother," then the national president of Satan's Choice. Mother's real name was Garnet McKuen, and he was about thirty years old. He was from Saint Catharines and had six convictions, including an assault on a cop and being caught with narcotics. With us was Drago Salajko of the Choice's Kitchener chapter.

In Miami we were treated like royalty by the president of the Outlaws, Big Jim Nolan. He and a guy named Pete of the Outlaws' Hollywood, Florida chapter picked us up and drove us to Nolan's house in Hollywood in a specially equipped van. The house was small, nothing impressive, but it was like a fortress. It was a two-bedroom bungalow that was very efficiently protected by

the latest in alarm systems. Big Jim had two huge Great
Danes who would just as soon chew you into pieces as
look at you. He always had a handgun in the living room,
and there were two or more high-powered rifles in other
rooms of the house.

Two girls were living there, one who worked in a
body rub place and was Big Jim's special girlfriend, the
other a broad who just worked and hustled for him. It
seemed to me at the time that almost every broad associated
with the Outlaws worked in body rub parlors, or topless
joints, screwing anyone and everyone willing to pay the
price. All the money they made went back to Outlaw
members like Big Jim, who provided them with places to
live, clothes, food, booze, and whatever drugs they wanted
within reason.

The Outlaws were making a fortune off women. They
had the body rub parlors and topless bars from Orlando to
Fort Lauderdale, in Chicago, and all across the country,
and they had an endless supply of women who danced and
worked as prostitutes. Those broads, hundreds of them,
were bringing in as much as $2,000 to $3,000 a week each.

Big Jim was an impressive man with an impressive
reputation. Only a few months before I met him he had
been accused of ordering the execution of three Hell's
Angels enforcers. He'd had them shotgunned to death in
April 1974. Their bodies were found in Fort Lauderdale,
face down at the water's edge, with their hands tied
behind their backs and cement blocks tied to their feet.

There were stories that Big Jim had personally skinned
other Hell's Angels alive. He certainly was big enough and
tough enough to do a job like that if he wanted to. He
stood about six feet eight in his stocking feet and weighed
about 250 pounds. Whether his reputation was true or
not—and he wasn't convicted on either story but for
something else—I found him to be a nice guy. It was
obvious he had lots of money—profits from the hustle of
his broads and from the sale of drugs by the club. On
every finger he had rings of all shapes and sizes—all gold

and diamonds, some big, some medium, but all expensive as hell.

Mother, Drago, and I stayed at his place for two days before moving on. Whatever we wanted we got, whether it was booze, women, or drugs. All the while we were there so was Big Jim's trusted bodyguard Pete, who roamed around the house carrying a fourteen-shot Browning semiautomatic handgun.

We were given the "honor" of attending the Outlaws' club meeting that week, but there wasn't much to it. It was short and sweet and to the point. Nolan introduced us to the membership and told them to treat us like we were one of their own. They did. We also got to see a clubhouse they had just rented and were rearranging. All the windows had been bricked in. Two bricks were left out of each at the middle as gun ports. They also had rattlesnakes around the place to keep out any unwelcome strangers.

In the time we were there, I met and talked to about ten Outlaws other than Nolan and Pete. They looked and acted like stone killers. They were really crude- and cruel-looking guys, let me tell you. They put a chill in your spine just lookin' at them.

After a few days we went to Key West with some of the Outlaws. We stopped at a house that was owned by their former national president, a guy they called Surfer, who I had met once before at a field day in Kitchener. While we fished, Surfer told me he had a job teaching school there.

Surfer was forty and he'd retired as a biker, but he entertained any of the Outlaws and their friends when they came through. I suspected the retirement was only partial. I figured they were moving things like guns and drugs through his area. They had plenty of bucks, those Outlaws. Some of them had to be millionaires with the kind of places they lived in and the businesses they owned.

Just before I left Florida I had a talk with Big Jim about bringing some girls from Canada with me the next time I traveled south.

"Can you get them jobs in your body rub shops?" I asked.

He burst out laughing. "You mean the massage parlors?" he answered. "Sure. You're welcome to come back anytime with any of your girls. I'll get them jobs, and you'll make plenty of money."

I tried to get a couple of the girls across the border in my van with one of my bikes, but I was turned back by immigration agents. I should have worked something out with one of Big Jim's people, but I wasn't trying to sell these girls. I just wanted them to work for me in Florida while I took it easy. It wasn't worth it to keep trying. I didn't want to get busted on some stateside white slavery rap.

Mother had a few broads that he'd shipped there from Canada to work in the joints the Outlaws controlled. One of them was named Cindy. A few months after I left, I found out she had died in a fire in a body rub place. When Mother came back he was a little shook up over it, but he never explained what had happened. We all figured she probably had seen something she wasn't supposed to see.

The last thing I heard about Big Jim was that he had come to Canada to have members of Satan's Choice hide him while he ducked a warrant. They eventually caught him and returned him to the States, where he was convicted and sentenced to a double-life jail term.

Some of the evidence and testimony that helped send Big Jim to jail came from a Canadian member of the Outlaws, a kid named Willy Edson, who had been one of Big Jim's enforcers. Before Edson became a protected federal witness in the States, he was supposed to have been one of the Outlaws who worked out a deal to supply the Chicago Mafia with women for its topless joints and body rub parlors.

When the law came after Edson, he hid in a number of Outlaw chapters in the States. Then they smuggled him across the border and hid him in Canada at Satan's Choice chapters in Windsor, Kitchener, and Montreal. Choice members gave him phony new identification, weapons, and a radio to monitor police calls, but he got caught going to a liquor store in Kitchener and was deported.

In November 1982 there was a trial of some Outlaws and their business associates in Chicago. Five were convicted, including Robert Burroughs, a Canadian biker and drug supplier for the Chicago Outlaws. Burroughs worked for the president of the Outlaws' Chicago chapter, Thomas Stimac, who was also jailed in the case. Stimac, who was a friend of Big Jim and knew a lot of Choice bikers, was identified at the trial as one of those who met with members of the Chicago mobs way back in 1977.

One of the women the Outlaws had supplied to the mob was named Betty Darlene Callahan. She'd been kidnapped in North Carolina when her boyfriend didn't come up with money he owed the Outlaws for drugs. After killing her boyfriend, they raped her and forced her to become a prostitute for them in Chicago. Her story was like that of a lot of girls. The big difference was the Callahan woman became a protected federal witness like Edson. She was able to testify about the Outlaws handling millions of dollars in cocaine, marijuana, and Canadian Blues because she'd been around long enough to see a lot and she remembered. When she got her chance to make a break and talk to the feds, she did. It saved her life. If Stimac or the others had had even a hint of what she was going to do, they'd have killed her. Like I said before, women are the weak link of bikers.

6

Nothing Is Secret

If the police want to know what outlaw biker gangs are doing or what biker is dealing dope or stolen goods or women, they usually turn to their special biker squads. The squads have informers on the street and in biker gangs. The biker squad cops talk to street people—like pimps, prostitutes, burglars, bartenders, gamblers, and nightclub owners—people who see and deal with bikers regularly.

The information they gather from these people usually can't be used in a court of law. It's not evidence. It's what they call raw intelligence. That's hearsay stuff that can provide valuable leads to dope pushers, bookie joints, holdups, burglary rings, and extortions. It can even prevent murders or stop gang fights, or it can help cops find guys that are hiding out. Intelligence is what makes biker squads and other special police units tick. Without it, police wouldn't know a damned thing about bikers, or any other crime group for that matter. It's their eyes and ears on crime.

While cops use intelligence to catch crooks, bikers have their own intelligence system to help them survive on the street. The bikers' system is probably better than the one the cops have because bikers can do things illegally to get information about what the cops are up to.

We needed intelligence to keep tabs on each other as well as the cops. The truth is that there is very little trust among outlaw biker gangs and even among bikers in the same clubhouse. Yesterday's friend may be tomorrow's enemy, and it's best you have a record on him. When you know more about your enemy than he does about you, you win battles and you win wars between gangs. While the cops were using us, we were using the cops to get information and to eliminate our enemies either through firefights or the cops themselves. All biker gangs did the same thing. The Choice, the Outlaws, and Hell's Angels were the best at the intelligence game in Canada and in the States.

One of the best intelligence sources we had in Satan's Choice was one who had access to the Canadian police computer. Gary Cuomo of the Choice had acquired that source. Club members carried her number around in their wallets. All a member would do, if he was worried about the cops, was call her number. She'd access the police computer to see if there were any warrants on him. We could also see if there were outstanding fugitive warrants on rival gang members when we'd spot them. If there were, we'd have someone in the club call the cops and tip them off to where the rival gang member was and who was with him. We could also check out anyone's criminal record through that computer. That helped us spot people from rival gangs or from the cops trying to infiltrate us.

Biker clubs used the sergeant at arms to rap with cops and pump them. Sometimes we used club members cops had hassled a lot. The cops figured they had them hooked, afraid that they were going to go to jail. Whoever they were, they'd been told by club officers to cozy up to cops to get information, even if it meant giving some up themselves.

While the cops were pushing those bikers for information, the bikers were using them to find out who the cops were looking for, what bikers were in trouble, where cops were concentrating their power—all kinds of tidbits that would help bikers avoid arrests or other trouble with the cops.

For quite a while, members of Satan's Choice had a gal working in the police dispatch office of the Ontario Provincial Police. She tipped us for years about things like when they were going to raid a biker clubhouse or homes. A lot of guys were able to skip out before raids. Large amounts of guns and drugs were moved and hidden because of tips we got from her.

There were other ways we would gather intelligence. One of the most important was through pictures. Bikers were forever taking pictures of each other. They took them at parties screwing broads; they took them when they were high on drugs; they took them at field events and at funerals—pictures, pictures, pictures. They filled album after album of bikers. They filled desk drawers and closets in clubhouses. Cops grabbed them on raids and more pictures were taken. Why?

Pictures are a record of what a guy looks like. Descriptions are never adequate—they can't fill the bill like a picture can. If the day comes that you want to have a guy hit, and you need an outsider to get next to him, what's better—a picture or a description?

I had been looking for a former member of the Toronto Outlaws. The Last Chance club members hid him out. They wouldn't turn him over, and I was unable to break into their clubhouse because they had it secured so well. So I did the next best thing. I took a bat and smashed the windows of four of their cars, bending some of the fenders as well.

The Last Chance bikers never forgot. They had pictures of me that they'd gotten at a field event or some other affair. They had one picture enlarged and, I'm told, it now hangs in their clubhouse with big block letters saying, "Wanted, Dead or Alive—Reward $200,000."

Many outlaw bikers in Canada and the States have pictures of me in their clubhouses or in their wallets. That way they can recognize me if they spot me and inform club members so a death squad can come after me. There are a lot of pictures of every biker in every club floating around. Someday they may be used the way the Last Chance bikers and other clubs are using my pictures.

Every biker club has its friends, its associates and hangers-on, people the cops like to call their support group. The cops say that for every biker there are ten support group members that help them. I think they are low on the estimate. It's a lot more than ten.

When I was a biker some of that so-called support group were citizens we used to get us inside information. Some held key government jobs where they had access to special and sensitive information. Like in the Driver Suspension Branch of the Department of Transportation. For years, I have had a source there who could go to the computer and check out auto license numbers. It was helpful. We were able to identify RCMP unmarked cars and other people who were doing surveillances on us that way.

I never overused that source, and it never cost me that much. Cops would like to think big bribes are paid for such information. It's just not so. I used to have plate numbers checked out maybe twice a month, and all it cost me was a bottle of good booze. My source was just a good friend. You don't really have to pay off good friends.

My government source has been a lifesaver for me, even today. If I didn't have a source like that, I'd be in a lot of trouble, particularly if there was someone tailing me or watching my house to set me up for a hit. I could call cops I know who are supposed to be available to help me in an emergency. By the time I got to them, if I could find them, and had them check out numbers like that, I could be dead. It takes them a helluva lot longer to do a license check than it does me.

I wasn't the only biker with a source in the Department of Transportation. There were bikers from the Vagabonds, Satan's Choice, the Paradice Riders, and other gangs who had girlfriends or associates that either worked in the department or had contacts there. In one instance, the wife of one of the Choice bikers was working in a government office. The cops found out about it and had her fired. But since there were other wives of members working in that office, the cops didn't stop the flow of information.

What information we couldn't get from corrupt government employees we sometimes got from people we dealt with in banks, and Bell Canada, the telephone company. My banking source, for example, could check the records of any bank to find out how much some guy or gal had in his or her accounts. Information like that was very useful when I wanted to set up an extortion or put pressure on someone to take on a "new partner." It also gave me a way of finding out if a guy was really what he said he was in business. It stopped a lot of ringers from slipping through the cracks.

The tipster I had in Bell Canada was equally important. She could provide me with any unlisted telephone number in Canada within two hours after it was activated. She could get me the numbers and the addresses of people I wanted to check out. That made her very valuable, particularly when I wanted to harass or threaten someone in an extortion or when I wanted to be sure that I had the right address for a bombing target. A number of bikers that I know of had sources in Bell Canada. Some provided the information because they liked the biker, others because they were paid, and still others because they were afraid the biker would hurt them or their families.

Very often bikers need new identification—like driver's licenses and credit cards—to hide from the cops or just to run up tabs on somebody else's credit. While I was a biker, one of my best sources was a Canadian postal worker. He could come up with driver's licenses and major credit cards—like American Express, Visa, and MasterCard—whenever I needed them. he'd snatch them from the mails for me, and all he wanted for his troubles was a bottle of whiskey. Sometimes there were bonuses of twenty dollars for a credit card and fifty dollars for a license, but that was it.

At one time I had five different driver's licenses. I can't count the credit cards I got from him and used to buy thousands of dollars' worth of goods. Scores of other bikers had similar sources, who could get them the documents they needed for identity changes. Hell, we supplied other bikers, many from the States, with licenses and credit cards and other identity documents that they needed to hide from the cops.

There were other biker sources who gave up information for some drugs, like cocaine or speed or Quaaludes. Still others wanted to be entertained by women, and that's something all biker clubs had plenty of—women who did what they were told. Whatever the price, the bikers in every club had information networks that kept them aware of what the cops were doing and who they were looking for and what rival biker gangs were up to.

To hide from cops or rival gang members you needed more than new identities. Just as important were places to hide—safe houses. Every gang had safe houses, safe harbors, or cool-off areas that wanted gang members could hide out in.

Because of our relationship with the Outlaws in the States, members of the Choice had places they could hide out in North Carolina, Georgia, Florida, Tennessee, Indiana, Illinois, and in the Southwest. The Outlaws, in turn, could smuggle their "hot" gang members into Canada to hide in our safe houses in Richmond Hill, in Concord, or up in the remote areas of the North, where we owned farmhouses and other places under the names of people who fronted for us.

I recall one Choice member who was easily identifiable because of his tatoos. We called him Charlie Brown, but that wasn't his real name. Mother, who was a tatoo expert, changed all his tatoos. The club even got him a job for a transfer company in Saint Catharines and told him to keep a low profile and stay away from the clubhouse.

Charlie Brown did what he was told and stayed

hidden for a long time. It was as though he had disappeared from the face of the earth. Charlie finally broke the rules and was eventually caught and sent back to the States, where he was wanted for a number of crimes. If he had paid attention to the rules, the cops would still be looking for him. We knew every move the cops made in trying to find him through people we had who kept tabs on car dispatches, fugitive warrants, and police computer information.

Howard Berry of the Choice's Peterborough chapter was wanted in Ontario for shooting a guy in Peterborough at point-blank range with a .303 caliber rifle. Needless to say, the guy he shot died, so Berry took off. He was smuggled across the border and went to Georgia and a safe house of the Outlaws. I heard later Berry was tested by the Georgia Outlaws to see how tough he was. They beat him up once, but not before he'd beaten the hell out of some of them. They accepted him after that.

Berry had always been tough—one of the toughest of the Choice. But in Georgia he went bananas. He got involved in some homicides with the Outlaws, and he was charged with stealing military equipment—automatic weapons and a tank—from an army base. When the cops grabbed him, they found he was wanted in Canada for the shooting and he was deported. He got eight years. Like Charlie Brown, he didn't stay cool, so the cops caught him. I guess nobody can stay cooped up in safe houses for long. Bikers got to be out doing things—usually bad—and that leads to their downfall.

PART TWO

Hustling with the Rounders

7

World of the Rounders

Between the violent, undisciplined life of the outlaw biker gang and the secrecy and tradition of the Calabrian Mafia is a strange, independent criminal world the public knows little or nothing about—the world of the rounder. It's a world I grew close to early in my life as a biker and later as an enforcer–hit man for Calabrians like the Commissos.

In a sense, Canada's rounders are like the criminals that police in the States call crime associates, of the Cosa Nostra or the Mafia. They operate independently in gambling and loan-sharking, they set up dope deals and hijackings, and they sell their services to organized groups like the Mafia. In Canada the rounders, unlike stateside crime associates, don't owe allegiance to anybody but themselves, and they deal with all types of organized groups, whether Chinese tongs and triads, outlaw bikers, or Calabrian and Sicilian Mafia crime families.

The term *rounder* has been used in Canada for the last twenty years or more. A rounder is really a street person who knows hundreds of other people that operate around bars and clubs, that sell dope, gamble, and deal in stolen or hijacked goods. Rounders always dress well. No matter where you go, whether it's a high-class or average hotel, whether you barhop, whether you go to the best clubs, you'll find a rounder or maybe several, and you'll always find them in classy, expensive clothes.

They are the people with connections. They're rough, they're tough, and they know where to get the things you need and want. At one of the better bars, Joe the Rounder can get you a pound of grass at a moment's notice, if you got the money and if someone's vouched for you. And there's Ken the Rounder at one of the class hotel discos. If you come with the right word and enough money, he can hustle up an ounce or more of coke faster than you can reach for your wallet.

Rounders answer to no one—not to the Commisso brothers, not to Paul Volpe when he was alive, not to Vincent Cotroni before he died, not to Danny Mo of Toronto's Kung Lok Triad before he went to jail for robbery, not to members of Satan's Choice or Hell's Angels or any other gang. They answer to themselves. They're on the street to make money and to survive. They deal with other street people, but it's their connections—for guns, for drugs, for women, for gambling, and for stolen goods—that make them important to the criminal world.

Go to a racetrack where everybody seems to know each other and you'll see little cliques there, groups of ten guys or less hanging around, working out deals. These are the people that the Italian mobs would come to see if they wanted to find out something. They are the people that the cycle gangs would go to to learn about jobs, or places to deal speed, or people to unload guns and counterfeit currency with. They are the guys who can cut deals for anyone and everyone. They all think they know people in the mob. A lot do and a lot more don't, but they shoot the shit about it, and when push comes to shove they use the right connects to get the job done.

Rounders would rather stay away from bikers, but they can't because a lot of them were bikers before they became rounders.

One of the toughest rounders I ever knew was Andy the Rounder. He and two of his fellow rounders, a guy they called Bobby and a black man named Billy, were tough enough to take on eight of the toughest members of the Toronto chapter of Satan's Choice in a bar called The Trick. The Choice bikers dragged them into the parking lot, beat them and then ran over one or two of them. Andy kept on fighting, even though he was outnumbered four or five to one. He really mauled one of the bikers—broke his jaw with just one punch. When he got through wrecking him, Andy went after a biker who had tried to run him down. The biker finally escaped, but not before Andy had smashed the car's windows and windshield with his fists.

Andy the Rounder was about five foot nine and about 170 pounds with curly, blond hair. Sometimes he wore a beard and sometimes he was clean shaven, but he was always dressed in a suit or slacks with a sharp shirt and he was always neat. I personally found out how tough he was at a hotel up at Wasaga Beach. I was there with another rounder, who was a sort of friend and business associate, when I heard some loud yelling in a hotel across the street. I went over to see what was going on. I saw that the guy who was screaming all kinds of curse words at Andy was a member of the Toronto Choice.

Right then and there I should have turned around, walked back into the hotel, and minded my own business. I didn't, and suddenly the Choice biker jumped Andy, knocked him down, and began pounding his head on the floor. My rounder friend decided to help Andy. The next thing I knew I was in the middle. A friend of Andy's decided I was the enemy and took a swing at me. I knocked him out. Then Andy turned and came after me. He said something I didn't like, and I hit him as hard as I could—knocked him down. He got right up and I knocked him down again. This time I kicked him in the head to keep him down. It was like kicking a block of wood.

Whew! What a guy! No matter how many times I knocked him down, he got up. Now we were in the street, and cars were roaring by, and we were still swinging. I grabbed him and tried to push his head into the wheel of a car. It didn't work. By then the cops were on the scene, and Andy was fighting them.

I saw no point in hanging around. I took off to get away from the cops. What set Andy off that night? He just didn't like bikers, and he was in the hotel drinking when some members of the Toronto Choice came in. He decided he was going to fight them.

Funny thing. About a year after that brawl, Andy started hanging around with some members of the Choice that I knew, and they began bringing him to the clubhouse, where he started to make some friends. By then he had calmed down and was busy making dope deals with the bikers. He was handling a pound of speed and more at a clip that he bought from a biker who'd been a rounder and had organized a drug ring that manufactured hundreds of pounds of speed, selling it at $8,000 a pound.

Andy and the more important rounders during the late 1970s hung out at one of the bars at the Hyatt Hotel. The Hyatt bar was popular with the rounders because one of them, a guy I'll call Roger, had two waitresses working for him. Their job was to spot trouble, usually in the form of cops trying to slip in undercover. When they spotted the cops or any other people who might be there to cause trouble, they were to tip him off. He, in turn, would tell us and the rounders he dealt with so we could cool any deals we had working before the coppers got onto us. Only Roger knew who the waitresses were.

Roger controlled the distribution of cocaine to rounders at that club. It wasn't unusual to see a dozen or more rounders meet with Roger to make multiounce buys. Sometimes they'd buy even more. Sometimes Roger the Rounder was a buyer instead of a seller, particularly when it came to speed. He could handle two, three, or more pounds at a time. He wanted pure speed, not speed that had been stepped on, or cut.

Roger's demand for pure speed and the willingness of Satan's Choice lab suppliers to deliver it to him were what eventually brought a lot of heat down on everyone, costing a lot of people some really big money. Roger drew the attention of some crooked narcotics investigators. Eventually they caught him with a big load of the pure speed.

Instead of busting him, they took his supply as a patch or payoff and said good-bye. It was the beginning of a lot of patches for dope dealers after that. A patch means they took your proceeds from crime—like drugs, or illegal guns, or gamblers' money—and kept it and you said nothing about what they did if you wanted to stay out of jail.

Roger kept his mouth shut and took the loss as part of the cost of business. Later on, he went to jail on another big speed bust. Other dealers—most of them rounders—had the same business expenses, since the narcs started hustling everyone.

These payoffs went on for years in the 1970s. The favored technique was to hit a gambler or a drug dealer with a minor summary charge that could land him six months or more in jail. If the Rounder gave the narcs the patch without any trouble, they would either drop the charge in court or they'd make sure he got probation or a fine with no jail sentence. That way they covered their asses on the bust and no one was the wiser. It wasn't only narcs pulling that scam—there were other coppers involved, and none of them ever got caught to my knowledge.

One of those who had to shut his mouth about a patch was Jim Lyons before he was murdered. His patch was a little different from some of the others. He had been charged with assault and was facing a long jail sentence. One day some coppers told him they could help him out if he came up with six handguns for them. Lyons didn't have them, but he went to a lot of his friends to get them. I supplied him with a .357 Magnum, a brand-new one I had just gotten. Other bikers gave him some other handguns. I helped him put the handguns in a sandbox on the side of Woodbine Avenue, as he was told to by the cops. Then we sat back where nobody could spot us and watched the cops drive up and put the guns in their unmarked car. The charges against Lyons were dropped a short time later.

I recall one time when I was charged with a break and entry. The guy I had with me had picked the wrong place to hit—the home of a cop's sister. Someone spotted us leaving the house and got the license number of the car we were driving. Two weeks later I was arrested. That was the day I found out that the house I'd hit was that of the arresting cop's sister. Now this cop was no graft taker. He wasn't looking for a patch, but he played the same kind of game that some of the patch takers did.

"You know the house you broke into was my sister's," the cop said.

"No, I didn't know, honest," I replied.

"No, eh?" he grunted. "Well listen to me, Cec. You just make sure that everything you took gets back. If you do, I'll see to it the charges get dropped."

I got the message loud and clear. As soon as I got out of the courthouse, I gathered all the stuff that we'd taken and put it in a plastic bag. Then I placed it on the side of the road in front of an old Satan's Choice clubhouse and called the detective involved. He picked it up. A few days later I appeared in court in Richmond Hill and the charges were dropped. The detective told the judge that the police had no way of identifying me with the case and that, as a result, they wanted to withdraw the charge. And that's what the judge did.

A little over two years ago that detective was killed while he was on patrol. He was gunned down in front of a warehouse where somebody was involved in a break and entry. I was sorry to hear about that. He was a decent cop—one I could trust. He had given his word to me and when I delivered he kept his end of the bargain. He wasn't a crook. He just stretched the rules a bit to help his sister.

There were a lot of rules we played by with the cops that were unusual. There were times, for example, when we—whether we were bikers, rounders, or Mafia hoods—got caught cold turkey on a crime and we'd try to cut a deal through our attorneys before the preliminary hearing. We might want to plead guilty and take a six-month sentence rather than face a long jail term or an extended trial that cost a lot of money and took us out of circulation for a long time.

One time, six members of Satan's Choice and myself were charged with break and entry and the theft of motorcycles and other stolen property, including a handgun. I wasn't there when the cops raided the Choice garage and found the stolen motorcycle parts, but I got charged with a couple of deals. To make sure they'd nail me, the cops took my handgun, which they'd found in the raid, and wrote my name on the back of the holster. Our attorney told all of us after the preliminary hearing that we were cooked—that we'd better make a deal before the case went to a higher court for trial. If we fought it, we'd get a minimum two years in the pen. If we didn't fight it, we'd get between four and six months each.

It was clear to all of us we couldn't beat the charges. What evidence the cops didn't get they'd rigged. So we made the deal and I got six months.

One of the most active areas for rounders was and still is Toronto's Airport strip, an area filled with bars, motels, and hotels. There were several popular hangouts there in those days—Attilla's Cave at the Hilton Hotel and the Skyline Hotel—where most of the gambler rounders used to hang their hats.

One of the most active was Walter (Wally) Chomski, a professional gambler–loan shark who worked with a Greek gambler who always made sure Wally won in the high-stakes card games at the Skyline. Chomski and the gambler rounders worked a strictly nighttime operation, ending their games at five or six in the morning, after $50,000 or more had changed hands.

For a long time Chomski was close to Johnny (Pops) Papalia, one of Ontario's most important crime bosses. While he was operating around the Skyline and other rounder hangouts, Chomski got in some heavy trouble with Johnny Pops. The word among the rounders was that he owed Johnny Pops a lot of money. The next thing I knew, in December 1974, Chomski had his right leg torn off when a bomb that had been planted in his Lincoln Continental exploded. The cops said the force of the explosion ripped the transmission loose and sent it up through the car, tearing up Chomski's leg.

They never solved the bombing. There were too many suspects, they said, and no one was talking, least of all Chomski. I heard he took care of his problem, whatever it was. He must have. He was allowed to keep operating, and he had no more trouble with the mob. In 1984 he and his son were arrested on charges of running a $750,000-a-year loan-shark operation.

There were a number of rounder gambler operations going every night. Chomski and his partner might work the Skyline on a given night, while other groups of two to four rounders would be working games at the Cambridge Hotel across the street.

There were also other groups working games at banquet halls like the Casa Commisso, where one of the Commissos' uncles controlled the action. The uncle knew all the cardsharps, and sometimes he'd let them in, and sometimes he wouldn't. When he did, he'd tell them that they had to pay a kickback on all their winnings to the Commissos. Then he'd let the suckers sit down and get taken—all but his close friends and relatives.

The gambling rounders had games all over town—at the Royal York, the Care Inn, the Holiday Inn, the Bristol Palace Hotel, and the Constellation. Their general routine was to hang out in the hotel bars or the coffee shops to make their connections. They weren't big drinkers because they had to keep their minds on business. They didn't cut deals with the hotel employees or management because they didn't want to share their money with anyone. They trusted no one. I've seen them, after they'd played cards, search each other to see if they were cheating. It was crazy.

To set up their games, they'd get rooms to play in, sometimes through hotel security people, who they did pay off to make sure they weren't raided or ripped off. They would target particular hotels when they knew there were to be big banquets or conventions or stag dinners. Some of the rounders were members of Kiwanis, the Lions Club, the Rotary, and through those memberships they would get lists of upcoming events to hit. They would know a week or two ahead of time where to go for the action, whether it was Ottawa, Montreal, Saint Catharines, Niagara Falls, Saint Thomas, or London.

No matter where the gambling rounders played, they rigged the games, set the gaff. They always had a gaff for something. They used dice that were mercury loaded. The heat from their hands would make the mercury set on the numbers they wanted to turn up. Sometimes they switched dice so fast no one spotted what they were doing.

I remember one rounder playing a high-stakes dice game at the Beverly Hills Hotel in Toronto. He was throwing the dice out and everyone was losing. It was about 2:00 A.M. when he rolled the dice again, and this time three of the suckers came clicking out. His hands moved like greased lightning. He grabbed the fuckin' things so fast no one else noticed, but I saw it and I thought to myself—oh shit, nobody saw it because they were too busy drinking. He was palming two dice as he threw out dice to make the number he wanted, and that once, one of those palmed dice slipped.

There was a game where they spun a top. The way the rounder spun it he always won. The sucker always spun it the wrong way and lost. The cards were rarely marked. They didn't have to be. The rounders dealing could make any card they wanted come up, and I defy anyone to spot what they were doing.

One event stands out in my memory above all others. It happened on the Mariposa Boat, a place owned by Don Pressey, one of the Commissos' associates. The event was a stag party for a rounder named George.

George was one of several guys who had robbed a bank in Winchester more than fifteen years before, getting more than a million bucks in cash, money that was for the payroll of the Windsor racetrack. George and his friends were caught after they tied up all the bank employees. So he went to jail. When he was paroled, he was broke, so the rounders of Toronto decided to hold a stag and raise money to give him a new start.

At the time, I was working for the Commissos. They knew I was going to work with the rounders to help raise money for George. At the club were a lot of outlaw bikers from Toronto and Kitchener. Among other things, most bikers are degenerate gamblers. They piss their money away in games, and half the time they know those games are rigged. But in this case they didn't believe the games were rigged because I was playing, and I wasn't known to be a gambler—in fact, I had never played poker before.

I sat down at a table with one of the rounders I knew, who had given me some general instructions on how to play. I was sitting in the game for a rounder who couldn't make the party. A number of bikers were playing, among them Ernie, the president of the Toronto chapter of Satan's Choice. He was blowing $500 every hand. So were some others in the game. I just sat there drinking—almost drunk—as the rounders dealt me winner after winner— flushes, full houses, three aces, straights, you name it, I got it. Finally, Ernie stood up and started to leave, but before he did he looked me up and down and shook his head.

"Kirby," he said, "I never seen you play before, but I gotta tell you—you are the luckiest mother I ever saw pick up a card." Then he turned around without another word and left the club. He had dropped more than $4,000 in the game.

That night I won over $10,000. The other rounders in the game dealt me the hands that couldn't lose. They knew no one would suspect it was a crooked game with me as the big winner.

Several times they tried to deal me some losers so it wouldn't look too bad. I almost screwed up their strategy by drawing cards when I wasn't supposed to. A couple of times one of the rounders had to kick me under the table, hard, to make me stop playing bad hands that didn't have a prayer of winning and that I was supposed to fold with or only lose a small amount on.

When the game was all over, I met the rounders and gave them all but $100 of the money I'd won.

"Look," I told them, "just give me a hundred bucks and you keep the rest for George."

They all laughed, shook my hand, and bought me a few drinks. I was supposed to have kept half, but I'd had a helluva lot of fun and they'd really done all the work. It was worth it for me to see some of those bikers get ripped off, especially Ernie. He'd figured he was gonna clean me out in that game. It was worth it all to see the expression on his face when he left with his pockets empty.

Ernie should have known better in the first place. When you gamble with the rounder cardsharps, you'd better check to see if you still got your pants after a game. They can't play without cheating. It's in their blood. They've just gotta have that extra edge—they've gotta get something for nothing.

Ron the Rounder was like that. He was one of the best Italian rounders in the business, and he was an expert at gambling. I met Ron while I was a biker, and we quickly became friends. He had style, Ron did. He did everything with a flair. He made and lost literally millions of dollars in card games from Buffalo and Niagara Falls to Toronto and Montreal. He survived because he was close to the Italian mob, the Cosa Nostra in Buffalo, and the Calabrians in Niagara Falls. He played high-stakes card games with them, but Ron never cheated while playing with his Mafia friends. That's when he lost big sometimes, playing with them. They hustled him but he didn't hustle them. It wasn't healthy.

Because of his close association with the different Italian mob groups, Ron had a lot of action steered his way—suckers the mob dealt with but told him it was okay to work over. Of course, they expected and got a piece of his action.

Sometimes Ron worked the suckers with the best gambler in all of Toronto, Eddie Neuff. I could introduce you to a dozen gambler rounders and they'd all tell you the same thing—before he was killed, Eddie Neuff was *the best*. He was an independent, a rounder, but he lacked the protection some of the rounders like Ron had, who worked with different mobs. Eddie was well known in the States. He'd been barred from a number of casinos in Las Vegas and Atlantic City because he was too quick—a professional counter who could tell you how many aces or how many fives or whatever had been dealt and used that ability to make big bets on hands when the percentages favored him.

One of the suckers that Ron and Neuff really worked over was the owner of a prominent Italian food company in Toronto. The food dealer—I'll call him Giuseppe—was the kind of guy who'd bet on when the next raindrop would fall. He wouldn't listen to anyone—not his brother, not his family, not his friends—he just had to play in the high-stakes card games that Ron and Neuff were operating in a room at the Seaway Hotel.

Ron told me later that he had never played with a sucker for punishment like Giuseppe. Night after night he would show up and play, and each night Ron and Neuff would take him off for $20,000, $50,000, $80,000. It was a dream come true for them.

Then one night Ron told me that Giuseppe had paid off in tens and twenties the night before. "He had a bag full of cash," he said, "and when he left he still was carrying a lot with him, maybe twenty thousand dollars or more."

"Does he keep all that money at home?" I asked.

Ron looked up at the ceiling like he saw a pot of gold on top of the rainbow instead of at the end. He reached into his pocket, took out Giuseppe's address, and handed it to me.

"Why don't you break into his house some night?" he said. "There's a helluva lot of money in there. This guy always pays in cash, and he comes to the game straight from his home." He paused for a minute, letting what he'd said sink in. "You get into his place and sack it and whatever you get just give me half—the rest is yours."

I knew I couldn't handle it alone, so I called a biker friend named Brooks to help me and we headed for Giuseppe's home. No one was there and we broke in. We couldn't have been inside ten minutes when Giuseppe pulled in his driveway. We both ran out the back door, and as we ran Brooks shouted, "Cec, I got some money out of a fuckin' bag—I don't know how much. There was a lot more—but I didn't have time to grab it, goddamnit."

We got back to the car we'd parked near a school and started counting the money. There was over $8,000 in fifty- and one-hundred-dollar bills. We'd missed the big bundle, the big stash, because we hadn't made sure he was gonna be gone for a lot longer before we broke in. I gave Ron $4,000, and Brooks and I split the rest.

Ron laughed when I told him what had happened, but not so hard that he didn't take his cut. Later he told me that every gambling rounder in town tried to get in on the action, get a piece of this food dealer. Ron and Eddie had milked him for hundreds of thousands, but like all good things it came to an end. Giuseppe's family found out he was squandering their profits, and they forced him to stop. Not long after that, Giuseppe died.

Ron was so good that he started to run his own school for card cheats, particularly for some of his Italian mob friends—charging them $100 for each lesson. He got a lot of people hot at him for doing that. It was really stupid. He was teaching newcomers a technique that's supposed to be kept inside the gambler-rounders' organization. There were maybe thirty professional card cheats in the city who worked the big card games. For a lousy $100 a lesson, Ron was giving away the road map to a gold mine.

Neuff, on the other hand, wasn't so lucky. He became the target of a gunslinger rounder friend of mine who had also been a member of Satan's Choice for a while. Neuff ran into this rounder and his sidekick, a biker who was later killed because he knew too much about this particular rounder.

I'll have to call the rounder Billy and his sidekick Al. Billy the Rounder has a number of convictions, but none of them is for murder. He doesn't leave witnesses around. He's been involved in one way or another in at least six killings, but he always slips through the cracks. They never nailed him for the Neuff case. There was one guy who could have nailed him for Neuff and for some other cases, and that was Al. He was an eyewitness, but he's not around anymore. The irony is Al wasn't the kind of guy who would have become an informer against Billy. He thought the world revolved around that rounder buddy of his.

For years, the coppers thought that Neuff had crossed some Mafia bigwig or some other big organized crime guy and been knocked off. His body was found January 5, 1979, stuffed in the trunk of a car at the Toronto International Airport. He'd been shot repeatedly. It took four days to thaw out his body at the Metro morgue and figure out how he'd been killed.

The last he was seen alive was in a Toronto restaurant on December 12, 1978. He was supposed to be married three days later. Five years later they found the body of Toronto Mafia boss Paul Volpe shot and stuffed in the trunk of his car at the same airport. For a while some cops speculated that Volpe may have been killed by the same assassin. Maybe he was.

Al told me before he was killed himself that Billy the Rounder did Neuff, and I know he was telling the truth, although I wasn't there to witness it. Seems Al and Billy had a guy in New York who was giving them some terrific tips on football games—on what teams were going to win and by how many points. This guy was right about 90 percent of the time, according to Al. Al said that he and Billy were paying this tipster for his information. He got a kickback on the money they won by taking off all the bookies in Canada with their bets.

For weeks they were having a field day busting out a lot of bookies. One of those they busted took off before paying off thousands of dollars. Billy the Rounder and Al went looking for him. They searched for him at his home, at his clothing store, at all his regular haunts, but he was nowhere to be found.

Billy was furious. "I'm gonna get that bastard, Cec," he shouted one night. "So help me I'm gonna get that little fuck and bury him." I don't know if he did, but he also made one other promise that night. "The next fuckin' bookie that rips me off, I'm gonna fuckin' do him," he said.

Al told me that that next bookie was Neuff. They started betting heavily with him and winning. He smelled a rat and on the last bet wouldn't pay off. So they shot Neuff and dumped him to make an example of him. Bookies throughout Canada understood the message.

While rounders would turn themselves inside out to help a fellow rounder like George, a lot of the rounders I knew had a cheap streak, too. Most of them never paid a bill in a restaurant. They were good at this—really good. They had a technique that few people could follow. All but one of the rounders in a group would leave, and the last guy, the guy with the bill, would walk up to the register. The waitress would be watching him. But he'd stick the bill in his pocket and ask the gal or guy at the register for change for the phone. That was it. He'd be handed the change, the waitress would think he'd paid his bill, and he'd walk to the phone so the person at the register would think he was making a call. They'd stop watching him, and before they realized it he'd be gone. No one would figure it out later, either, because the bill would never turn up to show a cash register shortage.

Rounders, like a lot of outlaw bikers, were also boosters, store thieves who either acted like shoplifters or did the smash-and-grab bit at jewelry stores—smash the front window, grab what they can, and be far from the scene in less than three minutes. Ron was a great booster of Royal Doulton china and figures, and he was good at it.

One of the best smash-and-grab thieves around was a Satan's Choice biker, Armand Sanguigni, who was found dead with his girlfriend on October 15, 1984, from a heroin overdose—a hotshot that someone he trusted had given him. Whoever dosed him figured Armand was a junkie, and junkies sooner or later talk if they can't get their supply of dope. So a friend did Armand. It's always a friend who does you in this business. That's why you try not to trust anyone. Sooner or later, though, we all make that one mistake. I'm trying not to get suckered that way, but you never know.

Sanguigni was Italian. He'd grown up in Toronto's Little Italy. When he wasn't racing around on his bike with members of the Choice, or peddling dope, or hustling counterfeit bills, he was busy boosting from jewelry stores. It was a sideline that he made $3,000 to $4,000 a month at.

Sanguigni wasn't a particularly good fighter, but he sure as hell was no coward. He was only five foot seven in his stocking feet, and I can't remember him ever weighing over 145 pounds, even when he wore a heavy black beard and mustache and his hair long.

Sanguigni was a fast talker, and his main topic was always sports or gambling. He was always at the track when it was open, gabbing with friends and rounders and betting his shirt. One day in 1978 he and a friend of his, a rounder turned biker turned rounder named Kenneth Goobie, came to the house of a friend of the Commissos to pick up some funny money. I was at the house when they made the pickup—$300,000 in counterfeit U.S. twenties. The next day they had sold it all off—peddled it all over Toronto after paying the Commissos fifteen cents on the dollar.

It couldn't have been two days later before there was a story in the paper about the town being flooded with the counterfeits, which became so hot nobody wanted to touch them.

The funny thing was that the counterfeit money had been hot for a couple of years. The Commissos and the Calabrian Mafia had peddled the stuff around New York— particularly in Long Island and Brooklyn. And they'd pushed it in Connecticut through pizza parlors the Calabrian Mafia controlled or could influence.

They moved hundreds of thousands of dollars of the funny money in the States, and they moved a lot of it in Vancouver with the help of the Vancouver mob and an Italian friend of theirs named Carmelo Gallo. In 1976 the roof caved in on that operation because they sold the money to an undercover agent. They were all convicted.

Later Gallo was part of a plot they wanted me to get in on to take down an armored truck in Vancouver that was supposed to be carrying a couple of million bucks. That scam fell through, but Gallo was busted a short time later in an international heroin scheme. He got a life sentence, but he escaped before he could do his time.

For a while things cooled down over the money that Goobie and Sanguigni flooded the market with. But a lot of people—a lot of bikers and rounders—had to sit with thousands of dollars' worth of the phony bills. Andy the Rounder got stuck with a big bundle. Goobie even got burned. He gave $20,000 in bills to a biker they called Jerry, who was a member of the Last Chance. Jerry was supposed to sell it, but he ended up losing it. Rather than face Goobie, he took off.

Goobie tried to hunt him down. I even went with Goobie one night to try and find him. No luck. Goobie did the next best thing. He took Jerry's bike and sold it about a year later. I got about $200 out of the deal.

But that didn't end the tale of the counterfeit twenties. About a year later, in 1979, I did a favor for Cosimo Commisso, and he told me he had some counterfeit money I could have if I wanted it. I thought, what the hell, it's cool now, maybe I can move it and make a quick buck, so I said sure.

"You know, Cec," he said, "that money's been nothing but a pain in the ass. I got pinched with it. Remo, he got pinched with it. Everybody that's touched that fuckin' stuff's been caught."

Cosimo let it sink in. He was letting me know I could land in trouble if I handled the money he was offering me.

"When we first got this stuff," he said, "we had this whole room just piled high with the money. We had about twenty million bucks."

Cosimo didn't say where they had held the money, but he said he had a guy that was still holding $20,000. "You get in your van," he said, "and you drive down to this place on Bloor Street. You park your van in the parking lot, leave your doors unlocked, and take a walk for about an hour. When you come back, the money, she'll be waiting for you. But you be careful when you try to unload. It's jinxed."

I did what he told me, and when I came back the money was there waiting. It was the same kind of funny money that Goobie had gotten. I took it north to a cottage I had and buried it. About a year later I came back to move it. When I dug it up it was soaked, even though I'd wrapped it carefully and put it in a container.

I didn't let a little water discourage me. I took it back to the city, dried it out, and then examined it to see if it could be used. The bills must have been cut by a butcher. Some were short, some were long—it was terrible. I picked up, stacked, and wrapped it and brought it to Ron, who gave me $300 for the whole load. The last time I saw that funny money was in November 1980, when biker Gary Barnes came out of prison. He stopped by my house to say hello and pulled out a roll of the bills.

"For chrissake, Gary," I shouted, "where the hell did you get that shit? Get that crap outta my house. I'm tired of seeing it. It's the same stuff we had years ago."

Gary had gotten the money from Goobie and Sanguigni, who were supposed to be his friends. The trouble was, they didn't tell him how hot the money was.

It couldn't have been a week later when Barnes started passing the money. Somebody took a license number off the car he was using and the cops traced it back to him and busted him. I felt bad about that when I heard it. I liked Barnes. He was a pretty easygoing guy, not the world's smartest, but tough and a stand-up guy, who stood up with you in a tight spot. I remember when I came back from vacation in Acapulco in February 1978—he was sharing a place with me at the time—I had pneumonia. I was with my girlfriend and I drank a bottle of tequila. The next thing I remember was Barnes carrying me into the Humber Memorial Hospital in the West End of Toronto. I probably would have died if he hadn't taken care of me.

8

Call Them Treacherous

Burglary, safecracking, counterfeiting, murder, arson, extortion, prostitution, motorcycle thefts, insurance frauds, gang wars—all of that and more was a part of my everyday life as an outlaw biker. You either live with it, become part of the action, or you don't survive—you become an outcast and sooner or later you become very dead.

At least some of these activities provide a source of income to the biker. But for the biker who was ambitious and wanted to make a bigger buck, moving narcotics was where the real action and the big money were. It was also where the violence could always be found, where gang wars started and where killings were part of the territory.

I first got involved in the narcotics traffic through Ken Goobie. A lot of bikers that I knew dealt in narcotics, but, until I hooked up with Goobie, I'd pretty much steered clear of it except for smoking a reefer now and then. I never thought much of the dope dealers. I still don't. They can't be trusted and Goobie was no exception, although it took me a little longer than usual to realize it.

I first met Goobie in 1970. He was only twenty-two then, but he was big and tough, with a quick and violent temper that had already cost him more than a year in jail for assault. We took an almost immediate liking to each other because, I think, he was such a good fighter, and in those days he backed off to no man. He was six foot, 170 pounds, a little bald on top with long hair down the sides, and he wore a mustache—he was never without that mustache. He had done some amateur boxing, winning two or three matches while fighting at the Lansdown Boxing Club.

He had already earned a reputation as a tough rounder in the downtown area of Toronto, where he battled in bars, dabbled in selling small quantities of dope, ran around with lots of women, and burglarized homes whenever he was broke. He was forever joking around and shadowboxing with everybody in bars and restaurants that he frequented. Behind all that fun loving and kidding around was a cool character who had a brain that was always click-clacking—figuring ways to make a quick buck.

In the beginning, I went on some burglary jobs with him after a friend of mine, a gambler we called Johnny the Hat, told me Goobie was like a cat when it came to pulling a job. He was right. Whenever we were broke, Goobie would come up with some place we could break into that had coin collections or money stashes or some other gimmick. He had good connections who tipped him, and we used them to get some loot to fall back on. It wasn't always wine and women though. There were some tough times. I remember days and weeks when things were so bad moneywise that we slept in the car of another biker because we didn't have enough for a room. But that didn't last long.

In 1972 Goobie, after I'd introduced him to a number of members, decided he wanted to join Satan's Choice. He did his striking period, and within a year he'd stepped up the ladder to become one of the biggest outlaw biker dealers in narcotics. Two of his suppliers were my friends Harry the Hat and Patsy Perry, both gambler-rounders who had connections for large quantities of speed from biker methamphetamine labs on both sides of the border.

Harry the Hat and Perry, who's dead now, could come up with five to ten pounds a week for Goobie, who was paying them $4,500 a pound for the speed and selling it to bikers and rounders, to pimps and prostitutes in the hotels and bars around Toronto's West End for more than $8,000 a pound after he'd diluted it once or twice.

In the early stages of his operation, Armand Sanguigni was Goobie's number-one guy—his trusted courier and distributor. I became his banker and a sometime courier. Many times I would have to take the money that Goobie and Sanguigni were pulling in from the operation to a restaurant to meet Harry the Hat, pay him for dope that had already been sold, and insure future deliveries.

It was an operation with high profits and equally high risks. Typical of those risks was a period when a lot of American money was coming in to pay for drug buys. Goobie told me he and Sanguigni were selling quantities of speed to a rounder and safecracker known as Irish Danny. Danny had some kid working for him named Larry, who was caught by the Horsemen (the RCMP).

The Horsemen turned this kid into an informer, and before long they were buying the narcotics from Goobie and others using American money. Eventually, Harry the Hat, Perry, and Goobie were all busted for trafficking in speed, but Goobie beat the rap. They never got to me, although I was the one with the American money, and I was the one using about ten different banks to convert it to Canadian currency.

The Horsemen never knew, or never had enough evidence to prove I was involved, and they never charged me with anything. By then I was making better than $1,000 a week, which isn't a helluva lot to some big-time cocaine dealer, but in 1973 and 1974 it was more than most of the big industrial executives and politicians were making as salaries, and it was a helluva lot more than any of the Horsemen were making.

It wasn't long after that that the Horsemen got Sanguigni. The day he got nailed he'd been at my apartment. I watched him as he crossed the street to his car. He was throwing a gym bag he carried up in the air like a basketball—higher and higher—playing catch with himself. The bag was filled with speed, better than two pounds.

Call Them Treacherous

As I watched him I remember thinking to myself—what a dummy! He's walking across that goddamned parking lot throwing $13,000 up in the air like it's nothing. He got into his car and he made it almost to the heart of Toronto when the Horsemen stopped him—smashed into him and drove him off the round. That ended his effectiveness as a courier. He got two years in jail for it.

With Sanguigni in jail, I had to do a lot of the courier work for Goobie, and he had to watch over the money. By 1976 he had developed another major source of supply and he was selling big amounts to the Peterborough Satan's Choice, to the Kitchener Choice, and to some of the more trusted rounders, including one I called Roger the Dodger.

I made most of the big deliveries to Roger. I was storing the stuff in a gym that I bought later on and turned into a health club. I used to stash the speed in the boiler room on top of the vents—usually ten pounds or more at a time.

Goobie would make the connection with the buyers and come to the gym to tell me where to meet them. I'd take out the amounts he had sold and deliver them to a drop-off location. I'd make sure the buyers picked it up, but I never took any of the money. Goobie saw to it that they paid him. For every pound I transported I got a lousy one hundred bucks. Goobie was getting ten times that. I was being hustled by Goobie and I knew it, but I wanted the money and I liked the excitement.

Goobie had an almost foolproof system. With one exception, he never touched the dope he was selling. As his courier, I never met the guy who was delivering the loads. That was my insurance policy. Goobie would send me to a place like York University, to a particular garbage can where a bag containing ten or fifteen pounds of the stuff had been dropped. If the cops showed up, all they would see was another bum rifling through a garbage can looking for some chicken parts or something.

Of course I took precautions to be sure I wasn't being followed. Sometimes I'd use different cars for pickups, other times a van. When I made deliveries, they were to people who Goobie or I knew. We never made deliveries to strangers. I had to be confident enough to meet with a buyer. I had to have known him for at least two or three years. When you sell to people you know, it's less likely you're going to get caught. There's always that chance, but it's less likely. The best system in the world is to sell to those you've known a long time. If you're stupid enough to sell to strangers, you might as well go into the cop shop and give yourself up.

The speed we were getting was like a rock. It was being brought from a biker lab to drop-off points where Goobie would be notified it was stashed. Usually it was in a locker at Oakdale, or at the Hillcrest Mall in Richmond Hill, or I'd find it underneath the rear of a trailer in a private parking lot late at night or inside a garbage container or garbage can at York University. It was never at the same location—always someplace new, and each load would be ten to fifteen pounds, about the size of a briefcase. The most I picked up in one day was fifteen pounds in a suitcase left at the Hillcrest Mall. It was four inches thick and twenty inches long, and it was so hard I had to use a hammer to break it up for distribution.

I would put the stuff in a special briefcase, take it back home or some other place, and chop it up into five- and ten-pound pieces. Then I'd hide it at the gym or in a toolshed at my dad's or high in the rafters of a garage we had down the street.

Goobie never went near the dope himself except once that I can remember. He had decided to bypass me as a courier and save himself a couple of thousand. He sent the buyer to a parking lot off Yonge Street, telling him the load was stashed under a trailer. When the buyer got there he couldn't find it and came back to me and Goobie at the Beverly Hills Hotel screaming: "The stash isn't there, you bastard!"

"It's gotta be there," Goobie shouted back. "I'll get the shit myself."

Goobie calmed the buyer down and took off for the

parking lot with me. When we got there, Goobie got out of the car and spent nearly an hour crawling around under trailers and cars until he finally found the stuff. What had happened was that the guy who owned the trailer had moved it and parked another car in the spot where the load had been stashed. Goobie found it underneath the car. It was the only time I saw Goobie handle a load of narcotics himself.

By 1977 I was pissed off about getting only one hundred dollars a pound, and I told Goobie how I felt.

"Look, Kenny," I said, "I want at least two hundred dollars a pound to handle this stuff. I'm doing a lot of work here—taking a lot of risks. I want a raise to two hundred dollars."

He agreed to up the ante to $150, and I accepted it. It wasn't long after that—maybe a few weeks—that I was stopped by the cops as I was driving a black van I owned. In the van was better than two pounds. The cops searched and searched but didn't find a thing. The load was stashed behind the panel of a back door.

It wasn't the first or the last time I had a close call. I was once following Sanguigni's car with my van when he suddenly speeded up and got about ten cars ahead of me. As I tried to keep sight of him, he went through an intersection. I had to stop for the light. Within seconds two Mounties' cars went barreling through the red light after him. About an hour later I phoned him and asked what happened.

"Whaddya mean what happened?" he said. "Nothing. What should've happened?"

"Didn't you see the Mounties chasing you?" I asked.

"Hell no, there were no Mounties chasing me," he said.

"Armand—you're an asshole," I said angrily. I was transporting more than three pounds of speed. If the Mounties had stopped me after missing him I'd have been cold meat. I was lucky that time.

Later on Goobie and a guy from the Vagabonds developed a way to package speed that made it easy to slip by the Mounties and other narcotics agents. They molded the speed into a pie-plate shape—they called it pie-plate speed. It came in different sizes and weights, but the shape was the same. For a long time, the narcotics agents didn't realize that the "pies" that bikers were delivering and receiving were actually quantities of speed.

Goobie was making millions. I know because I was his banker. Every week I'd take $20,000 to $30,000 or more and move it through the banks, changing the money from Canadian to American currency. I can't remember ever being questioned by anyone at any of the banks. I'd usually change about $2,000 at each bank, never more than that, so they wouldn't ask questions. Once the money was changed, I'd arrange to wire it to relatives of Goobie's in the States, particularly California. I was just one of his couriers, and I handled over three hundred pounds of speed in a two-year period. That alone represented more than $2.4 million in sales, and Sanguigni must have handled double that or more before he was jailed.

What Goobie and Sanguigni didn't send across the border, they gambled away—especially Sanguigni. They were being taken like any suckers at a black crap table in the Yorkville area. Those blacks just loved Goobie and Sanguigni.

The games were rigged, of course, with loaded dice. Goobie dropped an average of $2,000 a night for months, sometimes more. He had the fever, and they kept his temperature high. You see, he wasn't smart enough to figure out why he was losing so much. He just had to throw those dice. He gambled in a lot of clubs in the area, and he bet his socks on football games. I saw him bet $10,000 in just one day. Sanguigni was just as bad. He was blowing thousands a week on bookies and the tables. It was god-awful to see.

You would have thought that making money like that would have satisfied Goobie. After all, he had the Satan's Choice colors—that meant he was protected. He wouldn't get ripped off. If an outsider tried, the gang would come after him. That protection was implicit while you were a member of the Choice. It was an insurance policy for the narcotics business. Of course there were exceptions. You could become the target of members of another motorcycle gang, who would rip off your stash, or worse, kill you doing it.

Dope rip-offs became a way of life in the narcotics trade, and outlaw bikers very often used techniques that they saw police use in busting dope rings. In Satan's Choice we had a number of techniques, but the most popular and successful one was to use a girl or someone known on the street to buy dope from the dealers we wanted to set up. That's the way the cops did it. They'd have an informer or undercover agent make a buy and when they got the signal that the buy had been made and the dealer was carrying dope, they'd bust in to make the arrest.

Well, we did a variation on that technique. Our "agent" would be sent in to make a buy from the dealer, usually an ounce of speed or cocaine, and leave, making an arrangement to buy a couple of ounces on the next visit. The agent would reappear in a day or two to make the two-ounce buy. By then the dealer had confidence in our agent and was ready to be set up.

The agent would then make arrangements to buy a pound or more on a special date and at a prearranged place. Once he or she went in to make the buy, we came charging in behind, our guns drawn, shouting "this is the police" as we flashed phony identification. The dealer would freeze without a fight. Convinced we were the cops, the dealer would surrender his gun and say nothing as we confiscated his narcotics and weapons. It was only when we tied him up and left that he'd realize he'd been had.

We all knew who the dope dealers were and what quantities they handled before we hit an operation. When I went on a job, I always made sure we had it thoroughly cased. Because of that we never had a problem on a dope rip-off. Others who handled rip-offs weren't always that careful.

There were always reports of a lot of shootings and beatings, like in the Rice Lake case I mentioned earlier. That started off as a drug rip-off, and two of the Choice bikers ended up shooting a guy who they believed was a dealer. He was hit in the spine and ended up a cripple. There were four witnesses in the case, and one of them just happened to turn up at a motorcycle shop that was used by bikers. Armand Sanguigni and another biker recognized the witness. They grabbed him and brought him up to the Satan's Choice clubhouse at 7 Woodbine Avenue, where I saw him tied up and gagged in the trunk of the car.

About a week later I read in the paper that they'd found the guy in Rice Lake. The cops came and searched the clubhouse for the rope they used and other things, but nobody was ever charged with anything.

To me it didn't make sense to get rid of just one witness, but Sanguigni and the others thought it would scare off the others. It didn't. They testified, and Bill Dollack and Bob Cousins were convicted of assault and jailed. The cops never did solve the murder of the witness they found at Rice Lake.

Goobie's biggest rip-off was one that didn't require a phony holdup, just a phony story. The guy he took was our supplier, the chemist who manufactured the stuff for biker gangs at a hidden lab up near Sault Sainte Marie.

Goobie's principal supplier was a former Vagabond who ran a pinball machine company. The guy was also a pilot, and he had access to a plane that was used to fly to speed labs throughout Ontario, pick up loads, and peddle the speed wholesale for the biker clubs to guys like Goobie. Goobie, in turn, sold it to dealers of various biker clubs on both sides of the border.

One of the biggest operations was on a small island in the bush at Sault Sainte Marie, where some members of Satan's Choice had a big lab that manufactured speed and PCP, a hallucinogen that was very popular among college and high-school students. The lab operators eventually got busted, and more than one hundred pounds of PCP and speed was seized.

In 1977, Goobie spotted a newspaper report that said that one of his biggest buyers, an associate of the Vagabonds, had been arrested at the Detroit Airport with a "large quantity" of speed. What the article didn't say was that the quantity was only two pounds. Goobie had just gotten fifteen pounds from our supplier. He told him that the buyer he'd sold the fifteen-pound load to had been busted and the entire load had been seized. He showed him the article and he bought the story. What really happened was that Goobie had sold off the fifteen pounds, including the two pounds, to his Detroit biker buyer, collected the money, and lost it all—more than $100,000—at the gaming tables. He lost so much at the black crap tables and with the bookies, in fact, that he fell behind in mortgage payments on one of his houses. The next thing I knew the house had burned down and Goobie had collected on the insurance. Funny thing about that fire. The only things that didn't burn to a cinder were about ten or twelve photo albums of his.

About a year later, the source Goobie had been using offered me the same deal he'd given Goobie. He'd provide me with the speed in whatever quantities I wanted and when I'd sold it off, I'd pay him. He wanted the same $4,500 a pound he was getting from Goobie wholesale. I turned the deal down. The risks were too great. After three years with Goobie and his crew, I knew you couldn't trust anyone you were dealing with. It wasn't worth it to me.

Until that happened, Goobie, Sanguigni, Mike Everet, and myself were a tight little clique in Satan's Choice. If one of us got in trouble, the rest would be there to help him. If one of us got involved in a fight, everyone jumped in to help, even when the odds were heavily against us. Sometimes we got into trouble helping a friend. Like Gary Barnes.

When Barnes got out of prison in 1978, he stayed

with me for a short time. He borrowed a .22 caliber pistol I had with a silencer. Barnes got himself in trouble shooting up a tent full of people in Peterborough. He didn't hit anybody, but he shot it up, and he was jailed for parole violation and then charged with possession of a weapon dangerous to public peace.

When I went to his place the day after to get the silencer, I found out he'd used my .22 to shoot up the tent. I talked to Goobie, Everet, and Sanguigni about what had happened and about the witnesses that were stacked up against Barnes. We decided to see if we could help him by trying to persuade some of the people he was charged with shooting at not to testify in court.

When we got to the place where one witness was staying, we ran into trouble that we didn't expect. We hadn't threatened him yet—we were just talking to him through a partially opened door, but I could see that he had a friend with a gun trained on us.

"Look," I tried to reason with him, "tell your friend we just came here to talk. We don't want trouble—we just want to talk."

The guy wasn't listening. His friend kept the rifle in his hands pointed at my belly. Then he started shouting at the four of us. I knew that if we stayed around it could only end up in a shoot-out, so I told the guy that we were going to leave and that we wanted no problems with him.

Two months later, in early 1979, we were charged by Terry Hall and some other biker cops with attempted obstruction of justice and attempted murder. We were all acquitted in a trial before a jury.

Under ordinary circumstances, we might have pleaded to a lesser charge, but a source I had knew a cop in Toronto Metro Police who was involved in the investigation. The cop, a detective from the Thirty-first Division, had talked to some people about the case before we were arrested and said we were going to be charged with a crime. He didn't say exactly what the crime was. The cop also predicted after we were bailed out that we'd beat the case if we fought it—that there wasn't much evidence against us. My source heard about it and told us all we had to do was get a good lawyer. It was another instance of our sources being better than the cops'—good enough to help us beat charges that might have cost us a jail term.

There was a lot of drug smuggling going on in the late 1970s between motorcycle gangs in the States and Canada. One of the more profitable businesses that I knew about involved hashish smuggling from Jamaica to Toronto. It was run by members of the Last Chance and the Toronto Outlaws, who later became the Rebels. At that time moving cocaine wasn't as big as it is now, and bikers zeroed in on things like grass, hash, and speed.

Three of the bikers, including a former president of the Toronto Outlaws, had each invested $10,000 in the business. They'd send one of their girlfriends to Jamaica, where she'd pick up the load of hashish and hash oil, strap the stuff to her legs, and fly back via New York, where she'd change flights.

Once they sent three girls down, after giving them $15,000 each to pay for the loads they were to bring back. The girls left Jamaica without any problem, but en route to the States they started partying and a sharp stewardess noticed that one of the girls had something taped to her legs. The stewardess, with the help of the pilot, tipped off customs before they landed in New York, and the customs agents pulled the girls off the plane, had them searched, and confiscated the hashish loads.

The bikers who had the big investment wanted to have the girls killed because they'd been so stupid, but they didn't. Two of them got tried in the States and got three years. The third girl was never extradited or tried, but the bikers lost one profitable smuggling business. Hash oil, in 1979, was selling for $500 a vial, an ounce, in Canada. The bikers were buying the stuff for $500 a pound in Jamaica, and each trip they were moving twenty pounds— loads worth $160,000 in Canada. That's a helluva return on a $30,000 to $45,000 investment.

A couple of years before I got out of the narcotics business with Goobie, I gave up my membership in

Satan's Choice. It all happened in March 1976. At the time I was vice president of the Richmond Hill chapter.

The Choice was involved in insurance frauds that used phony thefts of motorcycles. What we would do was have some guy register motorcycles in his name. He'd then report them stolen, and the insurance company would send him a check, of $7,000 or more each, to cover the loss.

One of the front men we were using was a young guy who was rooming with a black kid. I'd had some trouble with both of them and had been a little nasty to his roommate. I didn't like blacks then—still don't. Outlaw bikers don't trust blacks, and it's rare to see a black biker riding with white bikers. You can say we're prejudiced. We do business with some of them, but we don't ride with them.

Anyhow, I'd chewed out this white guy for being late on some payoffs to us. He'd noticed, I guess, that I didn't take to blacks, and he decided to use that to get me. A week or so after I'd had problems with this kid, my wife started getting threatening letters and phone calls. The letters were written in a way to make her and me think that they were from a black.

I was wild. No black was going to threaten my wife or me. So I went to this black's house, but before I left I tucked a gun in my belt and went to the Choice clubhouse to get some backup. There was just one guy there, Billy the Bum.

"I'm going down to face this nigger," I said to Billy, "and I wouldn't mind having you back me up in case something happens. All you gotta do is sit out in the car and keep an eye open in case some other people show up."

This bearded giant of courage looked up sort of lazily from where he was sitting and said, "Gee, Cec, I can't leave yet. I just ordered a pizza."

That blew my mind. I had helped this guy out of a few jams and never hesitated. I was steaming. It was a club rule that you always helped a fellow biker when he was facing trouble—you stood with him and fought with him. I'd always lived by that rule.

"You son-of-a-bitch," I shouted. "You just stay where you are and eat your fuckin' pizza. I'll do what I gotta do without you."

So I went alone that night to this black kid's boarding-house. He'd moved to a different room after he and his roommate had a fight. I went there and talked to him calmly, all the time fingering my gun in case I ran into trouble.

First I pulled out the letters my wife had received. He looked them over and shook his head vigorously.

"I didn't write no letters to your wife," he said nervously. "I got no reason to."

"Maybe you did and maybe you didn't," I said. "You willing to give me a sample of your signature and hand-writing and come to the clubhouse later? I'll make sure your ex-roommate is there and make him sign a piece of paper. I think he might have written them and tried to get you in trouble for it."

"Sure," he said. "I got nothin' to hide."

We set a time to meet, and as I left six big black bucks were out on the street waiting for me. Each of them had a gun. If anything had happened with the kid, they were going to gun me down. They let me pass without any trouble.

The next night the black kid and his ex-roommate showed up at the clubhouse. The white guy's girlfriend waited for him in a car outside. I shoved a piece of paper in front of the white kid and made him sign it. He was shaking like a leaf, but he signed his name. It was a match to the handwriting in the letters.

I grabbed a .410 shotgun, pulled the hammer back, and pointed it right in his face. As I did that he pissed all over himself.

"You're the bastard who's been writing letters to my wife—not this kid," I said, pointing to the black. "I should blow your fuckin' brains out right here. Now there's the door. You better get outta here while you're still alive. I ever see you in the West End again doing anything, I'll put you in the hospital for a year."

The kid ran out of the clubhouse, wet pants and all, straight to the car with his girlfriend and drove off like his life depended on it.

I met the next night with the chapter president, a guy we called Monk.

"Here's my colors," I said, throwing them on a chair in front of him.

"What's the matter, Cec?" he asked.

I pointed to Billy. "One, you see this guy here?" I said. He nodded. "I was in trouble and I asked him to help. I'd helped the bastard before when he was in tight spots. He was a fuckin' coward. All he said was he was gonna eat some pizza. He's not a man. I won't be associated with someone like that." I paused a minute, letting what I'd said sink in. "You want me to stay?" I asked.

"Hell, yes, we want you to stay," Monk answered.

"Well, then, throw the bastard out," I said.

Monk took a vote of the chapter's membership, but there weren't enough—you need 90 percent—to vote him out. Only seventy-five percent wanted him out. He had some friends who depended on him to get them dope that he was buying from some dealers including Goobie.

So I quit. I was the vice president and the road captain of the chapter at the time, but I quit. I just walked out after the vote and threw my colors on the chair as I left. The irony was that a year later he quit anyhow.

It wasn't long after that that I teamed up with Cosimo Commisso and the Calabrian Mafia to begin a new and even more violent career in crime.

PART THREE

Mafia Enforcer

9

The Enforcer

Ron the Rounder paved the way for me to start working for the Commissos. It wasn't something that was planned. It was just a question of timing, and need. I was the right person to fill a need, and Ron was around to recommend me. It was as simple as that.

In the spring of 1976, Ron found out that I had left Satan's Choice. I hadn't seen him for a while. At the time, I was busy hustling a buck in a part-time job as a tractor-trailer driver for a construction company. Ron had been out of town working high-stakes card games for the Niagara Falls Italian mob. We bumped into each other at one of the rounders' hangouts in Toronto's West End.

"Where have you been hiding, Cec?" he asked. "I've been looking all over town for you for some friends of mine."

"What friends are you talking about?" I asked.

"The Commissos," he answered. "They'd like to have you working for them."

Now I had heard about the Commisso brothers. Anyone who worked the streets as I had had heard about them. They were the bosses of a rough-and-tumble outfit that was shaking down contractors and businessmen in a large segment of Toronto. The guy who was their godfather, so to speak, the head man of respect for the Calabrians, was an old-timer named Mike Racco.

Racco, his real name was Michele Racco, ran a popular bakery shop in Toronto. It was particularly popular with a lot of the old so-called members of the Calabrian Honoured Society or Calabrian Mafia. They all used to meet there.

Racco was the Carlo Gambino of Toronto. I remember reading about Gambino playing the role of the godfather at a popular bakery and confectionery in New York's Little Italy. The old and even some of the young Italians would come from all over New York to get Don Carlo's blessing and help. Well, Racco was like that in Toronto. Everyone who needed the help of a godfather in the Calabrian community, including the Commissos, would come to the bakery to see Don Michele.

The Commissos bossed their own family, but they took their orders from Don Michele when push came to shove. So did the bosses of two other Canadian Calabrian families, police and underworld friends of mine have told me. Racco, before he died in January 1980, was the Capo Crimini, the boss of bosses for the Calabrian Mafia in Canada and the United States. Later I was told there was no one higher than him among the Calabrians, not even the Calabrian Mafia bosses in Siderno.

Nobody in Satan's Choice had ever dealt with someone like Racco or the Commissos because, up to that point, they lived in different worlds. Calabrians stuck with Calabrians and kept to their own traditions and secret society. There was a frame of mind among mafiosi like the Commissos and Racco and his son, Domenic—bikers and the Mafia don't mix.

With that in mind I wondered out loud why the Commissos would want to hire an ex-biker, and an Irishman to boot. I certainly didn't fit their mold. I also wondered what happened to the guy that was their former enforcer. Where had he gone? Had he been killed?

"Come on, Ron. What the hell would the Commissos

want with me?" I said. "I'm not Italian. And worse—I was a biker."

Ron shook his head. "Look, Cec," he explained, "they've heard of you—they've heard a lot about you. I've been talking to them about you." He paused for a minute, looked around to see if anybody was listening to us, and then kept talking. "You got a good reputation as a solid person—a solid rounder. They want me to bring you to the Casa Commisso. If things work out you could make a lot of money." He reminded me that for years members of the Niagara Falls Italian mob, as well as people like himself, had worked with members of the Saint Catharines Outlaws in drug deals and occasional beatings that had to be given to street people.

So I agreed to go with Ron to meet the Commissos the next day. I was a real fish out of water there. I'm certain, now that I think back on it, that I was the only non-Italian in the damned place. It didn't bother me at the time. I expected it to be that way.

The three of us sat down at a table near the kitchen, where Cosimo felt nobody could listen in, and Ron introduced me. Then Ron got up and walked over to some other men so Cosimo and I could talk privately.

"How you like to work for me?" Cosimo asked in heavily accented English.

"Depends on what you have in mind and how much it pays," I answered matter-of-factly.

A trace of a smile crossed his face before he answered. "Ronnie, he says you can be trusted. He says you're tough—you do good work. I give you some jobs—we see how good you are." He was giving me the once-over as he talked. I think he was wondering what happened to the long hair, the stubbly beard, and the dirty jeans and black leather jacket he expected a biker to be wearing. I had changed that look even before leaving the Choice. I'd shortened my hair. I'd shaved the beard. All I had was a mustache, and I was always cleaned up and dressed up when I went out. So I suppose I was a surprise to him and to his brothers, Remo and Michele, who had joined us at the table.

"Fine, but what about the money?" I asked.

"You'll be paid well," he said. "We put you on the payroll when we see how you do the first job."

I suspected they would test me on a few minor jobs before giving me any major assignments, if they ever did. Ron had told me I'd probably make about $500 a week to start, but that the money would escalate if I did well for them. I had other concerns besides money. I wondered where I would stand if there was trouble with other mobs as well as with the cops.

"Look," I said, "before I jump into this I'd like to know something for my own protection. Just who is running Toronto? The Raccos, you, Johnny [Pops] Papalia, Paul Volpe? I don't want to get done myself 'cause I don't know the players."

Cosimo looked around and motioned to his brothers. "We run this area," he said. "We run it all. We control Toronto."

He and his brothers weren't saying they shared things with anybody or that they answered to anybody. He was saying they were running things and that Toronto was their pie. They were saying if I worked for them I wouldn't have trouble with other mobs.

I was impressed and I nodded in agreement. "Okay, that's fine," I said. "I just wanted to know what position I'm in. What if I get caught doing anything for you in the future?"

Cosimo looked at his brothers and, still smiling, answered, "We have a lawyer for you and we pay all your expenses. We'll look after you."

With that we shook hands, and I gave them a number where they could reach me. "Just call," I said, "and I'll meet you someplace to talk about whatever job you want done."

Cosimo nodded. "We'll be in touch."

In early August 1976, I met with Cosimo and received my first assignment. A contractor owed him money, and Cosimo wanted me to give him a message to pay or else. He gave me the contractor's name, the location of his office, and a description of what he looked like. His instructions were to deliver a message, not to hurt anyone, yet.

So I located this guy's office—I don't recall his name now—and I went up to see him. I just walked into his office, up to his desk, and laid it on the table to him. No open threat, just a subtle intimidation.

"I don't want to say this more than once, my friend," I said. "You owe a friend of mine a considerable amount of money. Now I suggest you pay him, because I don't want to have to come back." I looked at him real hard, the muscles in my jaw twitching. "I hope you're smart enough to understand."

The contractor understood, but as I left I decided to leave a reminder—just in case. I flattened all the tires on his car. Cosimo never said how much the contractor owed, but when I saw Cosimo a couple of days later, he was obviously pleased.

"You're on the payroll, Cec," he said.

The next job was on a bookie. It was sort of a spur-of-the-moment thing. I was in a pool hall one evening when Cosimo walked in.

"There's this fella over here," he said. "We want him to pay the money to us, but he needs the persuasion." He pointed to a middle-aged bookie who I'd seen operating at the pool hall quite often and who was pocketing better than $10,000 a week in profits without paying anyone for the privilege. "That's him," Cosimo said. "Persuade him."

I walked over to the bookie and pressed him pretty hard. He was up against the wall, shaking like a leaf as I sort of whispered in his ear while I jabbed him hard in his lower gut. He got the drift and that night started paying the Commissos a percentage of his daily take.

He wasn't the only one to get a message from the Commissos that night. They had me come with them to visit a boxing promoter they called Bernie, who had been holding out on them—not paying them a percentage of the money he was taking in promoting fights and shylocking some of his own fighters.

The Commissos laid it on Bernie pretty heavy. While I held his arms they stuck guns in his face and cocked the hammers. Suddenly Bernie smelled like a miniature cesspool. He'd crapped all over himself in fright.

All of these assignments were tests. There were four before I got a major assignment, but not all went off without a hitch. The last of the tests had a few twists and gave Cosimo a big laugh.

My job was to beat the hell out of a guy who apparently owed them a bundle of money. Cosimo had given me the guy's address and his phone number, and I called to see if he was in. I couldn't tell him who I was or why I really wanted to see him—not if I wanted to get him out of his apartment. So I came up with a tale I thought would make him come down.

"This Mr. Smith?" I asked.

"Yeah, you got him," he said.

"Look, I'm sorry, Mr. Smith, but I just backed into your car down in the parking lot," I said. "You want to come down and look at the damage and figure out how much I owe you?"

"I'll be right down," he said, anxiously.

I already knew where his car was parked because I'd cased his operation pretty well beforehand. When he arrived at the car I was standing there, my head bent over to hide my face. I whipped around suddenly with a blackjack in my hand and clobbered him across the head, knocking him cold. Then I worked him over good.

Several days later I went to see the Commissos, and Cosimo greeted me. He handed me $500 and was laughing like hell.

"You didn't do the right guy," he said, still laughing.

"I don't get it," I said. "If I did the wrong guy, why are you so happy?"

"It's all right," he said. "You did his partner. This smart ass. He sent his partner to meet you. The partner that you did, he's gonna spend two months in the hospital. So the guy we wanted done, he's paying up. He doesn't want to go to the hospital the same way."

My target had gotten suspicious, knowing the Commissos were after him, and had sent his partner to double-check the car damage, believing nothing would happen to him. I had a description of the guy I was supposed to beat up, but it was dark, and so the wrong guy got worked over. The blackjack I used on him was made in Brazil—eight or nine inches long, flat, thick at the end. It didn't leave a muscle that wasn't blackened, not to mention a few broken bones.

While the wrong guy had been put in the hospital, the results were the same. The Commissos had gotten their money. I was now ready, they were convinced, for bigger, tougher assignments. I didn't know it at that moment, but I was about to become their new top enforcer.

People like me aren't concerned with history. We probably should be. If I had known as much about the Calabrians as I do now, I probably would never have gotten involved with them, and I wouldn't be in the kind of situation I am.

When I agreed to work for the Commissos, I knew very little about the Calabrians. In fact, all I knew were some stories I'd read about the arrest of an Italian named Francesco Caccamo. Toronto Metro had raided his home back in 1972 and found some guns and explosives. But more important, they'd found some papers that were supposed to describe the initiation ritual that Calabrian Mafia members—the Honoured Society—have to go through.

Those documents—they came to be known as the Caccamo Papers—were the first real evidence, I'm told, that the public was given of the Calabrian crime organization. Caccamo was no informer like Joe Valachi in the States, but those papers were as important as anything Valachi had to say about the Cosa Nostra. Valachi could describe how he was "made" as a member, a soldier of the Cosa Nostra, when he testified before the U.S. Senate in

1963, but he had no document that spelled out what he was talking about. Caccamo didn't say anything, but the documents the cops grabbed said it all—more than he could have—and made it more believable. There it was in black and white.

That was history and I didn't know much more about it. If I had, I would have understood more about the first major assignment that the Commissos gave me. It was in October that Cosimo called me to the Casa Commisso. It had been quite a while between jobs, and I figured they were still testing me. I was living a fairly straight life then, still driving the tractor-trailer. Working for them was a sideline.

The target for this job was a salesman by the name of Antonio Burgas Pinheiro. He was about thirty-eight years old, and he lived in Brampton, Ontario, with his wife and four kids when he wasn't working for the Appia Beverage Company of Queen Street, West Toronto.

"We don't want this man hurt," Cosimo explained. "Just blow up his car or his pop truck. We'll take care of things from there." Remo just sort of stood there, nodding in agreement, letting Cosimo do the talking. Cosimo always did most of the talking.

I found out later that Italian soft-drink beverage companies, according to the police, had been at the center of some serious extortions by the Calabrians from Siderno in the late 1960s. A couple of murders and the bombing of the Appia plant in 1972 were involved. Two officials of the Cynar Dry Ltd., an Italian soft-drink company that employed a relative of the Commissos, had been murdered.

The first one was Salvatore Triumbari, president of Cynar. He was gunned down as he left his home in a Toronto suburb in January 1967. The next guy killed was Filippo Vendemini, who was from Calabria. He had been involved in delivering illegal alcohol for some big Calabrian Mafia hoods, like Paolo Violi from Montreal and Vincenzo (Vincent) Melia. I had to deal with Melia later in a murder plot in Connecticut. Vendemini was shot three times in front of his shoe store in Toronto.

The reasons behind the murders were never made

clear, by police or anyone else. It was part of a Calabrian problem and a fight for control of the Italian soft-drink market by people like the Raccos and Commissos.

I found it interesting that Violi was picked up and questioned about Vendemini's murder. Just as interesting was the fact that somebody had spotted a Montreal license plate leaving the area at the time. Cosimo told me later that the cops traced the license number and the car to a place where the car owner was supposed to be staying. The car owner was there with Cosimo and Remo playing cards. He was grabbed, but they had to release him because there was nothing to prove that he was driving the car. The Commissos weren't charged with anything either. Still, it was quite a coincidence that they were all together and that they all had connections to Vendemini and Cynar employees.

Knowing that history in advance would not have made a difference in how I approached the job, except maybe I would have wanted more than the $1,000 they offered me for it.

On October 23, 1976, I drove out to Brampton. Pinheiro's truck wasn't there that night, but his car, a 1974 Chevrolet, was in the driveway. After parking my truck where no one would notice it, I went back to his car with two sticks of dynamite under my coat and a five-foot fuse.

In a matter of minutes, I placed the dynamite between the frame and gas tank of his car, stretched out the fuse, lit it, and drove off in my truck. I was far enough away when the bomb went off that I didn't even hear it—but half of Brampton did. It exploded at 11:00 P.M. and caused more than $1,000 damage to the car. Later that evening I called Pinheiro's home and threatened him. The cops taped the call but could never identify my voice. They stayed that night, and watched him for a couple of weeks after that because he was so badly shaken.

Pinheiro told them that he didn't have any idea who was behind the bombing. Maybe he didn't, but his boss, Liberato Simone, told the press that the people behind the bombing were trying to drive him out of business. He never identified the Commissos or anyone else. His problem was that his soft-drink company was competing—the Commissos wanted to control the business.

The Commissos were more than happy with the way I operated. They were busy shaking down people all over the city, using the bombings and beatings I had handled for them to intimidate others. Sometimes they worked, and sometimes people needed personal object lessons. A drywall contractor, who the Commissos said needed such a lesson, lived in an expensive neighborhood in King City.

I got the call to meet Cosimo and Remo at the Casa Commisso. As usual, I parked my car in the nearby parking lot of a Kentucky Fried Chicken store and came in through the banquet hall's rear entrance so I wouldn't be spotted if the cops were watching.

The guy they wanted shaken up was Andy Pozzebon. He owned the Pozzebona Construction Company. They told me that Pozzebon owed a large plastering bill to a friend of theirs.

"If you do a good job and he pays his bill," Cosimo said, "you gonna make ten thousand dollars."

I smiled at that figure and nodded. "Sounds good," I said, looking at Remo to see if he was in agreement.

Cosimo said he would go with me to show me the location and what he wanted me to do. We drove to Pozzebon's home and to the business so I would have a good feel for the area. He told me he wanted me to put a stick of dynamite in Pozzebon's mailbox in front of his home and then to call his office.

That's exactly what I did on November 11. I told Pozzebon's secretary that my name was Thompson and that she should call her boss at home and tell him to look in his mailbox for a special message that I'd left in it. She called Pozzebon, and when he went to the mailbox he found the dynamite. He called the York Regional Police.

A couple of days later I called the Pozzebona Construction Company again and talked to the same secretary.

"Did Mr. Pozzebon receive my message?" I asked.

The woman was nervous—obviously upset—and she struggled to answer, stuttering a little. "Ye-e-s, he, he got your message," she said.

"Good," I said. "Now tell him he better pay his plastering bill, or the next time I'll blow up his car."

She delivered the message, and Pozzebon must have paid the Commissos. They paid me $1,000 with the promise of more to come. I never got the extra, but they were famous for that.

Extortion, bombs, beatings, threats—they were becoming routine. But in December 1976, the Commissos changed the routine. This time murder was their game.

10

The Contract Is Murder

The push and shove, phony names, and telephone threats came to an end at a meeting between Cosimo and me at the Casa Commisso.

"Cec, I want you to do a guy for me," Cosimo said. "It's worth ten thousand dollars."

I was still ticked off about the payoff the month before, and I let him know it.

"You mean ten thousand dollars, like in ten thousand dollars you were going to give me last month for Pozzebon?" I said. "Come on, Cosimo. No more bullshit."

"Cec, that was not my fault, not Remo's fault," Cosimo explained. "We don't get everything we're supposed to get. When we get it, you get it. You have my word."

"Okay, okay, Cosimo," I said shaking my head. "Who do you want done?"

"This fink, this Dennis Mason," he said. "He's a witness against a friend of mine. I want him shut up—permanently and fast."

Mason was a relatively young guy who worked in a place called Pizza-Pizza in a shopping plaza. He was a witness against a Commisso associate who had been charged with possession of counterfeit money. It was the same junk that had put so many of the Calabrians, their friends, and bikers behind bars. It would even cause the attempted murder of another witness, Long Island pizza parlor owner Giuseppe Magnolia, who was shot six times in 1978 by a couple of Canadian Calabrian hit men who screwed up their job.

He was involved in a lot of deals, but in this one he was facing long jail time because of Mason's testimony. He had supposedly sold $2,000 worth of counterfeit to Mason.

Cosimo gave me Mason's address, and we drove first to his home and then to his pizza parlor. After we split up, I began stalking this guy—planning his murder.

It was cold, and it snowed during the next couple of weeks as I watched this kid. I watched him drive home, drive to work. I followed his routine until I had it down pat. There was a pattern to his work. Most of the time he delivered pizzas to private homes. That became the frontpiece of my murder plan. The pizza delivery.

My initial plan was to gun him down from a wooded area across the street from a home where I planned to have him deliver a pizza. The location I had selected was perfect. It was under the large branch of a big Christmas tree.

It was snowing the night I called the pizza parlor from a phone near the Prince Hotel. I parked the van and sat underneath the Christmas tree, waiting for Mason to show. It was very dark, about midnight. I was almost certain he would be the one to deliver the pizza because it was so late. I sat under this tree for thirty, forty minutes. Nobody saw me. The delivery vehicle showed up at the house.

A young guy stepped from the truck and rang the doorbell. Just as he delivered the pie and turned back toward the truck, I got ready to step out and blow him away. As I looked down my gunsight at the door, I could see it wasn't Mason—it was someone he'd sent.

I tried a couple of other ambushes, but they didn't work either. Finally I decided on a bomb. I was going to blow this kid to kingdom come the day after Christmas in his mother's driveway.

The dynamite I was using had been given me by

Cosimo. I should have known better. I took the sticks he'd given me and a stick I had, wired them to the dash of Mason's car, and rigged it so that when he turned the ignition key it would go off. The hookup was relatively simple. One wire went to the windshield wiper fuse under the dash, and the other was wound to a bolt connected to the master cylinder. The wiper fuse remains inactive until you turn that ignition switch. Once it's on, an electrical circuit is made, and *boom!*—off goes the bomb.

After wiring the car and making sure everything was set, I left for home. A day later, the front page of a newspaper had a story about a guy who got minor injuries in a car in a bomb explosion.

Minor injuries! Jesus Christ, I shouted, how the hell can you get minor injuries with six sticks of dynamite? This kid had to have had a guardian angel sitting on his shoulder that day. All he got out of it was some minor cuts. One stick of dynamite should have killed him. The five bad sticks that Cosimo gave me and the stick I had just gave him some cuts.

To add insult to injury, the kid I had been stalking and almost killed, was the *wrong* Dennis Mason. Cosimo had not only given me bad dynamite but bad information. He'd screwed up from start to finish. For all my troubles I got a lousy $2,000, but then I hadn't done Dennis Mason, the witness. As for Commisso's associate, he went to court two weeks later and the real Mason showed up to testify. When the associate saw him, he pleaded guilty in a plea bargaining and got two years out of the deal.

In addition to murder contracts, I was responsible for a homicide. It happened May 3, 1977, when I blew up the Wah Kew Chop Suey House in Toronto's Chinatown. The murder was accidental, but it was a murder nevertheless. It could have been avoided if the Commissos had done their homework before handing out the contract.

The Commissos, I learned later, had taken a contract to blow up this place through members of the Kung Lok Triad, the Chinese crime syndicate that controls gambling, extortions, and drug peddling in Chinatown. The Kung Lok is kind of a Chinese mafia, a secret society, complete with bloody initiation rituals and secret oaths, that came to Canada from Hong Kong and, like the Calabrians, shakes down the people of its own community.

Restaurant owners, gambling dens, tailors, all kinds of small shops pay some sort of extortion to members of the Kung Lok. Those that don't get visits from their enforcers. The next thing you know, merchants and customers have been beaten up and sometimes killed. That triad has Chinatown locked up tight.

Even the old Chinese tongs that used to run Chinatown and its merchants knuckle under to the Kung Lok and hire their enforcers for protection. All the Oriental gambling dens in Toronto are supposed to be protected by the Kung Lok.

One of the gamblers who wasn't paying for protection was a big shot at the Wah Kew Chop Suey House. Cosimo told me that this guy had been using the place for some gambling, running phony dice games and Chinese games after hours without the Kung Lok's permission. In fact, he was cutting into the business receipts of one of the gambling dens the Kung Lok were providing protection for.

Because the Kung Lok was under pressure from the Toronto police, they decided to get somebody outside Chinatown to handle the job for them. When Cosimo got the contract in late April, he called me in to tell me about it.

"You gonna get paid fifteen thousand dollars for this job," he said. "When you do the job, make sure there's nothin' left. Level it. Do it at six in the morning. Nobody be there then." Remo stood there nodding. He was certain no one would be there when the bomb was to go off.

Famous last words!

I had to case the layout of the place. The next day I went to the Wah Kew and gave them a take-out order. While they were busy cooking it up, I walked around, looking for rooms where I might set the charge. Finally, I checked out the washroom. I noticed there were some loose ceiling tiles. After jamming the door to be sure no one would surprise me, I stood on the toilet seat and pushed the ceiling tiles up. It was perfect. Plenty of space to put a bomb and timer where nobody would spot it. I also checked to see when the restaurant emptied out. By 3:00 A.M., it was closed and everybody was gone.

The next order of business was to get the dynamite and the blasting caps I needed. I figured it would take about one hundred sticks with a couple of blasting caps made up into two separate but identical bombs. Each bomb was to have fifty sticks of dynamite, a blasting cap, a standard twelve-volt flashlight battery, a small clock, and a positive and negative wire that ran from the blasting cap to the clock. I drove to Windsor and got the dynamite from the Satan's Choice chapter there. They always had dynamite available because of extortions they handled and the gang wars. It was usually stolen stuff, but it was dependable.

At about 7:00 P.M. the night of May 2, I put on some glasses, changed my hairstyle, and went back to the restaurant carrying a gym bag and a briefcase with the two bombs. The idea of the two bombs with two clocks was if one didn't work, the other would—sort of a safety valve.

I ordered a couple of egg rolls and coffee to go and went back to the washroom with a doorstop in my pocket to jam the door while I worked. I stood up on the toilet seat again, lifted the ceiling tiles, and gently eased the bombs, one by one, into place. With each bomb, I left a wire loose—I always left a wire loose—the final wire that made the connection for the bomb to go off. I kept it loose until the last minute, just in case something banged or screwed up. It was lucky I followed that procedure. If I hadn't I probably wouldn't be around today.

One bomb was resting on a ceiling tile ledge that had a slight downward slant. I had something in my pocket—I can't remember what the hell it was—that I took out and dropped. I started to bend down to retrieve it. I had the bomb above me with the connecting device taped on but not hooked up. I took my hand off for a split second and then I saw it falling as if in slow motion—falling, falling—I said to myself, "Oh, my God." I heard it hit the floor. I blinked, involuntarily threw up my arms to protect myself—a foolish act in itself—and looked at the floor. There was a momentary silence, but I could hear my heart pounding like a sledgehammer. I thought to myself as I looked at the bomb, "Christ, I'm still here."

I was breathing again. When my hands stopped shaking, I wiped the sweat from my brow and my hands. Then I gently lifted the bomb and put it back on the tiles. When everything was in place, I set the clocks to go off at about 6:00 A.M. and hooked up the final wires, closing the ceiling tiles carefully behind me. Then I left, picking up my take-out order as I went.

I guess it was about 2:00 A.M. that I telephoned the restaurant just to be sure nobody was there. The phone rang and rang but there was no answer. If someone had answered I would have told them—"Hey, get the hell outta there—there's a bomb about to go off." But there was no answer, and after I hung up the phone I thought no more about it.

The bombs went off about a half hour early. Official reports said the explosion occurred at 5:33 A.M. The bombs tore the hell out of the place. Working in the kitchen, which shared a wall with the washroom, was a cook who was later identified as Chong Yim Quan. He was killed by the blast. Three other employees were injured. They had come to the restaurant in the early morning hours to begin preparing meals for the day's customers. I'll never know why any of them didn't answer that damned phone.

I heard about the homicide on the morning news, but I didn't see Cosimo and Remo until about a week after the bombing. We were in the Casa Commisso.

"Great information you and Remo gave me, Cosimo," I said. "I thought you said no one was gonna be in the restaurant."

"Ah, Cec, so what?" Cosimo said nonchalantly. "It's no big deal. It was just a Chink."

That was typical of Cosimo and his brothers. They didn't give a damn who got killed or who got hurt as long as the contract was fulfilled and they got their money. They didn't care as long as it wasn't their family.

I shrugged at his answer, and figured I could be just as calculating as Cosimo or his brothers. "You got my money?" I asked.

He nodded and shoved an envelope across the table. "Here's your money," he said.

I opened the envelope and counted it out. There was $18,000 in cash. For the first time he'd paid me more than he'd promised. I didn't ask why. I knew. I pocketed the money and left without another word.

I never found out how much Cosimo and his brothers got for the job, but the restaurant damage was estimated at more than $168,000. He probably pocketed twice what he paid me. But then that's what crime bosses do. They take the lion's share. That's why they're bosses.

If the murder of the Chinese cook was accidental, there was nothing accidental about the Commissos' plot to murder millionaire Montreal stock promoter Irving Kott in April 1978.

From the time I had first met the Commissos until May 1979 there had really been only two contracts for murder and a bombing that turned into murder.

The Mason hit was a case of mistaken identity and only faulty dynamite and a switch of deliverymen had saved his life. The planned Piromalli murder fell through because Piromalli died of natural causes before they could send me to Italy to do the job. If I had gone, I doubt I would have lived to tell this story or become a witness against the Commissos.

The murder of Kott was probably the most important hit assignment the Commissos had come up with, except for Piromalli. There were more significant hits they wanted me to handle a little later on, but by that time I had decided to bare all and become a secret RCMP informer.

For more than twenty years Kott had wheeled and

dealed in the securities business in the United States and Canada. In 1962 he'd been fined $10,000 by the Quebec Securities Commission for trading in unregistered stocks. Police then thought he was being financed by Montreal Mafia boss Vincent Cotroni. The Cotroni brothers, Vincent and Frank, were Calabrians and close to the Commissos.

In 1967 the Quebec Securities Commission ordered a halt to the sale of stock for a company known as Allegheny Mining & Exploration Co. of Quebec because its owners were dealing with Kott, who was involved in stock deals under investigation in Florida, New York, Denver, Toronto, Vancouver, and Montreal.

In 1973, while he was living in New York, Kott was sued in U.S. District Court for more than $8 million. A British tycoon, Iain Jones, claimed Kott had defrauded him out of a multi-million-dollar calculator business. A year later Kott and eight others were arrested for fraud in the sale of Somed Mines Ltd. stock to investors in Ontario, Quebec, and Europe.

One of those arrested with Kott was Stanley Bader, a swindler who became an informer against Johnny (Pops) Papalia, a Toronto mob boss, and Cotroni. Bader was shot to death in front of his guarded northeast Miami home in March 1982.

In 1975 Kott pleaded guilty to conspiracy in the Somed Mines case and paid a $500,000 fine, but not before he and eighteen others were charged in the $5.5 million swindle of Continental Financial Corp. of Montreal, an American-owned subsidiary of Industrial National Corp., the owner of the Industrial National Bank of Rhode Island.

Through all this Kott was supposed to be operating with the blessing of the Cotronis until 1978, when they were blitzed in one of his stock operations. I bring up this history because it explains why the Commissos, in particular Cosimo, went to such lengths to make sure I handled this job.

The price to hit Kott, Cosimo said, was $25,000. He said he was acting as a "broker" in the deal for Kott's partner, who would benefit from Kott's death. I never believed that was the real reason or source for the contract. I was convinced then, as I am now, that the Cotroni mob had given the Commissos the contract to kill Kott because they believed Kott had swindled them. Later on Kott's bodyguard, Michael Pozza, was gunned down in Montreal after he'd been subpoenaed in a Quebec crime inquiry into Mafia control of the garment industry in Montreal.

Cosimo gave the Kott hit plot a personal touch.

"This is a very important job, Cec," he said. "I'm gonna meet you in Montreal and I'm gonna show you where this guy works, where he lives. I'm gonna show you everything about this Kott." He paused for a minute and looked straight into my eyes. "I'm not rushing you," he continued. "You can kill this guy whenever you feel it's right, but we want him killed soon. *Capice?*"

I understood, and for $25,000 I'd put icing on the job if he wanted it. He was saying don't rush, but hurry. It's not good when you have to hurry jobs like this.

Cosimo's plan was for me to fly to Montreal. He was going to drive. The following day we were to meet in front of the Bonaventure Hotel.

We met, and for the next day or so, Cosimo drove me to every haunt of Kott's. He knew the guy inside out. We went to where he lived and where he had breakfast every morning at a small place not far from his home, which was in a Jewish neighborhood. While we were casing the house, Kott suddenly came out, climbed into his gleaming new Mercedes-Benz, and drove right past us. Cosimo was furious.

"If I had the gun," he shouted, "I'd've killed the no good son-of-a-bitch right then."

That told me there was something very personal in this contract. For Cosimo to say that he'd have handled the hit personally on the spur of the moment was extremely unusual. He wanted this done and done right to impress someone.

We didn't stick around too long after that. Cosimo

took me to an Italian district in Montreal, where we stopped at a coffee shop and had a sandwich.

"We'll just eat here and take off fast," he said. "We don't wanna hang around too long because people know me in the area and I don't wanna be seen in Montreal."

After we finished casing Kott's business location, his home, and his hangouts, Cosimo gave me the address of a girlfriend of Kott who was also his employee. "He stays at the girlfriend's sometimes," he said quietly. "Sometimes he stays the night, sometimes a couple nights."

Then we split. I flew back to Toronto to construct the bomb I'd need and get a .22 silencer to go with a special .22 handgun I'd acquired for the hit. I also went to a Mercedes-Benz dealership in Toronto to check out their cars and see the best place to put the bomb.

Before I was ready to handle the job, I traveled back and forth to Montreal a couple of times, staying a different place each time as I stalked Kott's every move. I wanted this guy down pat before I blew him away. The Commissos had given me $1,000 for expenses.

The first time I went I had taken the .22 and silencer and the dynamite with me—all ready to hook up to his car. I planned to go through a side window of his house and hit him inside. Just as I was going through the window, somebody walking his dog on the street spotted me. That caused a little unexpected heat, and I had to leave the area. Everyone thought it was a burglar.

I had to lay low for about two weeks. Then in late August I returned. This time I planned to attach the bomb to his car and rig it so it would explode when he turned on the ignition. Later I had to change that plan.

When I got to Montreal I found out Kott was in court. I parked near the courthouse and walked around most of the afternoon, trying to find Kott's car in the parking lot. It might have been in the underground garage, but I wasn't about to look. There were too many cops in the area, so I walked on by, got to my car, and left.

I was concerned about being seen. I remember driving by a cop at one point. It was early morning. I was figuring I might have to shoot the cop if he stopped me. He kept on going, never looked at me, so I just took off.

I had no photograph of Kott, just a good description. I'd seen a photo, but I never carried pictures of the victims I was after. Cosimo had handed me a piece of paper with addresses and directions. I memorized most of it. I had trouble memorizing the phone numbers. If I knew a number was in the telephone directory, I'd destroy it. If not—if it was an unlisted number—I'd keep it inside my sock.

Every time I went to Montreal to case Kott's movements, I stole a new set of plates off a Quebec car and put them on mine. I figured I had at least twelve to twenty-four hours before the theft was discovered and reported to the cops. It would take them another couple of hours to alert their cars to the stolen plates. In that time I could keep tabs on Kott's movements.

I took other precautions. I changed the type of clothes I'd wear and my appearance each day. Sometimes I'd comb my hair down, wear a baseball cap or a winter hat with a tassel. Sometimes I'd wear sunglasses or tinted eyeglasses and dark clothes. It always was different, and I'd always look for the quickest way to exit an area before parking or walking around.

One day I sat outside Kott's office for six hours, waiting for him to go to lunch. I didn't realize it, but he had a kitchen in his office and he'd usually have his secretary make his lunch.

The next day I called his office to make sure he was there, then I went to his place of business, the Highland Knitting Mill Inc., and spotted his car parked in an underground parking lot. I retrieved the bomb from my car, set the wiring, and returned to his Mercedes. There was a parking attendant maybe two hundred feet away from where I was. He never spotted me.

The bomb—five sticks of 75 percent nitroglycerin taped together—was placed on top of his exhaust pipe, almost exactly beneath where he sat. I ran electrical wires back to a battery that I hid behind one of the car wheels on the inside, below the axle.

I had a pressure-sensitive ignition starter button on top and placed it under his tire so that at the slightest movement of the tire, it would go off. Once it was in place, I slipped out quietly and drove back to Toronto.

I figured at most Kott would get into his car within a couple of hours, and *poof!* up he'd go. If he sat in his car on top of that dynamite, his asshole would be on the third floor of the warehouse of his firm. Wrong.

Kott never used the Mercedes. Instead, he climbed into his wife's Jaguar and drove to the airport. While he was away the parking attendant was sweeping under the cars and saw the button under the Mercedes. It was very dark. I still don't understand how he saw it. I should have put it on top of the tire, not under—it was my mistake. I hurried the job too much.

It was about 5:10 A.M. on August 28, nearly nine hours after I had set the bomb in place. The attendant looked at the button, pushed it, and *ba-boom!* it went off, sending him flying halfway across the lot. Another person who was walking nearby was knocked to the ground.

The attendant lost part of his hearing in the explosion, but he wasn't badly hurt otherwise. Neither was the bystander. Kott's car was demolished, and two other cars parked nearby were badly damaged.

I didn't know that Kott had escaped injury when I reported to Cosimo back in Toronto. He was pleased. Then he found out that Kott wasn't hurt.

I saw Cosimo about three weeks later. Surprisingly, he wasn't all that upset. I guess those who had ordered Kott hit weren't that upset either. Maybe the explosion had sent a message to Kott that he understood and, as a result, had taken care of their problems. Whatever happened, Cosimo handed me $3,000 more for my trouble. It wasn't the $25,000 I'd been promised, but then I hadn't nailed Kott either. I hadn't expected to get anything.

"Well, I guess Kott knows who's after him now," I said.

"Well," Cosimo said, "he knows who he owes money to—but there's others who are after him."

"You want me to go back and do the job right?" I asked.

"No. Never mind, Cec," he said. "Remo, he's going there to kill him."

I know Remo never went, and Kott is still alive. I never did figure out why Cosimo said that. Whatever the reason, I was $3,000 richer for botching a job. If they hadn't been in such a hurry to take him out—just as they'd wanted Mason done in a hurry—Kott and Mason might not be around today.

11

Everything Has a Price

Whether it was concrete or cement, plumbing or plastering, electrical wiring or trucking—if it had anything to do with the construction industry, the Commissos and their Calabrian Mafia friends had a hand in it somewhere, and usually that hand was reaching in and taking, either with threats or as part of a mob agreement.

Michele Racco and his family had a piece, Paul Volpe and his people were in it, and so was the Luppino crime family of Hamilton. The infiltration of the construction industry by mobsters, some of them from the Mafia, some of them associated with the Mafia, was so widespread that it even resulted in an investigation by a Royal Commission under Judge Harry Waisberg. There had been many bombings and shootings in the industry, which the commission documented in an investigation that lasted more than a year and produced a 770-page report. That was back in 1974.

What the report and the investigation didn't produce was public evidence of the Raccos' and Commissos' operations in construction. That was probably because the coppers knew little about the Calabrian Mafia at that time and even less about the Commissos. The Commissos were young then. They hadn't reached the status of bosses of a crime family that could rattle the cages of other mobs from Long Island to British Columbia.

The people who drew most of the heat for the bombings and shootings, the shakedowns of contractors, and the infiltration of unions from 1970 to 1973 were bosses like Paul Volpe, or Natale Luppino, or people representing the Stefano Magaddino crime family of Buffalo.

When I started working for the Commissos, I learned quickly that their big thing for making money was the construction industry. They probably made more from extortions in that industry than from their trafficking in heroin, and it was a helluva lot safer.

They had a lot of ways to make money in construction. One of their most successful was making the law that contractors depended on to collect debts work for them. It could take years for a guy to collect through the courts. In fact, contractors could and did go broke waiting for the law and civil suits to settle their claims. Even when the courts made awards favoring a contractor, he often found out that the guy he was suing had a dozen different corporations and the corporation he'd been dealing with was legally bankrupt. The debtor had simply moved his money from one corporate account to another.

What that did was make room for guys like the Commissos to become "collection agencies" for contractors. For a slice of the money owed, the Commissos would collect, and they didn't let legal technicalities or stalling tactics get in the way.

Take a major contractor—let's call him Builder X. To complete his project he subcontracts electrical, plumbing, and plastering work out to smaller, specialized contractors. Mr. X promises to pay these contractors $300,000 more or less to complete their work.

Now the electrical contractor finishes his job and comes to Mr. X and says, "Pay me." Mr. X doesn't have the cash right then, so he says, "I'll have to pay you later." The electrical contractor has employees to pay, supplies to pay for, bills to meet. He sues in court to recover his money. Maybe two or three years down the road he collects—

maybe he doesn't. Meanwhile, Mr. X has used the electrical contractor's $300,000 and similar amounts from the plumbing and plastering contractors to invest in some other project that makes him an even bigger profit.

That was the system for a long time. It took the Commissos to find a way to make big money out of it. Now the subcontractor goes to his friend down the street who knows "the Mafia, who knows the Commissos." The Commissos then go to see Mr. X or send someone like me to hassle and threaten him. They collect, they get a piece, and the subcontractor gets most of his money back. That's the way it's done here.

By 1978 I was getting a number of contracts from the Commissos to squeeze contractors who they wanted to extort money from, who they told me were not paying bills they owed to subcontractors. The first of these involved Ben Freedman.

Freedman was the main contractor on a construction project in Toronto. He had hired a couple of subcontractors to do some electrical work that cost more than $175,000. When it came time to pay, Commisso said Freedman suddenly came up with short arms and long pockets. There was no money, he told them, either wait or take him to court.

The subcontractors, both of them Italian, turned to Remo and Cosimo for help. They wanted their money and they wanted it now and they didn't care what had to be done to get it. That's when Cosimo called me in.

We met at the Casa Commisso on February 13, and then drove to Freedman's home in North York.

"Bomb his house," Cosimo said, "but don't hurt anyone. I just wanna shake this guy so he pays up what he owes."

The fee to do the job was $2,000. Originally Cosimo wanted me to put the bomb on the side door of the house. I didn't see any problem until I got there that night on my own.

I was in a jogging suit, which I wore so that anyone who saw me would think I was just another one of those health nuts jogging up and down streets in the area. People don't take much notice of joggers. The jogging suits I wore were usually black or dark blue, which made it even harder for anyone to see enough to remember. I also wore a cap.

I had two sticks of dynamite with me and a five-foot fuse that I connected to a percussion cap that I'd hooked to the dynamite. When I got to Freedman's house, I spotted some kids' bicycles and a baby carriage around the front. I decided against a bomb at the door. I didn't want some kids to get maimed or killed because they were playing at the wrong place at the wrong time. So I chose to bomb Freedman's car, which was parked in the driveway.

I put the bomb between the wiper blades and the windshield, set the fuse, and jogged away. I was long gone when the bomb went off. The next day I read in the paper that the car had been totaled, but that no one was injured.

A couple of days later Cosimo went to a public telephone booth and called Freedman to explain why the car had been blown up.

"Be smart, Mr. Freedman," he said, carefully speaking the words so his accent wouldn't be obvious. "Pay your bills. That way no one—no kids—get hurt."

Cosimo paid me the $2,000 and said I'd done a good job. Cosimo, however, had not kept his word. He had told me that when I handled these extortions for him, I would get a percentage, as much as one-third of what was collected as a result of my intimidation of the victims. I never got anything beyond the $2,000. It was another pipe dream.

Once the Commissos delivered for a subcontractor, they were in a position to muscle him or make deals to collect for him on other projects. In effect, they became his private collection agency and silent partner. That was the case with the electrical contractor who had collected from Freedman because of my bomb. There were other contractors who owed him money, big money, and the Commissos were going to cash in collecting those debts.

Everything Has a Price

The biggest of the targeted contractors were a pair of apartment and condominium building owners named Jerry and Roman Humeniuk. They were brothers and partners. In March 1978 I got the first of several assignments from Cosimo and Remo to force the brothers to pay more than $196,000 they owed. The contractor had done a lot of work at this exclusive and very expensive condominium complex and hadn't been paid for it.

Before taking on the job, I checked out the area to see what the best escape routes were and how many people were around at different times of the day and night. I finally settled on doing the job in the underground parking lot of the condo, where I figured it would be least likely to kill anyone.

I took two sticks of dynamite with a three-foot fuse which I'd gotten from the Commissos and lit the fuse a few minutes before 9:00 P.M. When it went off it blew out plate-glass windows that partitioned the parking area from an underground lobby.

Not long after, I telephoned some people who were living in the complex—people whose names I'd gotten out of a telephone book.

"Look, you don't want to get hurt, right?" I asked.

A woman in the room was crying and the man who was on the phone was asking, "Why us? Why are you calling us? We haven't done anything."

"Just tell that landlord of yours to pay the money he owes to his contractor," I snarled. "He'll know who I'm talking about. Tell him to give up the money he owes or I'm coming back and blow the fucking apartment house apart—and I'll blow up your fucking place with it."

The woman was hysterical now, screaming into a telephone extension: "He isn't here. Please! Leave us alone!"

"Lady," I answered, "just give him the message." I hung up.

The Commissos gave me $2,000 for the job. Two months later, they wanted me to go back.

"This building owner," Cosimo said, "he hasn't paid up. We want you to go back again—blow up his car."

This time he wanted me to zero in on the home of Roman Humeniuk in Oakville.

I drove by the place first to look around. There were kids in the yard and in neighboring yards. I didn't think it would be safe. Blowing up the car might cause a fire because the car was very close to Dr. Humeniuk's garage. Then the fire would spread to the house. I didn't want some kid trapped in that house by fire. So I figured out an alternative plan.

Early on the morning of May 15, I threw one stick of dynamite on the lawn and put a big hole in it with the explosion. I almost screwed up with that one. I used a short fuse, about a foot. That gives you about forty seconds after you light it to get the hell out of the area. I hit a red light just as that one went off at about 12:15 A.M. I could hear the explosion, feel the van rock a little, as I waited to get on the Queens Expressway. Humeniuk's house was just a short distance from the expressway exit.

Still nothing. The Commissos were mad as hell. Humeniuk hadn't paid, and the contractor was pressing them for results. So in July I went back to the condominium again, this time to the other side of the garage, where there were two concrete supporting pillars. I rigged a bomb with four sticks of dynamite, a six-foot fuse, and a blasting cap. When it went off at 12:05 A.M. the morning of July 21, it shook the entire complex and sent debris flying more than sixty feet onto the nearby golf course. The bomb was designed to cause more fear than damage, and that's exactly what it did.

I called the same tenants again and went through the same routine. The woman was almost a basket case by then. The idea was to get the people to tell the Humeniuks to pay what they owed or they'd move out. When they moved out, the owners would lose money. Rather than lose money and have an empty condo, they'd pay what they owed.

I don't know if it worked. The Commissos claimed the

Humeniuks never paid up, but they never called me back to squeeze them anymore either, which made me believe that their contractor was a satisfied customer. I figured they were just trying to get out of paying me any part of that $196,000 that the Humeniuks owed the contractor. All I got out of all my work was about $3,000.

It was apparent to me that by the time I got the Humeniuks' extortion contract the Commissos had a lot of the construction industry subcontractors lined up, ready to pay them to do what the courts weren't doing. Even while I was handling the Humeniuks' bombings, I got the nod to start extorting money from developer Max Zentner and his millionaire partner, John Ryan, the owner of the engineering firm of John Ryan and Associates.

In May, Cosimo told me to try to go after Ryan and Zentner, who he said owed an electrical contractor "friend" of his more than $200,000 for work he'd done on a project. The contractor was supposed to be suing Ryan in court to recover the money, but Ryan's lawyers were stalling.

Cosimo showed me Ryan's home in Hamilton, his Cadillac, which was usually parked in the driveway at his home, and his office in Toronto. He said I should also muscle Zentner, who lived in Montreal.

"Break his legs," Cosimo said of Ryan. "You break his legs and rough him up good."

So in May I went to Ryan's home at about 5:00 A.M. and flattened the left rear tire of his car. I waited in my car for him to show up. I figured I'd waylay him when he tried to fix his tire. The trouble was, by 9:00 A.M. he still hadn't come out of his house. So I left. About five days later I returned. I changed my facial appearance with a mustache, a wig, and glasses, walked up to the front door, and knocked. When he opened the door, I knocked him flat with a blackjack to his face.

I then traveled to Montreal and telephoned Zentner, telling him to get his partner to pay up or he'd get the same treatment Ryan had just gotten. Nothing happened, but Cosimo paid me $1,000 in cash that Remo pulled out of his pocket. The money was to cover my expenses.

About two weeks later, I returned to Hamilton. It was about 1:30 A.M. when I got there with two sticks of dynamite and a five-foot fuse. I spotted a 1977 Firebird in the driveway that I knew belonged to Ryan's daughter. I set the bomb on top of the rear tire, set the fuse, and took off. I heard it go off just before I hit Main Street in Hamilton. It sounded like two trains colliding.

Later I saw a picture in the *Hamilton Spectator*. The car was wrecked. Pieces of it were found two or three houses away, and the bedroom window of a neighboring home was cracked, but no one was injured. The Ryans and their daughter were staying at some cottage near Parry Sound. A witness said she'd seen a sports car leave the scene when the bomb went off. Hell, I was driving a sports car, but she couldn't have seen me. I was about a mile away when that bomb went off. Witnesses sometimes have vivid imaginations.

After the bomb went off, Cosimo wanted me to call Ryan and tell him that the next time a bomb went off, his son or his daughter would be in the car that was blown up. I tried getting Ryan, but his secretary never let me talk to him. I was never certain that he'd paid the $200,000 to the contractor, but the Commissos didn't ask me to go back. They just paid me the $2,000 they said they'd pay and that was that.

One thing that drove me wild with the Commissos was that they were full of promises of big money, but rarely delivered. Sometimes I'd get so pissed off that I'd pull out of jobs I'd promised to do unless they paid me the money up front. Take the case of Alphonso Gallucci, the owner of Gallucci Construction in Toronto.

The Commissos said Gallucci owed a friend of theirs more than $54,000 and had stalled paying. Cosimo's face was flushed with anger when he told me what he wanted.

"You break this guy's arms and legs," he said angrily. "You break them slow so he feels the pain longer."

"How much am I going to get for this?" I asked.

"We give you a percentage," Cosimo said.

Everything Has a Price

"No good, Cosimo," I said. "I'm tired of promises. I want my fee up front. Like the Chinamen say, 'No tickee, no shirtee.' No money, no legs broken."

Finally, after a lot of arm-twisting, I said I'd do the job, and Cosimo drove me to Gallucci's home and to his business. In October 1980, after a couple of months of haggling with Cosimo and Remo about up-front payment, I pulled out of the deal. As far as I know, Cosimo never got anyone else who was willing to do the job.

Shaking down contractors to make them cough up money owed builders and subcontractors they were collecting for produced only a small part of the Commissos' take from the construction industry. They were also very active in bid rigging on municipal contracts, like hydroelectric projects, buildings, or highways. When they wanted to rig bids, the Commissos would threaten the competition facing the contractors they were dealing with. Once their man got the bid, they became his partners, and their people—plasterers, electricians, plumbers, cement suppliers—would be used on the job. They'd inflate the cost of the job, pocket the profits, and run like thieves while the public or business paid the price.

I recall one dam project that the Commissos wanted to control in British Columbia. They wanted to use a friend of mine to do it. The friend was "Charlie Tuna." That wasn't his real name, but he didn't do anything wrong, so I'm not going to name him. He was the son of the owner of one of Canada's largest construction companies, which had bid on the project.

They wanted me to shake down Charlie Tuna, rough him up if need be, to put pressure on his old man. I refused. Charlie Tuna was a friend of mine who eventually joined the Rebels motorcycle club. He used to work out and hang around at an athletic club that I owned and operated. I remember trying to talk Charlie out of getting involved with the cycle gangs.

"You're a nice guy, Charlie," I told him at the gym.

"You don't want to join a motorcycle club. You'll just wind up in trouble."

Charlie Tuna's father ran a big outfit. They had millions, and Charlie used to drive around in a souped-up Porsche and a special truck that was worth $40,000 or $50,000. He was a big, strong kid, about five foot ten. Long before he teamed up with the Rebels bikers, he rode around on a Harley-Davidson.

Charlie Tuna and some of his Rebels friends were grabbed one day at the border by customs or immigration. They were hassled but they never got into any real trouble. Charlie finally got out of the biker clan and went back to working for his family. It was the smartest thing he ever did.

When Cosimo wanted me to make a move on Charlie Tuna I said, "Look, I don't do friends. I'm not extorting him or his family."

"Cec, don't say no," he said. "Think about it."

"There's nothing to think about, Cosimo," I said. "I'm not shaking down Charlie or his family. That's it."

"Okay, okay, Cec," he said. "We gotta see if we can get through to this company some other way, work something out with them."

He smiled as he looked at me. "If they don't cooperate, I'll get my friends in the unions in British Columbia and we'll close this company down with a strike. You'll see. They'll fall in line."

I don't know if they did fall in line or if the Commissos got a piece of the pie at the dam project, but there was no doubt in my mind about Cosimo's influence with the unions, particularly the plasterers' union. One day Cosimo gave me the address of their union hall and told me to go there and sign up. "Once you sign up, you'll be a member," he said. "You'll get a check for five hundred dollars every week."

I said no to the offer. I knew that if I went to that union and signed up, the guys in the union would sooner or later know who I was working for and start talking. One night the guy who ran the union would come to me and say, "You're Cosimo's friend. I want you to burn this house or break this guy's head." It would have been stupid. I could have taken down an easy $500 a week, but why take the chance? It wasn't worth it.

The plasterers' union was only one that the Commissos had their hooks into. Just before I began working as an informer, I'd heard them talk about forming some sort of protection union for the construction industry.

Their plan was simple. They were going to use this union to shake down contractors who were being shortchanged by companies they did work for. For a fee or a percentage of what was owed, they would send union goons to the company that owed the money. The company either paid up or faced beatings of employees by union muscle, wildcat strikes, and other forms of intimidation. I never found out what union they took over or whether they actually put the plan into operation. By that time, I'd become a witness against them and was no longer able to get that kind of inside information.

The Commissos were also busy controlling the mobile lunch trucks that provide workers with sandwiches, coffee, soda, and other goodies at construction sites. It's a damn good way to make a buck if you're sitting at a catering hall, like the Casa Commisso, pressing all the buttons while everyone else does the work.

The mobile lunch truck business is so lucrative that the boss of the Joseph Bonanno family in New York, Philip (Rusty) Rastelli, got into it and wound up in jail after a federal jury in Brooklyn found him guilty of extortion. Rastelli was more than once a guest of mob members in Toronto and Montreal, where the Bonanno family had a lot of friends and connections for their narcotics business and for other rackets they were involved in in Canada.

The Commisso version of Rastelli's racket was geared toward the construction sites themselves. The Commissos and the Raccos controlled most of the catering trucks in Toronto. When there were rivals, they usually didn't blow up their trucks or threaten them, they went after the construction site superintendent and squeezed him—made him keep the competition off the site.

Cosimo brought me to the owner of one of the mobile catering companies, who was close to Michele Racco. He was having a problem with a construction site superintendent who was letting a rival company service the workers.

"What my friend wants," Cosimo said, "you do for him. You'll get paid well."

I didn't trust this friend of Cosimo's and Racco's. He wanted me to rough up the site superintendent—break his legs if I had to—to make him open the site to his lunch trucks. When I was through with that, he said, he wanted me to burn some trucks of another catering company in another part of the city. There was something about the way this guy talked—the way he wanted to grind his competitors under his heels—that made me uneasy. I figured he'd double-cross his mother, let alone me, so I refused to handle his work. Cosimo wasn't happy about it, but he didn't press me. He knew I'd made up my mind. The lunch company caterer was greedy. He already had trucks operating all over the city—at construction sites, industrial complexes, garages, you name it—and he wasn't afraid to handle hot goods to increase his profit margin.

Some time after I turned down that assignment, Cosimo told me that the lunch company caterer's trucks were going to handle a $100,000 load of cigarettes, stolen from the Imperial Tobacco Company, that I was arranging to sell to Cosimo for some friends. The cigarettes were from a trailerload that Ken Goobie and Armand Sanguigni were trying to peddle for $40,000 through a middleman named Richard Corbett. Cosimo finally agreed to take the load for $30,000.

With all those lunch trucks, he said, they could move a trailerload of stolen cigarettes in a day and no one would ever be the wiser, least of all the cops.

Funny thing about the hijacked cigarette deal. At the last minute Cosimo had second thoughts about his friend. When he got the cigarettes, he arranged to sell them to another mobile lunch company owner—a rival. This guy

promised Cosimo a bigger profit than the guy Cosimo'd
wanted me to work for. That was always Cosimo's downfall—
his greed.

In the end, the whole deal blew up in Cosimo's face.
After paying about $12,000 of what he owed on the
cigarettes, Cosimo lost everything when a sharp-eyed
citizen spotted his Calabrian flunkies unloading 127 of the
original 317 cases of cigarettes in a rundown garage in
Toronto. The citizen called the police, who seized the
cigarettes and arrested four men who later pleaded guilty
to possessing stolen cigarettes. The Commissos had to
provide lawyers, bail money, and expenses for the four. It
was a fiasco for the Commissos; for Goobie, Sanguigni, and
Corbett; and for me. I'd expected to make a good piece of
change out of the deal, but all I got for my troubles was a
headache and a lousy $100.

12

Hustling a Buck

Working as an enforcer and hired assassin for the Commissos had some good paydays, but it wasn't exactly lining my pockets with enough gold to live on easy street. The money I received for blowing up the Chinese restaurant and for contractor extortions and the attempted murders of Mason and Kott went fast. Too fast.

There was a new Corvette, there were a lot of fast women, and there were even more slow horses. I went to the track too often and bet more often than not on the wrong nag.

I had recognized early in my relationship with the Commissos that I'd have to supplement my income with side deals of my own. For a while, I continued operating as a courier for Goobie's narcotics. I also handled a number of drug rip-offs with some bikers that added thousands to the stash in my safety deposit box. I was averaging $75,000 to $80,000 a year, but it wasn't nearly enough. I had become a rounder of sorts myself, and I was always looking for new ways to make money.

Through a chance meeting with two international gambler friends—I remember them only as Bob and Roman—opportunity came knocking. Roman was a good friend of Eddie Neuff, the murderer gambler, and he was pretty close to Ron the Rounder, who had introduced us.

Hustling a Buck

We'd all done some drug rip-offs together. On this particular night, we were at a hotel in downtown Toronto tossing down a few when Roman asked me if I'd be interested in taking a trip to Bogotá.

Roman's objective was to locate a source for cocaine that he and Bob planned to smuggle into Canada. They had a front they were convinced would get them through customs. They were leaving for Colombia to have some parts made for a plumbing operation they were running. Their plan was to have the parts produced on a massive scale and smuggle coke inside some of the parts being shipped to them. It wasn't a foolproof plan, but it was successful for them.

I decided to go along for the hell of it. I'd just finished blowing up the Chinese restaurant, and I wanted some high living without worrying about coppers or the Commissos or anyone else looking over my shoulder. I wasn't the least bit interested in smuggling narcotics. I considered that too risky.

We spent about a week living it up in the city and sightseeing. During that stay, we met a high-ranking official of the Bogotá Chamber of Commerce at a Colombian bank where we were changing Canadian currency into pesos. One thing led to another—before I knew it the discussion went from pesos to plumbing supply parts, cocaine, and finally to guns.

"Can any of you get guns?" he asked. "We need guns, all kinds of guns—rifles, machine guns, bazookas, ammunition."

Roman and Bob were dumbfounded. They were trying to set up a supply source for a cocaine smuggling operation and here this guy was talking about reverse smuggling— moving guns from Canada to Colombia. They both shook their heads, figuring that their lack of contacts for weapons was going to cost them in trying to set up the drug-smuggling operation. At that point I surprised them with an offer of help.

"There's a guy I know," I said. "He's sort of a friend. His name is Chuck Yanover." Roman's face brightened as I spoke, and the Colombian business official leaned close to listen to what I had to say.

Of course I knew Yanover, but we weren't close friends, just sometimes business associates. Like a lot of members of Satan's Choice and other biker gangs, I had sold stolen motorcycle parts to Yanover for years. I'd lost track of him for a while, but after he was in prison he apparently graduated to the big time. He got hooked up with Nathan (Nate) Klegerman, a convicted diamond swindler and international con man who was Paul Volpe's right arm. In 1974 the Royal Commission that investigated the construction industry identified Yanover as part of the Volpe mob that was shaking down and bombing contractors. Two years later he was busted with Volpe, Klegerman, and three others for trying to smuggle $1.5 million in diamonds into Canada.

With all that, Yanover still managed to get an arms dealer's license. He used to brag about that to me whenever I saw him. He was the Ontario agent for Fabrique Nationale, a Belgian arms manufacturer. The joke was that as the agent for the Belgian supplier he was helping arm the Ontario Provincial Police. He said he was negotiating a contract to sell the police a special rifle they were after. When Yanover told me that, I didn't know whether to believe him or not. Chuckie was always bragging, talking about million-dollar deals and international plots to take over countries.

From the tip of his balding head to his pudgy feet, from his thick glasses to his weasellike face, there was nothing about Yanover to remind you of a cold-blooded mercenary capable and ready to kill whoever stood in his way. Yet that was exactly what he was. And he had a lot of mercenary friends—gunmen for hire—he'd met while peddling arms for the Belgians.

Yanover was full of schemes in those days. He was living on the fifth floor of a building owned by Volpe. We used to meet there occasionally, usually in the boiler room of the building, when I wanted to buy some diamonds or some guns from him. It was at one of these meetings that Yanover offered me a murder contract.

"I got a couple of things for you to do if you want some work, Cec," Yanover said.

With Yanover you never knew what to expect, so I was cautious in expressing interest.

"Yeah, well, what have you got in mind?" I asked.

"First of all," he said, "I can guarantee you a million bucks if you'll handle a contract to kill Fidel Castro."

I looked at Yanover as if he'd lost all his marbles. "Come on, Chuck, you're not serious," I said.

"I sure as hell am," he snapped. "The only thing is it's going to take a helluva good shot. You're going to have to take the shot at him from a quarter of a mile away. That's as close as you'll be able to get."

I started to chuckle, but I saw Yanover getting almost beet red with anger, so I coughed and frowned and speculated that the job was a suicide mission.

"Chuck, be reasonable," I said. "I don't speak Spanish. I wouldn't last ten seconds there after taking a shot at Castro. The people would tear me apart. Even for a million bucks I don't think I'd be interested. I don't have a secret desire to kill myself—not yet."

He never said much more about it, but I got the impression that the plan to hit Castro was something hatched up by some mob guys who wanted to get back into the casino business in Cuba. Castro had cost the Italian and Jewish mobs millions when he took over their hotels and threw them out of the country. Since then the papers and U.S. congressional committees have reported a number of plots to kill Castro, some sponsored by the Central Intelligence Agency, who wanted to use the mob, others planned by stateside mobsters who had dreams of getting back their casinos.

When I turned Yanover down, he didn't bat an eye.

"Okay, maybe I got something else for you," he said. "I got something personal you can handle. I'll give you ten thousand dollars and all your expenses will be paid."

The target of his vendetta was some poor slob who

was working a Caribbean cruise ship. The guy had made the mistake of taking off with a girlfriend of Yanover's. Yanover didn't like people chasing his women, even if he was chasing three or four at a time himself.

"You go down to Miami and you get on this cruise ship," he said. "You grab him and just dump him off the boat and forget about it."

"Let me think on it, Chuckie," I said. "Maybe I can do something."

Later on he had a guy he wanted me to get rid of in Switzerland. I don't remember his name, but he wanted this guy hit in the worst way. Friends of mine and the cops told me later that some guy who was a witness against Yanover was shot in Switzerland and nearly killed. I never was certain whether that was the guy that Yanover wanted me to hit.

It was about a month after we'd talked to the Colombian businessman that I arranged a meeting with Yanover at the Prince Hotel. Roman, Yanover, and myself sat down. I was acting as sort of the middleman, figuring I'd collect from both sides on the deal.

"I have this Colombian," Roman explained to Yanover. "He wants to buy automatic weapons, bazookas, tanks, and whatever else he can get his hands on, and he's willing to pay whatever it takes to get them."

Yanover sat there nodding, wiping his glasses. "You just have him send the money up and I'll ship them whatever they want—planeloads of tanks, guns, munitions—you name it, I'll get it, and the prices will be right."

Both Roman and Yanover sort of glided over the costs. Nobody got specific about the price of a tank or a machine gun or anything. They just talked in generalities.

"How are you going to get weapons like that to them in the quantities they want without attracting too much attention?" Roman asked.

"Look," answered Yanover with just a hint of anger in his voice. "I've handled shipments like this lots of times before. We just report the plane lost at sea after we deliver the weapons. Just go back to Bogotá and have them draft some money to a bank here and we'll start delivering the guns and tanks they want."

Roman never went back and he never saw Yanover again to my knowledge. The last I heard he was living in England.

As for Yanover, we kept on dealing together. From guns and cocaine to arsons, from a plot to overthrow a Caribbean island called Dominica to a plan to assassinate the president of South Korea. The government overthrow plots happened later, when I became an informer and witness. In the late 1970s Yanover's biggest value was as gun supplier.

He had a supply of handguns and machine guns available on almost a moment's notice. He could get anything I wanted—grenades, machine guns, plastic explosives, antitank guns, even tanks themselves. His suppliers weren't just the Belgian manufacturer. He also had sources in New York and Chicago, sources he didn't talk about. I used to buy a lot of guns from him—guns that I sold to bikers, to the Commissos, to rounders I knew.

Cosimo was always in the market for guns. If he wasn't buying them from me, he was getting them from two Italian gunsmiths who had a shop in downtown Toronto. The gunshop owners themselves were in the market for special guns, even those that were hot. I recall selling one of the owners a collector's Winchester carbine. It was hot—stolen in a burglary—but they didn't care. They had a customer who wanted it, no questions asked. Cosimo sometimes bought hot guns from the youngest gunshop owner. On one occasion, the owner promised Cosimo he'd have ten guns coming in from a source he had in the States within a couple of days.

Collectors' guns—any guns—were always wanted by bikers, who were constantly checking out gun collectors and gun stores that they could heist later. There were times when everyone in Toronto seemed to be in the market for a gun of some kind and no one asked questions. Bikers and rounders in particular were always either buying or selling guns. I didn't have to go look for them. They would come to me to sell their wares. If someone really wants a gun, he can always buy one on the street—whether it's in Toronto, Montreal, New York, or Miami. They are out there for people who know people, and it doesn't take too much to find and get to know the right people.

When I was dealing heaviest in guns between 1978 and 1980, I always had two or three of my own just sitting around for possible sales or jobs. Keeping guns around sometimes got me in trouble. I already described how Gary Barnes took a gun of mine and shot up a tent full of people.

The worst incident I can recall resulting from my trafficking in guns came out of my giving a .32 caliber handgun to James Munro, a rounder friend of mine, in May 1980. Munro was short on money and he was an old associate. So when he asked me for a gun and said he'd take care of me later, I didn't ask what he planned to use the gun for. It wasn't any of my business. Munro was a hustler. I knew he handled burglaries and heists, but that was his business.

On May 14, Jimmy and his brother, Craig, tried robbing George's Bourbon Street Tavern, a Toronto nightclub. A Metro cop, Constable Michael Sweet, interrupted the robbery and was shot. That brought out an army of cops, and for a couple of hours Craig, who was older and crazier than Jimmy, held the cops at bay with the gun I'd given Jimmy. All that time, Constable Sweet was bleeding. He bled to death from the shots that Craig later admitted firing at him. Both Craig and James Munro got life for murder. I was never charged in the case, because the Munros never implicated me. When I became a witness and got immunity for past crimes, I admitted giving Jimmy Munro the gun just one day before the shoot-out. I felt bad about Sweet. He was a good cop with a wife and three kids. He was just in the wrong place at the wrong time.

While I was moving deals on the side with people like Yanover and the Colombians, I was still very active with the Commissos. In 1978 alone I handled seven arsons and bombings, some of which I've already described. Probably the most violent and the one that was supposed to bring me the most money was that of the Laramie Sports Store in Guelph, Ontario.

It was strictly an insurance blowout, set up by the store owners, Bruno Spizzichino and his partner, Armando DiCapua, with the help of another Italian friend, Rocco Mastrangelo. Mastrangelo was the connection to the Commissos. He knew Remo very well. I'm not sure whether the connection was through friends in Italy or from contacts in the Calabrian community of Toronto.

Their plan was to bomb and set fire to the store, collect the insurance, and pay the Commissos $20,000 for the job. DiCapua and Spizzichino went to Italy to borrow the $20,000. Then they flew to Las Vegas and then, after a short stay at one of the casinos, to Guelph. The idea was to make it look like they had won the $20,000 they were bringing into Canada while they were in Las Vegas. Once in Guelph, they deposited the money in the Bank of Commerce and, after a short wait, took the money to Mastrangelo. He, in turn, paid Remo and Cosimo for the job.

I found all that out later when I wore a body mike and recorded their recollections of what happened after the Commissos had been arrested and jailed. In 1978 all I knew was what Cosimo told me, and that wasn't a helluva lot.

I was working out at a gym in early June when Cosimo called me and told me it was important that I come to see him at the Casa Commisso. When I arrived he said he had a job for me.

"I got friends in Guelph," he said. "They got a business that's not good. They wanna burn it—blow it up and collect the insurance."

"How much is my end, Cosimo?" I asked.

"Eight, maybe ten thousand dollars when the job's done," he said.

The next day we met at a pool hall and Cosimo told

me he wanted to drive to Guelph and introduce me to the owners. I didn't like the idea too much, but Cosimo said that the owners were friends of his family and that, for my protection, he would identify me only as "George."

I finally agreed to go, but I said I'd drive. The following afternoon, Cosimo and I drove to Guelph in my Corvette. When we got to town, I parked the car about a block away and then walked to the store, where Cosimo introduced me to DiCapua.

DiCapua gave me a tour of the store and the building. He showed me a disco and an after-hours club on an upper floor and a karate club in the basement. Then he took me to a storage area in the back of the store and showed me a door that he said led to an alleyway. While I was there I studied some gas pipes that led downstairs, and I told him that I would probably place the bomb downstairs near the pipes to set fire to the place.

"I'll be back in about a week with the materials I need," I said to DiCapua.

"Okay. I'll be waiting for you to return," he said.

On the way back to Toronto, Cosimo made a promise. A few days after I had finished the job, I was to come to the Casa Commisso to collect my $10,000.

Before I returned to the store I ran into a problem. I'd gone to a cottage I owned to get the dynamite and blasting caps I needed. All told, I had twenty sticks of dynamite. But I had no fuse, and I knew it would be difficult to get fuse, do the job, and not be identified later by inquisitive cops as someone who had bought fuse at some store. My biker friends didn't have any fuse and neither did the Commissos. My alternative was to try using a sparkler, the kind you see used at fireworks displays.

I went to a nearby novelty store and bought a large package of long sparklers—about two feet long. I had no way of being certain my idea would work without testing it, so I returned to the cottage, took a blasting cap, and went out in the backyard. I put a sparkler in the blasting cap. It fit perfectly. Then I lit my makeshift fuse and watched, timing how long it took for the sparkler to reach the cap and blow. It took about two minutes.

That afternoon, June 20, about 6:00 P.M., I arrived in Guelph. It was sunny and hot, and I was sweating as I looked at the package I had filled with the dynamite lying beneath the glove compartment of my Corvette. I was a little nervous, partially because of the heat and its possible effect on the dynamite. I drove around the block where DiCapua's store was. As I drove by, a police paddy wagon passed me. I pulled over to the side of the road a considerable distance from the store, parked in a lot next to a fire station, and waited to be sure the paddy wagon wouldn't return.

At a little after six, I walked back to the store with the dynamite in a gym bag. I was wearing my gym clothes and driving gloves. The door of the store was locked, but as I turned the doorknob, DiCapua appeared and let me in.

He was fidgety—something I didn't need at a time like that.

"I was expecting you last night," he said. "You never showed up so I phoned this man—Rocco—to see what was keeping you."

"I had a problem getting some materials," I said, "that was all. This Rocco—I never talked to him."

As I spoke to him, I unzipped the gym bag and showed him the contents. His eyes sort of bulged out a bit, and he seemed to be shaking, but it didn't stop him from chattering like a magpie.

"Wait till late, till about one in the morning before you start the fire," he said. "I need plenty of time after I close the store to get home."

Then he walked me to the back door again, opening it to show me the main street behind the building.

"This isn't an alleyway like you told me before," I snapped. I was angry—more at myself than anything for not casing the place better on my own the first time.

DiCapua was clearly afraid, but he kept his head. He gave me the telephone number of the karate club that was adjacent to his store basement.

"Please," he said, "phone them about ten or eleven tonight. Make sure no one's there."

"Don't worry about it," I said. "Of course, I'll check. I don't want anyone in the building any more than you do. Nobody's gonna get hurt. Don't worry."

With that he left, and I went to the basement and sat in the storage area for nearly three hours, listening to the people at the karate club work out. I could hear them through the wall as they kicked the heavy pad, threw each other down, and shouted their so-called battle cries.

When I didn't hear any noise for a while, I dialed the club's number on the phone. I let the phone ring for a long time, hung it up, and then phoned back to be doubly sure no one was there.

While I was listening to the people in the karate club work out, I had carefully pulled the dynamite from the bag and taped it together. I'd also put in the blasting caps with the sparklers inserted. Before I set the bomb, I walked quickly up the back stairway leading to the door and pulled one of the bars open to make certain that the door would open when I came running back up the stairs. I checked my watch—it was about 12:30 A.M. DiCapua had had plenty of time to establish his alibis. I went back downstairs and started two fires in the storage room area.

As the fires burned, I went to the boiler room and placed the bomb inside. I wanted it to blow the cast-iron boiler and hit the gas main next to it. That would trigger still another explosion and blow the place sky high. Later I learned I had blown open a one-and-a-half-inch gas line that just sent out puffs of flame.

When I set the bomb in the boiler, I placed newspapers around one of the sparklers. As I left, I lit a match and touched the sparkler to the newspapers. They were burning as I dashed from that room, passed the storage room where the other fire was burning strongly, and ran up the stairs and out the back door.

Just as I came out the door I spotted the police paddy wagon I'd seen earlier. It was pulling into a parking lot across the street, and two people were walking up the street toward me. I slammed the door with my right foot, uncertain whether it closed tight or not, put the hood on my gym suit up, and started jogging up the street as if I were working out.

I had used three sparklers to set the bomb off. That gave me six minutes to get out of the area. I jogged down the street, hurdled some guardrails, ran across the railroad tracks and down the street to where my car was parked. By the time I reached the fire hall parking area and my car, the alarm bells hadn't gone off, so the fire hadn't been spotted. It had taken me about a minute to reach the car.

My palms were sweaty, and there was a chill along my spine as I started the car and drove off unhurriedly down some city streets to Highway 7 and then to Route 401.

I went to see Cosimo two days later at the Casa Commisso and collect my money.

"You got the money you owe me, Cosimo?" I asked.

He shook his head. "I'm sorry, Cec," he said. "I gotta go to Guelph and get the money from these people. Come back in few days."

So I did, and he handed me $2,500.

"Where's the rest you promised me?" I said angrily.

"That's all they gave me," he said. "They say the fire department, she come, put out the fire—the building, it no burn."

I didn't believe him. A few days later I drove to Guelph to check. I noticed as I drove by that the windows were all black, and those that weren't were all boarded up.

I then drove around the side of the building to the other block, where a hotel was located. I checked the outside wall and part of the sidewalk—they were intact. The bomb hadn't worked as planned. It had blown the boiler apart and destroyed the room it was in, but it had missed the gas line it was intended to set off. I didn't learn until later that I had just missed by a few feet the city's main gas line, which for some strange reason ran through that building. If I had hit that, blown it up, I'd have taken a whole city block and probably killed a lot of people— something I hadn't even thought about.

The building had burned all right, but not to the ground. The store was destroyed and there was $100,000 damage to other shops in the building, but the building wasn't leveled the way they had planned. Fire investigators never realized the place had been bombed until years later, when I became a witness. They had thought all along that the fire was caused by a gas explosion. No one had even suspected arson or a bomb.

It took me nearly four years to find out that the Commisso brothers had stiffed me on that job. They had collected the $20,000 from the store owners up front. Among crooks on the street, there is a code of honor of sorts. When it came to the Commissos, there was no honor. There was more of a code of honor among biker gang members than with the Commissos. Two sixteen-year-olds breaking into a house had more of a code of honor than these Mafia men did. The only code they had was to look after their "family." I was an outsider. I wasn't Italian or Calabrian, so they stuck it to me.

13

Shaking the Disco Beat

The Commissos once pitted me against bikers. From the time I became a biker and before, nightclubs, bars, and discotheques were the targets of shakedowns, of extortions, of biker-run prostitution. It didn't matter whether we were in Orlando or Fort Lauderdale, Montreal, Toronto, or some small suburb, the bikers singled out night spots and hotels for all sorts of money-making schemes.

Talent agencies run by bikers or biker associates supplied the topless clubs and the strip joints with strippers and topless dancers. More often than not, the places where the bikers sent their women became centers of prostitution and muggings, and frequently attracted violence between rival biker gangs. Since I had "officially" left the street and biker clubs, nothing had changed except the names. Bikers still had talent agencies, still supplied women, and still muscled clubs that didn't want to do business with them.

The women who work for these agencies don't realize what they're getting into when they go to them for jobs. They think they're dealing with legitimate agencies. Most of them are young, just out of high school. Some of them are girlfriends of bikers who are told to go to the agency and work or else. Still others are starry-eyed kids who think that the agency is really a talent agency, a stepping-stone to stage or television or movies.

Once they start dealing with those running the agency, they're hooked. They're told they have to pay an agent's fee and give a percentage of their salary to the agency so that the agency can provide them with protection while they strip or dance. Most of the girls don't object. Those who do either get roughed up or find they can't get jobs.

Some of the clubs that the girls dance and strip in are owned by bikers. The Outlaws and the Pagans owned a lot of topless bars, discos, and stripper joints in Long Island, Philadelphia, and Orlando. They were hidden behind corporate fronts, biker relatives, or biker associates, but the club members were the real owners. The vast majority of clubs where bikers' women worked, however, weren't owned by bikers. They were extorted and shaken down by bikers and forced to use biker women as their performers.

Biker club members would go to a nightclub, a small bar, or a disco. They would promise the owners a kickback of the money they collected from the broads the bikers supplied. They'd also promise to look after the broads.

Now the bar owners would go for those tales, those promises because they didn't want bikers to come in and break up their places, and that threat was implied by the bikers.

"Look, if you don't want my women in here, fine, but tomorrow night there may be twenty-five Vagabonds here having a r-e-a-l good party," the biker would say.

So hundreds of bar owners all across the United States and Canada signed contracts to hire dancers, strippers, and entertainers that were supplied by the biker agency. If it was a small club or bar, the owner was also usually invited to use the shuffleboards, pinball machines, and video games that the bikers or their friends owned or controlled. The bar owners still made their profits, and they avoided violence and damage in their clubs and attacks on their employees and patrols.

The biker agency meanwhile put ads in the papers for

more dancers. The bikers also muscled in on the talent that other agencies provided for the hotels, bars, and discos on both sides of the border.

A good example of what I'm talking about involved the owner of a disco in Toronto. He was a Greek who went by the name of Cosmo. I was introduced to him by Cosimo.

"Cosmo, he's having trouble with the bikers," Cosimo said. "They been causin' fights, damage in his club. They even raped his waitress and one of his customers."

"Which bikers?" I asked.

"The Paradice Riders," he answered. "They cause him lotsa trouble." Then he added, "You talk to them—get them to stay outta the place for a while. If they do, this guy, he'll pay—we'll all make some money."

"Okay," I said, "I'll see what I can do, but tell your friend it's probably going to cost him. Bikers don't do things for nothing, and you know I don't."

So I went to see a friend of mine at the Paradice Riders—one of the top officers—and I talked to him about the problem and about the rapes. I told him one of his biker members, a guy named Terry, and some of his friends had raped this waitress twice and one of the customers.

"Look," I told my friend, "stay out of the disco for a while. The guy, this Cosmo, is willing to pay me money if you do. We'll all make money."

At first my friend was against the idea. "Hell no, Cec," he said. "We don't want any fucker tellin' us to stay outta his place. Nobody tells us where to go."

"Okay, okay, I understand what you're saying, but just stay out of there for a while—as a favor to me," I said. "I can make a few bucks. You know, one hand washes the other."

So he agreed. I offered him a kickback—a couple of hundred bucks for him and some of the boys to have a night on the town—but he refused. He was doing it as a favor, and you don't get paid for favors. I told him to tell

Terry I'd get the girl off his back—stop her from testifying against him.

With the deal cut, I went back to Cosimo, and we sat down with the disco owner.

"My friend here," Cosimo said, "he's talked to the bikers. They know him and they're gonna stay outta your place. But it's gonna cost you. Nothing's for free."

Cosmo understood. He came up with several thousand dollars to pay for the protection that Cosimo was providing through me. He also had a long talk with the waitress. She agreed to forget what Terry and his friends looked like. Terry never came back. He went into hiding in the States with another biker gang because the coppers had warrants out for his arrest on that rape and some other similar assaults. And the club—it burned down a couple of months later. I was never sure whether the bikers did it or it was an accident. I didn't care. I'd collected the money and Cosimo had kept maybe $500.

In May 1979 I set up the Superior Fitness Centre. I bought the club from a friend of mine who wanted to get out of the health/fitness business. I wanted in because I needed a business as a front and because I thought I could make some money out of it. It was a dumb move.

It wasn't long before I was commingling gun smuggling, bombings and arsons, and plots to shake down discos in the health club. I didn't pay attention to the business, and as a result I lost money on it.

I soon found out that I wasn't a particularly good health club businessman. By August 1980 I'd sold out and just about broken even on the deal. For over a year, it did provide a good front for my operations and for meetings with the Commissos and others I had criminal deals with.

Early in the summer of 1979, not long after we had straightened things out for the Greek disco owner, the Commissos told me they were convinced there was gold to be mined in Toronto's discos. Because I was an ex-biker with a lot of contacts among biker gangs and the rounders, I was the key to the plan.

Shaking the Disco Beat

The idea was simple—use biker gangs to break up clubs and muscle club owners and then, for a fee, promise them protection from biker intimidation. Of course, the bikers would get some of the profits, and they would only be asked to stay away from a club that was paying for protection *temporarily*. After a few weeks or months they could go back and terrorize it some more, and the Commissos would collect all over again. It was the first real semialliance between some of the biker gangs and the Calabrian Mafia. It was at best shaky, because no one trusted anyone, and for good reason.

The first test of the extortion alliance, as I'll call it, came when Cosimo came to see me at the health club. He knew a disco owner named Mike who ran an after-hours club. The place had become a target of the Vagabonds, who the owner had mistakenly tried to keep out. They kept coming back to break up his club and harass his customers.

"I don't know, Cosimo," I said. "You don't tell bikers to stay out of places. They don't care about the money. It's a matter of pride."

"Try, Cec," he said. "See Mike. See what you can work out."

I set up the meeting with the disco owner at Harvey's Restaurant and talked to him about his problem.

"Maybe I can get the bikers to stop breaking up your joint, Mike, but it's going to cost you," I said.

"How much?" he asked.

"Two grand now—maybe some more later, but at least you'll be in business," I said. "The way things are now, you're just about shut down."

"Okay, see what you can arrange," he answered. Then he reached in his pocket and handed me $1,000. "Here's half on account."

I went to see a friend of mine at the Vagabonds and explained that I was rousting this disco owner for a quick buck.

"Look, get the guys to stay away from this joint for a few weeks, maybe a month," I said. "That'll give me a chance to make some money off the guy and I'll look after you. Besides, we've helped each other before."

My friend agreed. "Seeing it's you, Cec, okay," he said. "This guy's an asshole. When you've gotten what you want outta him let me know. Then we'll go back and break his lousy club up again."

I laughed, slapped him on the back, and left. For the next two weeks I collected $1,000 a week from Mike. I was supposed to split with Cosimo, but all he asked for was $500 and that's all I gave him. He figured I was splitting with the bikers. I gave my friend some, but I kept most of it.

There were other clubs we shook down the same way. Some worked, but one didn't—a place called the Peaches on Pears Disco. It was owned by a guy named David Freedman, who I knew through the gambler friends that I'd gone to Colombia with. Cosimo knew about Peaches on Pears and he knew about Freedman, who he said had plenty of money and would be an easy extortion.

Freedman had helped me out a few times, and I wasn't about to shake him down for Cosimo. While I gave a nodding agreement to Cosimo to handle the deal, I secretly called Freedman at his apartment in Hyde Park to warn him.

"Look, Dave, some people want me to lean on you, you know," I said. "Remember that other place, that disco that burned down not far from your place? Be careful— you don't need their kind of trouble."

Freedman was quick to show he had no fear of the implied threat that I was trying, in my own way, to warn him about.

"I don't know what you're saying to me, Cec," Freedman said, "but if anyone is trying to put the arm on me, they're gonna get nothing. If they burn my place down, they'll be doing me a favor."

"Dave, forget it," I said. "I'm just trying to give you a friendly warning—nothing more. Just make sure your insurance premiums are paid up."

I went back to Cosimo and said to him, "Forget about

Freedman and his club. No way are you going to extort the guy. He's not going to pay up."

Not all of the disco owners were targets for shake-downs by the bikers and the Commissos. At least one, Harold Arviv, had his own ideas about how to make money and get rid of business partners.

Arviv pleaded guilty in 1986 for his role in a conspira-cy to blow up his disco on January 9, 1980. That's when Gi Shik Moon, the Korean ex-sergeant and partner of Yanover, took thirty sticks of dynamite and blew the disco sky-high, causing over $700,000 in damage. Yanover and Michael Gerol, who supplied the dynamite, were convicted when Moon testified against them. Moon said that Arviv offered him $10,000 "front money" and 25 percent of the insur-ance to blow up the place. Moon agreed to do the job after talking it over with Yanover, who was in prison at the time and was to split the proceeds. I'd introduced Yanover to Arviv—but I'm getting ahead of myself.

I first met Arviv in November 1977 through a Satan's Choice biker friend of mine, Frank Lenti, who frequently worked out at the health club that I kept in shape in by lifting weights.

Lenti at first told me that he had a million-dollar burglary setup that he wanted me to go in on. The burglary was to be that of a house owned by a Jack Mamann. Arviv and Mamann had been business partners in a place called the Hippopotamus Restaurant, which I later robbed, on January 15, 1978, for Arviv.

Lenti said that the information on the setup came from Arviv, who wanted us to rob Mamann's house and split the money we found with him. I agreed. The terms were I would take 50 percent of whatever we got, and Lenti and Arviv would split the other 50 percent. I was taking the lion's share because I had the experience and I'd be doing most of the work planning and executing the job.

I did a surveillance on the house and kept track of the people who were in and out at different times. On the day

I decided to break into the place, I telephoned to be sure there was no one in and then donned a postman's uniform I had in the trunk of my car.

I drove past the house again, making sure no one was around, parked a few blocks away, hoisted a mailbag with a crowbar inside over my shoulder, and walked to the house. I rang the doorbell, waited a minute or so for an answer, and, when there was none, went to the rear of the house and broke in through a glass sliding door.

I searched the den, the bedrooms, the whole damned house for about seven or eight minutes before the phone started ringing and ringing. I had a feeling I might have been spotted by a neighbor who was calling to see if someone was home or if I was in there alone. So I left—empty-handed.

I was steamed over finding nothing, and a few days later I told Lenti. He went back to talk to Arviv, who claimed that there was money in the place and that he wanted me to go back and try to find it.

I told Lenti the only way to do the job now was to stage an armed robbery. In December 1977 I recruited a couple of friends who had just come out of jail to handle the job, Gary Barnes and a friend of his.

I took them to the house, showed them the layout, and told them what I wanted done. Then I supplied them with two balaclavas—handcuffs—and one revolver, a P-38 that I gave to Barnes. His friend had his own gun. I drove them to the house that evening. I parked about two blocks away while they went to do the robbery.

They got inside when someone opened the door and handcuffed one of Mamann's older sons. Mamann was not at home. They said the family was upset—the kids were crying, so was the wife, and she denied that there was a big stash of money in the house. All they got was some jewelry and a few hundred bucks in cash. When they met me at the car, I drove off, checked the jewelry, and found Mamann's name engraved on a gold bracelet. There were also some rings. I told my friends to keep the money, but the jewelry I threw out over the roof of the car into a vacant lot near a car-wrecking lot.

When I saw Lenti again he told me that Arviv had told him that Mamann had taken the money out of his house two days before the robbery and had had it deposited in an account in a Swiss bank.

I wasn't too happy about all the trouble I'd gone to for nothing, and I told Lenti that I wanted to see Arviv personally. A meeting was arranged at Arviv's disco, which was under construction at the time. It was early January 1978.

When I went to meet with Arviv, I was carrying a .22 caliber High Standard automatic with a silencer in the front of my pants, hidden by my coat. I was prepared for anything. Arviv, Lenti told me, was a former Israeli army commando. I suspected that he could be violent and might have armed himself for the meeting.

Arviv didn't know me as Cecil Kirby. Lenti had never told him or his contacts who I was. He knew me only as "George," a name I used frequently when Cosimo introduced me to some of his "clients."

"You owe me some money, Mr. Arviv," I said. "You owe me for a B&E and a robbery—and I figure those two jobs were worth twenty thousand dollars."

He agreed that he owed me money for what I'd done for him and said he'd pay me $10,000. There was a problem, however. He said that because his expenses were running high at the disco he was building he'd have to cover what he owed with several payments.

All the time he talked, I felt the gun cool and hard against my gut. Because of the way it was positioned in my pants, it was damned near impossible for me to sit down, so I paced up and down slowly, keeping my jacket on to conceal what I had. If he made a move—tried anything—I was ready to blow him away right where he sat. But he didn't. He didn't give me a hard time at all.

The next day we met at the Hungarian Gourmet Restaurant, where he paid me $2,000 in cash and later, at another meeting, paid me another $1,000. It was then that he told me he had a friend that was the manager of an after-hours club and that he would talk to this guy to arrange a fake robbery of the night deposits. He figured I'd get at least $10,000 from the job, and I could keep that plus the money he'd already given me.

On January 15 I held up Yvo Sajet, the manager of the Hippopotamus—the club Arviv told me to hit—using his description of Sajet and his European sports car.

I parked about a block away from the parking lot of the Hippopotamus and waited for a couple of hours. First, some women who appeared to be waitresses got into a car and left. I walked back down the street cautiously and stood at the edge of the parking lot, about seventy-five feet from the manager's sports car.

I saw a man come out of the club and walk to the car carrying some boxes, which he put on the car roof. I appeared out of the dark behind the guy. He was about six foot three, 210 pounds—a big man.

As he opened the car door, I said, as Arviv had told me to, "You have something for me?"

Sajet hesitated for a minute, then answered: "Yes, I do." One box was still on the roof of the car. He pointed to it. "This is what you want."

"Turn around and bend down a little bit," I said, disguising my voice as best I could. As he did I hit him with a blackjack I was carrying. The blackjack flew from my hand in front of the car. Sajet was semiconscious, lying on the ground. I grabbed the boxes, and as I walked around he said there was still something in the car. I looked inside, saw another box, grabbed it, and then walked to the front of the car, picking up my blackjack.

"Give me about ten minutes," I said to him, "then call the police." Then I jumped the fence, ran behind some apartment houses, down the street to my car, and opened the trunk, throwing the boxes inside. When I checked the boxes out I found only $4,800 in cash and some charge receipts.

When I saw Arviv again, I told him he still owed me $2,000—that his friend wasn't carrying as much as he'd promised. Arviv said he realized that, but he couldn't pay me the $2,000 right away because he was short on cash. In the months that followed, Arviv kept his word and paid me what he owed. He seemed to be a gentleman among the criminals I had known.

There was an attempt at extortion after that. One of my original contacts and some other guys, one biker from Satan's Choice, went to him and tried to shake Mamann down. They hadn't talked to me about it—it was something they did on their own, and they were caught by the cops.

Arviv really hated Mamann. He never really explained why. He said he had started the Hippopotamus and that Mamann and his brother were his partners. After a bitter separation, Arviv went into a clothing business that went under. He said he tore the store down and then started building the disco on money he borrowed from lawyers and other people. I couldn't figure out why he was having so much trouble getting money. His father-in-law was Louis (Lou) Chesler, a multi-million-dollar Canadian financier who was chairman of both the General Development Corp., which sold Florida homes and lots through the mails, and Universal Controls Inc., a big electronics firm. Chesler had also worked in the Bahamas as part of a group that developed a gambling resort at Freeport.

In October 1978, when I was on a diamond-buying visit to Yanover, Chuckie asked me if I knew Arviv. I told him I did and he said his friend Gi Shik Moon had lost a ring of his in a fight at Arviv's Disco.

"You want me to see if I can get the ring back?" I asked.

Yanover nodded.

The next night, Lenti and I picked up Yanover and went to the Oriental Palace, where we met Moon, who told me what happened at the fight. Leaving Moon behind, the three of us went to Arviv's Disco and sat down with Arviv. I introduced Arviv to Yanover and told him about Moon losing the ring. Arviv said he had found the ring after the fight and had turned it over to the police because no one had claimed it. While we sat there drinking his booze on the house, he sent one of his flunkies out to the police and within an hour had the $3,000 ring back in Yanover's hand. That meeting was to lead to the Moon contract to blow up the disco for Arviv.

Maybe ten months later I brought Cosimo to the disco. Arviv had told me he was tired of running the place and wanted very badly to sell it. Since Cosimo wanted to get into the disco business while he was using me to shake down most of the owners in town, I told him that the disco was for sale and that it might be an opportunity for him. He could use a front man to operate it.

Cosimo had other ideas. He tried to strong-arm Arviv and shake him down for the business. Arviv was too smart for that. He suggested that if Cosimo wanted the place he come up with a million bucks and, lacking that, be a nice guy and sip the free champagne. Cosimo backed off on his extortion try after that—I was never certain why, but it could have been because of Arviv's father-in-law. Chesler had some heavy friends—people like Meyer Lansky, the American syndicate's financial wizard, and Trigger Mike Coppola. Those friendships and the respect Chesler had with mob people probably made Cosimo think twice.

A couple weeks after that, in the middle of August 1979, I returned to the disco and Arviv told me that he couldn't sell the business so he'd decided to blow it up.

"Can you do the job?" he asked.

"For fifteen thousand dollars I can do it," I said.

"Make it ten thousand dollars, after it's done," he said. "I'll get the money to pay you then."

"I'll need money for the dynamite," I said. "It'll take a big bomb here in this room." The room we were in was at the rear of the bottom floor.

At first he wanted to supply the explosives, but I told him no—I wanted to buy the dynamite and be sure of the stuff I got. He gave me $300 to make the buy. The bombing was to be done within a few months. I did buy some dynamite, but I never went back to see Arviv or deal with him. In 1981 I turned the dynamite over to the Ontario Provincial Police after I had become an informer.

On January 8, 1980, Arviv's Disco blew sky-high. Nobody was hurt. For a while I couldn't figure out who had done the job. I thought I was the only bomber in the city. In 1983 the truth came out. Moon pleaded guilty and got a five-year sentence. He testified against Yanover, who got nine years, and Gerol, who got seven.

Arviv at first fled the country and holed up in Miami. He finally was extradited to Canada, where he was freed on bail put up by his mother-in-law, Molly Chesler. She put up $250,000 cash, a $250,000 surety bond guaranteed by a condo. There were two more $100,000 bonds guaranteed by property owned by a popcorn company executive and a real estate executive.

As an added guarantee, Arviv had to surrender both his Canadian and Israeli passports. He's still awaiting a trial that I'm supposed to testify at, but it's been stalled for more than two years by his lawyers. Moon and Yanover were convicted and jailed—even Sajet was jailed for thirty days for misleading police with the false robbery report. Arviv pleaded guilty in April 1986, just before I was scheduled to testify at his trial. He was to be sentenced in September. There's still more than $100,000 on my head and a lot of people standing in line, waiting for an opportunity to get me out in the open once more.

Cosimo too often acted on impulse. It was a part of his personality that often seemed to cause him problems, and where his family was involved the impulse could be violent. An insult to his family could have an injurious if not fatal impact on the lives of innocent people. One incident in particular involved a restaurant in downtown Toronto.

There was fire in Cosimo's eyes when he began pounding on a table and cursing in Italian as I entered the office at the Casa Commisso.

"Hey, Cec," he said. "I got a job for you."

"Whatcha want me to do, Cosimo?" I asked.

"I'll give you two grand to blow up this *ristorante* downtown," he said. "I want you to throw a bomb right through their fuckin' window, you understand?"

"Sure," I said, "through the window. But what place are we talking about?"

"It's this fuckin' Napoleon Ristorante," he shouted.

While he was talking—his face flushed—he was counting out $2,000 on the table in front of me. That was unusual and gave me a hint at the depth of his anger. He almost never paid for a job up front.

I asked him why he wanted the place hit and he explained that the night before his wife and his mother-in-law had stopped at the restaurant. While they were there his wife had an argument with the woman who owned the restaurant.

"This woman," he shouted, "she threw my wife and the mother out and my wife, she's very upset and insulted." He pounded again on the table. "Throw the bomb right through the fuckin' window."

"Suppose there's people in there," I asked.

"I don't care," he snapped. "You do it Sunday night, when the owner is there. I don't care if there's anybody else inside at all. Fuck them. Just blow the inside of the place right out, you understand?"

"Okay, okay," I said. He was very agitated, and it was no time to question him. "I'll do something similar to what you want," I said.

So I went to my cottage and made up a bomb that consisted of two sticks of dynamite, a battery, and a timer and brought it back that same night. I cased the restaurant and then parked my car on a nearby corner.

I slipped down the side of an alley on the east side of the restaurant and put the bomb on a window ledge. For a split second I took my eye off the bomb as I reached into my pocket to get something. I felt like I was suspended in time watching my own killing as I saw the bomb fall from the ledge to the ground. It took only seconds, but I thought it was in slow motion and that my hands were frozen to my pants. As it hit the ground, my heart literally stopped.

If I had had it wired to the blasting cap and I had had the cap in the dynamite, I wouldn't be here to tell this story. They'd still be scraping pieces of me off the buildings.

After I caught my breath, I picked the bomb up slowly, put it back on the window ledge, made sure it was firmly in place, set the timer, and left. I was in the North End of Toronto, about twenty miles away, when it went off.

The next day I read in the paper that the bomb had injured three women. Now that wasn't what I had intended. Despite Cosimo's orders, I had phoned the restaurant before I arrived to make sure that nobody was inside. I had let the phone ring about thirty times, and when nobody answered I figured it was safe.

When I placed the bomb, I couldn't see inside because the window was so thick and there were no lights on. But I guess the owner and two of her friends had returned to the restaurant after I'd left and were sitting inside when the bomb went off, sending glass flying through the air like razor-sharp missiles.

Police told me later that one of the iron bars outside the window next to the bomb was blasted loose and thrown across the room where the women were. The police said it narrowly missed the owner's head and struck the wall. If it had hit her it might have decapitated her. They were all hurt, cut up pretty bad. Later, they received awards for damages and injuries from the criminal compensation board, but they at least survived.

And Cosimo? He was pleased as hell over the results. He didn't give a damn about the women. The insult had to be avenged and it was. For a time, however, the papers blamed it on French terrorists. The bomb had gone off at 8:45 P.M. on May 4, 1980, the anniversary of Prime Minister Margaret Thatcher's taking office in England. She'd opposed French separatists' plans to have the Province of Quebec declared a separate country.

* * *

There was one other club owner, a restauranteur really, that Cosimo put the arm on. He wasn't trying to collect for himself on this one—he was trying to collect a debt that Willie O'Bront, the French rackets friend and money launderer of crime boss Vincent Cotroni, said was due him. O'Bront lived in Hallandale, Florida, where he was accused by U.S. drug agents in 1983 of operating a $50-million-a-year narcotics trafficking ring.

In early July 1980 I went to see Cosimo about the job. The target was Maury Kalen, then the owner of Mr. Greenjeans Restaurants in Toronto.

"This Kalen, he owes money—a hundred thousand—to a friend of mine, to Willie O'Bront," Cosimo said. "I want you to send the message to him with a bomb."

Now I knew who and what O'Bront was, but I knew nothing about Kalen, so I took Cosimo at his word. I also took his word that he knew where Kalen lived when he gave me the address of his house in Toronto. I had a description of his car and the locations of his office in Village Grange and of the restaurants, one on Lombard Street and the other in the crowded Eaton Center. The Greenjeans Restaurants weren't anything elaborate, but they were popular for their salad bars and food.

Cosimo wanted me to set off a bomb in Kalen's house or his car, but on looking over the area, I figured the best thing to do was drop a couple of sticks of dynamite taped together without a fuse in the mailbox at his home.

I ruled out bombing the car as being too dangerous. The restaurants were out as far as I was concerned because there were too many people around them. I figured the bomb in the mailbox was as good a message as any explosion, and that way no one would get hurt. If something more violent was needed later—well, that was another story.

The job was worth $2,000, and Cosimo paid me the fee. Late on the night of July 7, I dropped the two sticks in the mailbox. I learned later that two guys in a room where Kalen was supposed to be saw the two sticks land inside their mail cage by the door. They called the cops, and early on the morning of July 8 the Metropolitan Toronto Police Explosive Disposal Unit came out to remove the dynamite.

A week later I got a call from Cosimo and met him again at the banquet hall.

"Cec, this Kalen, he moved from Heath Street just before you put the dynamite there," he said. "I want you to go to his new home and bomb it. I'll give you two thousand more."

The new location was the Palace Pier.

"Cosimo, that place is crawling with security guards," I said. "It's too tough to hit."

Cosimo smiled broadly. "Don't worry, Cec," he said. "I'll take care of the guards. I know people there."

"You mean that the security guard will let me in to place a bomb at the fuckin' door!" I said.

"Well, maybe not," he said.

I told him I wouldn't handle the job, and later I learned from police that it wasn't Kalen that owed O'Bront money, but supposedly his father. Not only was Cosimo stupid about what he thought could be done, but he did lousy homework on addresses and his victims.

14

False Hopes, False Starts

Today, Montreal's Mafia is supposed to be run by a Sicilian "man of respect" who they call Nicholas Rizzuto. He divides his time between Canada and Venezuela, where he has a business. I don't know Rizzuto personally. I do know that he and the Commissos were close. I also know that for many years before Rizzuto took over, Montreal's Mafia was ruled by Vincent Cotroni and the three Violi brothers—Paolo, Rocco, and Francesco. All of them had two things in common. They were Calabrians and they had gotten to where they were in Montreal because of Carmine (Lillo) Galante.

Galante was Joseph Bonanno's underboss before he was killed in July 1979. While he was with Bonanno, he was sent to Montreal to organize a branch of their New York crime family. That, along with other things, caused Buffalo mob boss Stefano Magaddino to complain about Bonanno ignoring other mafiosi to plant "his flags" all over the world. I'm told that the Cotroni brothers and the Violi brothers were, like Galante, among the most vicious killers and Mafia men ever to walk the streets of Montreal.

Galante's top men at first were Giuseppe and Vincent Cotroni. The youngest brother, Francesco or Frank, moved up later. At the same time, the Contronis' closest supporter and enforcer was Paolo Violi. The only guy who wasn't a

Calabrian was Galante—he was born in the States. His father was supposed to be an immigrant fisherman from Castellammare del Golfo, the same Sicilian village that Bonanno came from.

They formed a Bonanno family branch that ruled Montreal and provided a smuggling route into the United States for heroin that was imported from Sicily and Marseilles. Public hearings in the States and narcotics agents later confirmed that.

The Montreal Bonanno branch then became a full-fledged Canadian crime family run by Vincent Cotroni. Galante eventually became Bonanno's successor and got greedy. He tried to take over the narcotics supply routes of some other bosses of the American Cosa Nostra, and they had him knocked off by his own people, replacing him with Philip Rastelli, who had a lot of friends in Toronto. Before Galante was killed, Cotroni went to jail for a couple of years and Paolo Violi became the acting boss of the Montreal family, according to a Quebec crime commission inquiry.

I first became aware there were problems between the Commisso brothers and the Violis on February 11, 1977. That was a couple of days after Francesco Violi, the youngest brother, was killed at the headquarters of a Violi importing and distributing company. He was supposed to have been backed against a wall and shot in the face by a shotgun. Another killer made sure he was dead by pumping some bullets into him from a handgun.

Cosimo called me and told me it was very important I come as quickly as possible to the Casa Commisso. When I arrived, Cosimo was pacing up and down and Remo was nowhere to be seen.

"So I'm here," I said. "What's the big hurry?"

"I need some guns—some pistols and shotguns, and I need them fast," Cosimo said.

"How many?" I asked.

"I need five, six, maybe more if you can get them," he said. He was very agitated.

"What the hell you need them so fast for?" I asked.

"You ask a lotta questions, Cec—maybe too many," he snapped.

He looked at me, his eyes flashing a bit. I was starting to get pissed off myself now, and I made sure he knew how I felt.

"Oh for chrissake, Cosimo. You want guns I'll get you guns," I said sharply. "I don't really give a damn why you want them."

His voice softened, and for the first time he sat down. "I'm sorry, Cec," he said. "You see the stories about Frank Violi?"

"Yeah, sure," I said.

"Well, the people in Montreal, they think me and Remo killed him," he said. He paused and lowered his voice. "We may have to go to Montreal to kill the rest of the family—like we get this guy."

Had he and Remo killed Francesco Violi? I had only what he said that morning and the way he was acting to go on. Just because he said they got Francesco didn't mean they did, but he was desperate for guns at that moment. I didn't press him any more on what had happened. Within a day or two I had acquired all the guns he wanted. When I was ready to deliver them, I called the Casa Commisso and asked for Cosimo. He wasn't there, but Remo was.

"I got that package ready that you need," I told him.

"Forget it, Cec," he said, "we're not going to need them."

Almost a year went by before the Violis made headlines again. This time it was Paolo who hit the front page.

"Blood spilling is feared after Mafia boss killed," was the headline of the January 24, 1978, *Toronto Sun*. The story was about how Paolo Violi was killed in his Jean Talon bar and restaurant on January 22 when two masked men burst in from the street to gun him down while he played cards. Both of the killers were using shotguns, a favorite Italian Mafia weapon. Four men, Sicilians, were arrested and later convicted of conspiracy to murder Violi.

Were the Commissos involved? I remember going to their banquet hall the day after the murder. We were

constantly meeting at that time, handling hijacked cigarettes, arsons, extortions, assaults.

"Where's Remo?" I asked Cosimo.

"He's in Montreal," Cosimo answered.

"Wasn't that where Violi was killed in his restaurant?"
I asked.

"Yeah, isn't that funny?" he said with a smirk on his
face.

It was funny, all right, but I found something else that
was strange. Both the Violi brothers had been gunned
down with shotguns. Remo's favorite weapon was the
shotgun. He loved skeet shooting, but he also said the
shotgun was his favorite weapon in Italy. They were also
close friends of Rizzuto, the guy who took over the Montreal
mob from the Violis.

On October 19, 1980, the last of the Violi brothers,
Rocco, was killed by a single shot in the heart while he sat
at his kitchen table with his wife and two children in his
home in the east end of Montreal. The cops said the
shooting was by a professional killer. I remember wondering at the time if the Commissos were involved. It was
their style. They wouldn't hesitate about killing a guy
in front of his wife and kids. Any family that would kill
whole families in Italy, including a baby in a crib, would
kill a rival in front of his family. They had no ethics—no
honor about murder—when it came to wielding power.

For some reason, 1978 and 1979 were years when a
lot of the Commissos' extortions and arsons went wrong. It
had to do with their lack of planning, their rush to do
things without checking them through thoroughly. Some
Calabrian friend would want them to burn down his place
right away to collect insurance and they'd hand me the job
and say go do it without even looking it over. If someone
got hurt or even killed because they were careless, they
didn't care.

The Avala Tavern was typical. It was located in Toronto
and was owned by a friend of the Commissos who was
never fully identified to me. Remo, who could speak the

King's English when he wanted to or pretend he needed an interpreter when he was in court, just handed me a key to the back door and told me to use garbage bags filled with gasoline to start the fire.

I'd never been in the place before, never had a chance to see where things were, so when I got there on the night of July 6 it was like groping in a dark unfamiliar closet.

I was carrying a jerrican filled with a mixture of kerosene and oil. Wherever I went in the damned place I kept banging into things. I finally found my way to the basement, where Remo wanted me to start the fire, but when I got there I couldn't find a light switch. There were none. I couldn't find the damned door to the upstairs either. I left the can lying behind me and I was lighting matches, trying to see where I was going, because like a dope I hadn't brought a flashlight. From the beginning, this assignment had been a disaster because it hadn't been planned.

I finally found a couch downstairs, and I took the jerrican and poured the stuff I had in it all over the couch. Now Remo wanted me to shut the back door to the basement behind me and lock it. What that did was cut off all the air. Since I couldn't find the upstairs door to open so the fire could spread to the upper section of the tavern, this fire had nowhere to go but out.

At 4:38 A.M., the Metropolitan Toronto Fire Department was called to the scene by a police constable who spotted the fire. The damage was limited to the couch, and the blaze had virtually gone out by itself by the time the firemen arrived.

The Commissos only paid me about a hundred dollars because the place hadn't burned down. Even if I'd burned the place to the ground, I would have gotten only a few hundred bucks. Later on some young Italian was hired by someone to go back to the tavern and torch it. The kid got caught in the fire he set. He was convicted, but he needed a lot of medical treatment first.

A month later the Commissos had another arson

scheme that was almost as bad. This time the place was a restaurant and banquet hall in Niagara Falls called Vaccaro's Italian Gardens. It was owned by another of their Calabrian friends.

This time I went to the restaurant with Cosimo. He drove while his driver, Vince, sat in the backseat. It gave me an uneasy feeling, like it was a setup, but I shrugged it off as my imagination. It was.

I went with Cosimo because I wanted to plan appropriately. I wasn't going to get caught groping in a dark basement without a light again. When we got to the restaurant, we all took a tour, outside and inside. I went up to the roof and looked around, noticing a giant Ferris wheel nearby, and I checked other buildings in the area. When I was through, we all sat down to a dinner with wine that had been prepared by Cosimo's friend. We talked first in general terms, then more specifically. Even then I felt uncomfortable, because stragglers and wise guys were coming in and wandering around while we talked.

What bothered me most was the way Cosimo's friend wanted it done. He wanted me to bomb the building next door so that his place would catch fire by mistake.

"That's too dangerous, Cosimo," I complained. "It'll take too damned much dynamite to do what he wants. If I put dynamite between the buildings, I can't guarantee that it'll work properly, and somebody could get hurt."

"Don't worry," Cosimo said. "It's worth ten, fifteen thousand dollars if you do the job right."

"I'm telling you, Cosimo, it's too risky to do it the way he wants it," I said. "I can take this place down good if I put the bomb in the kitchen. And there's less chance of somebody getting hurt."

Cosimo's associate wasn't sure he could pay the price. He wanted time to check his insurance policy and told me to come back again later.

A couple of weeks went by, and I didn't hear from Cosimo. Finally I asked him about it.

"Forget it, Cec," he said, "it's all been taken care of."

I learned later that the restaurant had burned to the ground. I never did find out how it was done, and I didn't care.

Sometimes I think carelessness was the Commissos' middle name. They were forever making mistakes, mistakes that injured innocent people or damaged the wrong location. They were reckless. They were like the gang that couldn't shoot straight. The only difference was they could shoot straight, they just didn't shoot or beat up the right people.

As careless and stupid as they seemed to be even to me, they were still making millions, whether they did nickel-and-dime extortions or rattled the cages of a whole industry, like construction. For them there was nothing too big or too small to make money from.

Typical of the nickel-and-dime jobs they managed to screw up was one involving a business called Cook-O-Matic, a pots and pans distributor that operated three miles from the Casa Commisso. The owner of the business was a man named Frank Mauro. Cosimo and Remo had tried a number of times to extort money from him without much success. So they turned to me and I, in turn, went to a friend of mine, a kid I'll call Jimmy Tires.

Jimmy was a young hustler and tough who wanted to make some money on the side, so I told him I'd pay him a few bucks if he hassled Mauro for me while I handled some other work. Jimmy did what he was told. He went to Mauro's business location, flattened all the tires on the guy's car, and then poured paint over it. Then he made some threatening calls to Mauro. It wasn't enough.

Cosimo complained that Mauro still wasn't paying. Finally, one night in December, Cosimo and I drove by Mauro's business. Two men were standing in front of the office loading boxes into a parked car.

"That's him," Cosimo shouted, "that's the fuck that refuses to pay."

"Which one?" I asked.

He pointed to one guy holding a box. "That's him,"

he said. "I want you to break his arms like this." He angrily snapped a toothpick between his fingers.

"Screw it," I said. "I'll do it right now." With that I parked the car around the corner, got out, and walked toward the man that Cosimo had identified as Mauro. My head was down so neither man could make out my face.

I caught him cold turkey on the chin. He was bleeding as he fell back and hit his head against the wall. I took off in a dead run around the corner, jumped in the car, and drove off.

It wasn't until years later I found out it was the wrong guy. The guy I'd banged around was the warehouse manager of Cook-O-Matic, a man named Peter Antonucci. I'd hit the guy Cosimo pointed out, but he'd pointed out the wrong man.

Maclean's magazine on June 21, 1982, identified Carmelo Gallo as a key figure in what they called "the Italian Connection" of a multi-million-dollar international opium, heroin, and cocaine smuggling scheme that stretched from Italy and the Middle East to Vancouver and Southeast Asia. They described him as a thirty-five-year-old "cheerful grocer" who had singlehandedly extended the 1981 narcotics trial by four months when he escaped from a Vancouver hospital bathroom during the trial. He was sentenced to life for conspiracy to traffic in heroin, and they gave him another twenty years for conspiring to deal in cocaine. The cops didn't see him again until January 1983, when he gave up to appeal his conviction.

I knew Gallo by a different standard and a different name. When I met him in March 1979 with Cosimo, he was introduced as Carmen Gallo, their "family" man in Vancouver. He was not only their main West Coast connection for heroin, but since 1976 he had been their primary source for counterfeit money. It was the same counterfeit American money that caused so many Calabrians and my biker friends to get either busted or shot.

I met Gallo at the Casa Commisso. He was nicer than most of the Calabrians that I'd met at the banquet hall or with Cosimo. He was a little guy, sort of quiet, always smiling, with a sense of humor and the kind of laugh that made others laugh. He was only about thirty-two years old at the time, with wavy brown hair and brown eyes. That was one thing about the Commissos' Mafia family. They were almost all young. There weren't any old-timers, any of what they call the Mustache Pete types.

When Cosimo introduced me to Gallo, he told me that after Gallo returned to Vancouver, he would be calling to arrange for me to join him on the West Coast.

"Carmen's gonna give us information for a big robbery that you're gonna handle," he said.

Cosimo went on to describe what they had in mind. It involved a courier who left an underground location in downtown Vancouver carrying a bag full of money—$200,000 to $500,000.

"They've been doing this for years," he explained. "They got no security—no guards, no cops, no gun, nothin'. This courier, he just takes the bag of money—he brings it out to the docks and pays the fishermen. They do it for one week steady, every day and that's it. We get only one shot at the jackpot."

"Okay," I said, "I'm ready to leave any time. Just get ahold of me the usual way."

A week or so later I got a call and flew out to Vancouver, where I met Gallo again, this time at an Italian restaurant. He took me to a twelve-dollar-a-night hotel in the Jewish section of town and got me a room.

"I'll be back in the morning to take you down to the place we want to hit," he said. "I'll have a driver to get you there. You'll have a gun, handcuffs, everything you need for the job."

I should have known right then to case the courier and the location on my own. The trouble was they had never given me details on the location, what route the courier followed, the times he left and arrived—nothing.

The next morning Gallo showed up at the hotel. There was no driver with him, no gun or handcuffs, and he wasn't smiling as he usually did.

"We missed it. We missed the last payroll yesterday," he said dejectedly. "I tried to call Remo but it was ridiculous. He wouldn't listen. You can't talk to him."

With the right information and the right time it could have been a simple job. I would have just had to flatten the tire on the courier's car and when he changed the tire, knocked him out, thrown him in the trunk, and left with the bag of money. I'd have been back in Toronto by the time he got out to report the heist.

I was supposed to get one-third of whatever was in that bag. Gallo was to get a third, and the Commissos would have gotten a third. The truth is, I'd planned to take half to make up for all the money they still owed me. It was just another false hope, a false start on another plot that failed.

Probably the worst arson plan of all was the one carried out at the Dominion Hotel in Acton, Ontario. I was supposed to blow it up, but like with Vaccaro's Italian Gardens I insisted on certain preconditions, so I didn't handle the job.

I was upset by the plan from the beginning because Cosimo had brought the client, the owner of the hotel, to the Casa Commisso to meet me. That was unusual, and it made me nervous. I didn't like meeting the people who were hiring me through him even though I was always introduced to them as "George." Meetings gave Cosimo a two-on-one edge if any arrests should result from the crimes. The worst part of it was I always had the feeling that I was being set up or used. I never knew if a so-called client was what Cosimo said he was or some Calabrian getting ready to do me in.

As George I met with the hotel owner, Cosimo Mercuri, in early August, just before going to Niagara Falls. Cosimo identified him as Cosimo Val-Currie, not Mercuri. They talked some in Italian first, which I didn't understand, then the hotel owner, who I later testified against as Mercuri, said he wanted me to burn the hotel down.

"I'll come up and look at it and tell you the best way to do the job," I said. "Maybe it can be bombed, maybe burning is best." Then I added a word of caution. "There are two things I want to be sure of. I want to be certain there are no people inside, and I want ten thousand dollars up front before I do any planning on this job."

Mercuri admitted there were people living in the hotel, but he didn't seem concerned about it.

"Then they have to be taken out somehow," I said. "You got to make some arrangement so there's no one inside when it goes up—maybe a phone call saying there's a bomb in the building."

"I don't know," Mercuri said. "I don't have the money right now. Give me a week to get the money."

I never heard from him again, but on August 19, 1979, the Dominion Hotel burned to the ground. A fifty-nine-year-old guest named Howard Gibbons was trapped in the fire and died.

Mercuri and two others—Michael McCrystal, one of his hotel employees, and Leonard Cripps—were arrested. Cripps was acquitted, but Mercuri and McCrystal were convicted after I testified about Mercuri coming to me with Cosimo. Mercuri went to jail for twenty-five years while McCrystal got two years.

Vaccaro Gardens, Mercuri, and a dozen other plots that I never got paid to do—they were all part of an increasing mistrust that was developing between us. I had been screwed out of more than $30,000 in promised fees in 1979 alone.

Up to then I had pretty much trusted the Commissos. I knew they had been cheating me, but that wasn't all that unusual in the underworld. Everybody chisels. Everybody's hustling. That's the way of the street. Even so, there was always a nagging feeling at the back of my mind about why they had chosen me as their chief enforcer. I wasn't Calabrian. I wasn't a sworn member of their Honoured Society. I played by my rules, not theirs.

I had always figured that the Commissos had gone outside their group because they didn't have anyone within the group who was straight enough, with the capabilities I had—the experience—to handle their jobs. Yet I knew that there was a possibility, a likelihood, that they might eventually kill me because I knew too much about their operations, had handled too many jobs for them.

While that uncertainty bothered me, it didn't concern me enough to fear for my life. In truth, I didn't really worry that much about living or dying. The day I started working for the Commissos, I had been divorced by my wife. It was my own fault for fooling around with other women. I had lost her and my daughter, and I really didn't have a handle on where my life was going.

I remember asking Cosimo when I started working for him in 1976 about my predecessor.

"I know you had to have somebody working for you—doing what I'm going to be doing," I said. "What happened to him?"

"Oh, he went back to Italy," Cosimo said. "He didn't want to stay in Canada."

I didn't really believe him then, and I still don't. I figured that the guy had been killed and that sooner or later that was what was in store for me.

I think what made it jell more for me mentally was seeing one deal after another go down the tubes and fewer jobs being offered. The uneasiness was the worst when I saw how Cosimo dealt with other people who worked for him, like Anthony Carnevale.

Carnevale was a drug dealer, a street punk, a guy who robbed card games and pool halls for the Commissos with other street hoods. The Commissos would set up the games and promise to provide protection for them. Then they would turn Carnevale and his thugs loose to hold them up. The robbers would take from $3,000 to $20,000 or more from people who were so-called friends of the Commissos. Carnevale and his men would take the piece allotted to them and give the rest to the Commissos, who planned the jobs. The Commissos made hundreds of thousands of dollars from holdups like that, many of them never reported to police, all of them handled by their stickup men.

On January 12, 1980, Carnevale was killed by a shotgun blast through the window of his parents' home. His girlfriend, who was with him, was badly wounded but she survived. I heard that Cosimo had been tipped that Carnevale was a police informer, yet he'd done nothing to hurt the Commissos or anyone involved in the dozens of robberies they had arranged.

PART FOUR

Government Witness

15

Let's Make a Deal

He was tall and gangling and there was something that reminded me of Jimmy Stewart in the way he walked and talked. Beneath his cap was a shock of dark brown hair and a mischievous Irish face. His eyes sort of sparkled with excitement when he talked. When he had something to say, I knew I was listening to the voice of an honest man.

I liked Corporal Mark Murphy from the first moment I met him under a phony name in the parking lot of the Casa Loma. There was nothing devious about the man. He was what he said he was—a tough, dedicated Royal Canadian Mounted Policeman who wanted to fight organized crime in Canada more than he wanted to eat, almost more than he wanted to be with his wife and children, who he really was devoted to.

He had been an important investigator in Operation Oblong, a big RCMP intelligence-gathering mission aimed at the crime organization of Paul Volpe. He was familiar with and had worked on Nate Klegerman, Volpe's top lieutenant in the loan-shark rackets, and he knew Chuck Yanover and what he was up to almost as well as I did.

Murphy and the investigators he worked with had spent thousands of hours looking at Volpe's rackets— loan-sharking, diamond smuggling, casino investments, arson, you name it. Their investigation had led them to Las Vegas, to New Jersey and Atlantic City, and finally to the convictions of some of Volpe's flunkies—Yanover, Murray Feldberg, and Jimmy Bass—for extortion.

His knowing all that and more about organized crime made my meeting with Murphy all the more important. It was a freak—a stroke of luck that changed my life and is probably the reason I am still alive today.

By November 1980 I knew it was only a matter of time before I would become one of the Commissos' victims. Assignments were coming fewer and farther apart, and each seemed to be more reckless than the last. It was almost as if they were handing me jobs that they hoped would result in my getting killed or caught by police.

My initial suspicions, as I said earlier, were raised when they wanted me to go to Italy to murder Momo Piromalli, the Calabrian Mafia boss. The Commissos swore they had a plan for my escape, but in the back of my mind I knew they didn't, I knew I was going to be wasted by some grubby little roadside in Italy and buried in some field where I'd never be found.

In May 1980 Cosimo insisted on bombing Napoleon's Restaurant, a stupid act of pure vengeance that nearly resulted in the death of three women because Cosimo's wife had been insulted. And then in October, there was what I considered his reckless order to bomb Maury Kalen's apartment despite heavy security. If I'd carried out that plan the way he wanted me to, I'd have been killed by one of those security guards the moment the bomb had gone off.

There were also a lot of little things, things I couldn't put a handle on, but that nevertheless made me uncertain. I could enter a room at the Casa Commisso and talk would stop. Cosimo, Remo, and I could be talking about something in English and when a friend of theirs entered the room, someone I knew spoke and understood English, the language suddenly turned to Italian. Remo was using cousins and relatives to contact me at the health club for meetings or to deliver messages and money to me. I had the feeling they didn't trust me and yet I'd never, up to then, talked to a cop or done anything suspicious.

Being cheated out of money I had coming to me was causing friction, arguments. I knew it wasn't healthy for me to protest so loudly about the money they owed me or to refuse to handle their assignments. There was no room for a rebel in the Commissos' organization. It might give younger, impressionable members ideas about discipline and whether Cosimo should be a boss.

With all these insecurities, I was also facing the likelihood of a long jail sentence for an old break and entry that involved an assault and extortion. The Commissos had always seemed suspicious about the delays my lawyers got in the case. There was something in their questions about those delays that made me think they thought I was whispering in some cop's ear. There was also no better place for the Commissos to have me wasted than in jail. A prisoner with a shiv, a prison fight—suddenly I'm history and they've got no one to worry about.

I had to find a way out, to protect myself, to cut a deal, and to work something out with someone in law enforcement. If I could trade important information for help in getting my sentence reduced or even dropped to probation, I'd have breathing space and maybe a chance to survive.

My first attempt had been with Terry Hall of the Ontario Provincial Police. I told him that his life was in danger, that the Vagabonds had a contract to kill him. He didn't even say thanks, let alone talk about seeing what he could do for me on the charges I was facing—charges he and Ron Tavenor of Toronto's Metro Police biker squad were responsible for.

There was little chance of my getting anywhere with them. They'd take whatever I gave them, but they wouldn't help me make a deal. If I couldn't talk to them, who could I talk to? I had to be careful, very careful.

On November 10 I dialed the number for the RCMP National Crime Intelligence Section.

"RCMP, can I help you?" the voice at the other end said smartly.

"Who am I talking to?" I asked.

"Corporal Murphy, Corporal Mark Murphy," was the reply.

"Look, Corporal Murphy, we don't know each other, but I can help you," I said. "I can solve a lot of cases for you, maybe even some murders."

"I'm listening," Murphy said, "but you haven't told me anything yet."

I told Murphy I was a former member of the Satan's Choice and that I could give him information on robberies that had happened and were about to take place. I also told him that if he played it straight with me I could give him information about organized crime, particularly the Commissos.

"All I want is someone to put in a good word for me when I'm sentenced on a B&E. For that you get a lot of heavy stuff." Then I added: "If you're interested, meet me in a half hour in the parking lot of the Casa Loma. Come alone, and no wires or we don't talk."

"What's your name?" he asked.

"No names for now," I said. "Just be there."

The Casa Loma Castle is a tourist attraction in downtown Toronto. It was built in 1911 and took three years to complete. It's advertised in magazines as North America's "most famous castle," and they are probably right. I can't remember ever seeing a castle anywhere else that had gold-plated bathroom fixtures and porcelain troughs for horses. But that and its ninety-eight rooms weren't what made me select it as a meeting place.

The castle is set up in such a way that it's easy to spot people in the parking lot or coming from various vantage points. It's also not the kind of place that mafiosi or bikers come to too often. By getting there before Murphy, I could see if he was followed or if there was anyone else there that looked like a cop or a hood.

I watched Murphy come up from Austin Terrace and

pull into the Casa Loma driveway. He parked where I told him to, climbed out of his unmarked police car, and stood up, towering over the roof of the vehicle. I jotted down his license number so I could check it out through a friend later. When I was certain there was no one following him, I walked up behind him.

"You Corporal Murphy?" I asked.

"That's right," he said. "What do I call you?"

"Call me Jack, Jack Ryan for now," I said. "When we know each other better, I'll give you my real name."

As we talked, my eyes tracked the entire parking lot and the overhead terraces of the castle for anything, anyone out of the ordinary. I saw no one. I patted him down to see if he was wearing anything. He wasn't.

"It's not that I don't trust you," I said, "but cops aren't my favorite people, and so far the ones I've dealt with haven't been too trustworthy."

"Let's get on with it," Murphy said, a little annoyed by all my precautions.

"One more thing before we talk," I said. "I've already supplied good information to Terry Hall of the OPP. He double-crossed me on a case in court. I don't want to deal with him anymore. That understood?"

Murphy nodded.

"I'm not asking to have charges against me dropped," I said. "I just want you to assist me at my sentencing—put in a good word for me. I can't beat the B&E. I'm looking at two to four years. I just want to minimize the sentence."

Murphy understood, but he guaranteed nothing. "I can't promise you anything," he said. "If what you tell me is helpful, useful, I'll talk to my superiors—see what can be done for you. But you've got to produce."

"Good enough," I answered. With that I began to supply him with information on some drug deals, some armed robberies, and some burglaries. We talked about bikers, about the Mafia, and about guns.

"I'm in the business of guns," I said. "I sell them. I sell them to bikers, to rounders, I sell them to the Commissos. Some are handguns, some are rifles, some are machine guns, and I know where they are. Sometimes when I sell these guns, people are shot." Then I added: "Maybe if things check out the way you want, I can give you some unsolved murders."

With that I left, telling Murphy to take some time checking things I told him about. "I'll get back to you in a few days, and then we'll see where we go from there," I said. "Just don't double-cross me. I won't forget it. I may even have to come after you."

When we separated that day there were problems, some of which I was unaware of. I had given Murphy my true name, but when I called him I used the name Jack Ryan so that no one else knew that it was Cecil Kirby who was talking to him.

The veiled threat had made an impression on Murphy. So did the relationship that developed between us in the year that was to follow. He considered me dangerous, and he said so in a confidential RCMP report dated November 2, 1982: "[Kirby's] dual personality ranges from a very kind person to a vicious, hot-tempered violent individual who is quite capable of killing. He might also be described as an opportunist. I quickly perceived Kirby to be an experienced criminal who had tremendous potential as an informer."

Murphy was cautiously optimistic that I could be helpful to him, but Hall and Tavenor and some of their superiors didn't see it that way. On November 26, at another meeting with Murphy, I was secretly watched by Hall and Tavenor, who had put me under surveillance and tailed me to the meeting. They recognized Murphy.

Tavenor and his superiors at Metro called Murphy. They demanded to know what I had been talking to him about. Murphy told them, but warned Tavenor not to say anything because I had made a veiled threat to Murphy if he told Tavenor and Hall I was talking.

At the meeting I'd had with Murphy, I had given him information I'd just received from a rounder friend on a stash of one hundred pounds of hash hidden in a store.

"If you want," my friend said, "we can hit this place—rip them off. All we have to do is pull our guns, tell them we're cops, tie them up, and leave with the load of hash."

I told him it was a great idea, then I went to the meeting with Murphy to tell him. He said I would have to talk to a narcotics sergeant of the RCMP about it.

I talked to the sergeant, told him I'd stall my friend as long as possible. "If you hit it in the morning," I said, "be sure you have a cop outside and that he's visible."

"How the hell do you know it's there?" the sergeant said, a little testily.

"Look, it's there. I guarantee it," I said. "If you don't go, I'm going to fuckin' go with someone else and take it for myself!"

On November 28 my friend and I drove down to hold up the drug dealers. As we approached the store, I pointed to a uniform cop in front of the store.

"We better get the hell out of here," I said. "There's a cop there." We drove off as my friend cursed our bad luck.

The RCMP wasn't so unlucky. They had seized 42 pounds of hash, 900 hits of LSD, pornographic film, and a stolen stereo. The haul was worth over $150,000, and they had arrested three people to boot. Murphy suggested I be paid $2,000 for supplying the information. It wasn't unusual to be paid for giving such good information. It was done all the time. His request was turned down. I got nothing, and the narco squad took all the credit.

Less than a week later I was pulled out of court during my trial by Hall.

"You're talking to the Horsemen," Hall said. "Get this straight, Kirby. You'll get no help on these charges unless you talk to us."

"I don't trust you, Hall," I said. "I'm not dealing with you."

It wasn't that I thought Hall or his superiors weren't honest. As far as I knew they were. I just felt Hall wouldn't keep a promise. Telling him how I felt didn't help. For the next month or more, Hall, Tavenor, and the brass they worked with did everything they could to stop Murphy from helping me.

I was caught in a tug-of-war between rival agencies.

The RCMP has Canada-wide authority, like the FBI in the United States, and they operate with local agencies the same way. They like to operate on a one-way street. They like to take information, but they don't give it unless they have to, because either they don't want to share the credit for a big arrest or they don't trust the local agency they're supposed to be working with.

The result of all these rivalries and mistrust is that organized crime profits. Members of different mobs learn to work together because it means saving their own skins and making big money. That's something police at national levels haven't learned to do yet. Until they do, the mobs will always slip through the cracks.

In this case, though, the big hang-up was with the locals. They didn't want the RCMP in the form of Murphy coming in and taking over a case or a possible informant. They threw up every roadblock possible. It seemed to me it was more jealousy than anything else.

As far as Murphy was concerned, I had proved I could be a valuable informer. But it still wasn't enough for his bosses and for Sergeant Robert Silverton of Metro, who supervised the operations of Hall and Tavenor. Then I dropped information on another important case in Murphy's lap.

There had been a robbery of a jewelry store, the Dolly Jewelers in Toronto, on January 15. On the day of the robbery, I was maybe a half a block away from the store when I bumped into the two guys who'd held it up, Nicolino Pallotta and Richard Cucman. I knew them both from the street, and they told me they'd just held up Dolly's and had a bag full of jewelry.

"Sounds like you got a lot," I said, after listening to them brag. "Look, if you have any trouble getting rid of the stuff, let me know. Maybe I can help out."

As I talked, my mind was spinning with possibilities.

I could use what I knew about the robbery as a bargaining chip with Murphy and those he worked for, and maybe I could make myself some money by recovering the jewelry and selling it.

Less than a week after I'd seen them, on January 20, I called Murphy.

"You know that Dolly Jewelers robbery?" I asked.

"Yeah, what about it?" said Murphy.

"If I can get some help at the court, if someone will speak to the Crown for me, I'll solve their robbery for them," I said. "I'll give them the names of the holdup men on a silver platter."

"I'll see what I can do," Murphy said.

Murphy tried. He talked to Silverton. He said Silverton wouldn't even consider speaking to the Crown for me. He said he then asked two inspectors he reports to to intercede with Silverton's boss, Inspector Don Banks of Metro. According to Murphy, they refused.

When Murphy told me that none of the coppers involved with him or with my case were willing to go to bat for me, I was furious—not at Murphy, but at the people who he worked for, who were so goddamned narrow-minded.

"Maybe if you give me the names, some proof, I can get them to agree," Murphy said.

"I'll have to think about it," I said.

A few days later Pallotta and Cucman came to me with the bag of jewelry and asked me to sell it. I took it, but I couldn't sell it because they were asking too much for it. So I returned it to them. It was mostly junk jewelry, anyway, about one hundred diamond rings, gold chains, knickknacks. They also had about one hundred used watches they'd grabbed, and I told them to throw them down the incinerator of the apartment we met at or police would track the stuff back to them. I found out later on that they had tried to sell the jewelry to the Commissos.

Finally, I decided to give Murphy the names of the holdup men. The cops arrested them both, and they were later convicted, but it didn't impress Murphy's two superiors, particularly Inspector James McIlvenna, who was the boss of the Joint Forces Special Enforcement Unit that was later to provide protection for me.

Murphy said that McIlvenna told him he wouldn't touch my case "with a hundred-foot pole."

"McIlvenna and Inspector [J] Wylie said I should let you go to jail, Cecil," Murphy said. "I just want you to know I'm not giving up. So don't you give up."

I didn't and he didn't, but a year later Pallotta and Cucman pleaded guilty to the robbery. Their attorney, Earl Levy, charged, in a grandstand play to the press outside the courtroom, that I had "ripped off" $140,000 worth of stolen jewelry from them. Cucman, who got two years, made the charge because the Commissos told him to. They were trying to show I had lied as a witness.

It didn't take McIlvenna long to jump on the bandwagon after Levy's charge appeared in the press.

"Did you keep the jewelry from those two?" he roared.

"If I had one hundred thousand dollars in stolen jewelry, I damn sure wouldn't be here talking to you," I snapped back. "I'd be in Florida, where I wouldn't have to listen to your shit."

Pallotta, who got three years because he was carrying the gun during the robbery, wouldn't confirm Cucman's story. He told the cops that I did give all the jewelry back, and he took a lie detector test to back up his claim.

McIlvenna never once said he was sorry for suspecting me, but then he had never wanted Murphy or the Crown or anyone to deal with me. He wanted me in jail and, I'm certain, if he had had his way, I would never have become a witness. But because of Murphy, he and some other shortsighted brass hats didn't get their way. The trouble is that in the end Murphy paid a terrible price for being as supportive as he was.

When I took the step of calling Murphy, I never considered the possibility of becoming a witness. It also never dawned on me that the Commissos would call me in to have me handle a murder in the United States.

Just after I told Murphy that I knew who held up the jewelry store, I was summoned to the Casa Commisso.

"I got a job for you, Cec," Cosimo said. "It's very important."

Cosimo seemed edgy as he spoke. He paced from one side of the empty banquet hall kitchen to the other. It seemed as if he was avoiding looking directly at me as he usually did. Suddenly he stopped in front of the table where I was sitting and looked squarely into my face, his eyes searching mine as if what he saw would tell him something he didn't know.

"There's this woman in Connecticut," he said. "She's a big problem to some friends of ours. She's gotta be done and I want you to handle the job."

"Why me, Cosimo?" I asked. "Why don't your friends have an American handle the job? Why don't they do the job?"

"Because it's a family matter. It's gotta be handled by an outsider who knows what he's doing and who can do the job right," he said. "That's you, and it's worth fifteen, maybe twenty thousand to you."

"I don't know," I started to answer.

"We'll take care of everything," he said. "Your expenses, that gun, everything you need to know about the girl, we give you."

"Let me think about it, Cosimo," I said. "I need the money for the lawyers on the case that's before the court, but I don't know if there's time. Let me think about it."

We didn't talk much more about it for a while after that. For nearly two weeks I didn't say anything to Murphy. I was worried. I'd never killed a woman before, and I didn't like the idea. Suppose the whole deal was a plot to get rid of me? What better way? I go to the States, I blast this broad, and then I get wasted. There's no witness to the conspiracy, they get rid of the broad, and they unload me, an outsider who knows too much about their Honoured Society and its members.

Over and over something kept clicking in my head. "They're gonna waste you any day now. They're gonna bury you with this job. Do yourself and the broad some good. Call Murphy." Still I waited.

I guess I knew from the start that if I didn't handle the job they'd get someone else to kill the woman, which, in fact, they tried.

While I stalled Cosimo, he went to Ken Goobie, who he'd met through me, and offered Goobie $25,000 to kill the woman. Goobie went to Gary Barnes to handle the job, and Barnes told me about it later.

Finally, on February 17, I called Murphy to tell him about the contract. I didn't want to see the woman killed, but I didn't know how to prevent it without Murphy's help, so I called him.

"I've got a contract, Murph," I said, "and I don't know how to handle it. We've got to talk."

We met again at the Casa Loma parking lot. This time Sergeant Norman Ross was with him.

"Take the contract, Cec," Murphy said. "Find out who the woman is. I'll get office approval. We'll go to the States, see the woman, and remove her from danger. You can then return to Canada and tell them there was just too much heat and police around, so you couldn't handle the murder."

I didn't want to follow Murphy's suggestions, but I figured I had no choice.

"Okay, but don't hang me out to dry on this, Murph," I said. "I've got to meet Cosimo and someone else at two o'clock."

Murphy told me to go ahead with the meeting and he would go to his office to get money to pay for the trip to the States to save the woman.

"How about wearing a tape machine to that meeting?" Murphy asked.

I was taken aback at first and then I refused. "Look, Murph, it's too dangerous right now," I explained. "They got a habit of touching you, putting their arms around you.

And here I'll be meeting with some strange guy. He may want to check me out, pat me down. It's too risky."

"Where are you meeting?" he asked.

"On Dixon Road, near Faces [a discotheque] and Howard Johnson's," I answered. "One other thing, Murphy. I'm broke. I haven't enough to buy a drink right now."

Murphy had repeatedly asked his superiors for expense money for me. Each time they refused, although I had, by this time, given them inside information that helped them solve dozens of burglaries and robberies and a number of murders.

"Here, Cec," he said, reaching into his pocket, "here's ten bucks. It's all I can swing right now."

So I left with Murphy's personal ten dollars to finance what was probably one of the most significant meetings I ever had. I felt like a complete jerk. Here I was, about to deal with a mafioso on a $20,000 murder contract, and all I had in my pocket was a lousy ten bucks, enough to buy maybe one round of drinks.

It was crazy. Murphy was crazy and so was I. Only crazy people try to beat the Mafia this way. What kind of copper was I dealing with anyway?

At 2:00 P.M. I met Cosimo at Howard Johnson's. Antonio Rocco Romeo was with him. We sat down at an isolated table, and Cosimo began talking in low monotones.

"Cec, this here's Antonio Romeo," he said. "He's the man who's gonna put you together with a friend named Vince in the States. It's Vince who wants this woman done. Vince'll take care of everything. He'll show you the woman, get what you need to do the job."

While I was having no problems in negotiating with Cosimo, who I was supposed to meet again on February 19 to get final instructions and $300 to pay for the airline tickets to New York, Murphy was running into one roadblock after another.

He asked for backup to accompany him and me to the States. He told the brass that he had no way of knowing how I would react in the States. He said he didn't know how reliable I would be and pointed out that I was an ex-biker with a reputation for violence. His request for support people was turned down.

Murphy's troubles were only just beginning. Nobody told him it was illegal or against RCMP rules, so he decided to take his service revolver along for self-protection. He declared the gun at U.S. Customs. He didn't know it then, but in doing that he sealed his fate. Those who opposed him used that as one of the charges against him for what they called conduct unbecoming an officer of the RCMP. When he explained that he took the gun because he felt the need for protection since he had no backup, his excuse was brushed aside. He didn't realize it at the time, but powerful forces in the RCMP were at work to get him for defying past suggestions that he let me rot in jail. If I had known that then, I would have told them all to go to hell.

On February 19 Cosimo and I met again. He advanced me $300 and said that when I got to New York, I was to get transportation to Stamford, Connecticut. There I was to meet Romeo and Vince at the Marriott Hotel the next day at 9:00 P.M.

"When you meet Vince there," he said, "you'll get the gun, expense money, and five thousand dollars advance. You'll get the other ten thousand when you finish the job."

I just nodded and went to meet Murphy and buy my airline tickets. The next day we left. The tickets cost me $260, and Murphy had to give me $50 more out of his pocket so I'd have some money for expenses. Unless something happened, I would be going to jail on February 26. I was beginning to wonder whether I had been stupid in trying to make a deal with the RCMP and save this woman's life.

16

The Connecticut Caper

I felt the American Airlines jet engines roar to life as we hurtled down the runway of Toronto International. I looked across the aisle and to the rear. From the corner of my eye I could see Murphy looking past me as if I didn't exist. Not the slightest sign of recognition passed between us as the jet rose and headed toward La Guardia Airport.

My hands felt clammy and cold as I leaned back and watched the flight attendant pass out drinks. I ordered juice, and I remember looking out the window at the clouds wondering how in the hell I had been talked into this trip.

Nothing had been resolved about my sentence before we left. I was still looking at from two to four years, and no one but Murphy was in favor of suggesting to the Crown or a judge that I be given a break for helping police. Yet here I was, flying to New York with an RCMP officer, preparing to meet with Calabrian Mafia hoods who wanted me to kill a woman I'd never seen before in my life.

I had boarded the plane using my true name, but once I hit New York, I would be operating under a fictitious name with phony identification in a strange country among people I didn't know. I thought to myself, "Cecil Kirby, you've got to be crazy doing this." Even as I wondered if I'd lost my marbles, the warning words of Murphy kept echoing in my head.

"You know too much, Cecil," he said. "Sooner or later, the Commissos have got to dispose of you. They can't let you live."

"You're just working on my head," I remember snapping as we talked about what he expected me to do after I had taken the contract from Cosimo to kill the woman.

"Be realistic," Murphy said. "First, they owe you forty thousand dollars by your own estimate. Why should they pay that much if they don't have to? Second, you've become a liability to them. You're a non-Italian working for the Honoured Society. You're not one of them. You don't live by their codes. You could put them in jail for a long, long time. So you're a liability." Then Murphy struck a chord that made even more sense to me.

"Remember Ian Rosenburg?" he asked. "He became a liability to the Volpe crime group. So what did they do? They bailed him out of jail and killed him and his girlfriend. If you don't work with us, that's what could happen to you."

"You mean they might be setting me up for a hit on this Connecticut caper, don't you?" I said.

"It's a possibility. It's something to think about," he said. "What better way to get rid of you? They have you enter the United States under an assumed name. They get you to a small place like Stamford, and after you do in the woman, or even if you don't do her, they kill you. Who would really be concerned about an ex–Satan's Choice biker if, in fact, they ever found your body?"

Those words were still ringing in my ears as the plane dipped toward New York.

When we touched down I quickly passed through customs and caught a cab for the Holiday Inn near the airport. Once there I called a detective at the New York City Police Criminal Intelligence Bureau, leaving him my phone number and room number as Murphy had instructed. The name I used was Jack Ryan—the same name that I used to register in the hotel.

The Connecticut Caper

It couldn't have been more than an hour before Murphy was knocking on my door. With him were two FBI agents. Within minutes we were in a bureau car and on our way to Connecticut.

Just before we stopped at a hamburger place for a quick bite and a phone call to some agents in Darien, Murphy spotted a car with a couple of black guys in it counting bundles of cash.

"Did you see all the money they were counting?" he asked.

"Yeah," I said. "They probably held up a bank or just sold a load of dope."

Murphy jotted down the license number, but the two FBI agents, one of them was a guy named Nick Mott, registered no reaction at all. Mott had all of two years as a bureau agent, and he was from a Midwest farm. New York was obviously unfamiliar territory to him. Even so, what Murphy and I saw didn't excite him, and he made no attempt to call Connecticut State Police to give them the car's license number as Murphy suggested. It was like it was an everyday occurrence, and what the hell could they do about it anyhow?

When we arrived in Darien I was introduced to several other agents, including John Schiman, Donnie Brutnell, and David Cotton, all from Connecticut. I was brought to a room at the Holiday Inn, where I briefed the agents. I told them I was supposed to meet Romeo, who was coming in from Toronto, at the Marriott Hotel in Stamford at 9:00 P.M. He was supposed to be with some-one named Vince, who would provide me with the money, keys to the apartment of the victim, photographs, and a gun to kill the woman with.

I half expected either Murphy or the agents to ask me to wear a body mike to the meeting. I wouldn't take that chance. My main concern was to find out who the victim was, not blow the whole deal before it happened.

Just before 8:30, I took a cab to Stamford. I got out at the corner near the hotel and was met by Schiman and

Murphy. With barely a word passing between us, I walked into the hotel lobby and waited for Romeo to appear.

I sat there for several hours. Nothing happened. Finally I got up, hailed a cab, and went back to the Holiday Inn.

I had to find out what happened. There was a problem. How was I going to find out what it was? I had no idea of where to reach Romeo or his boss, Vince, and I hadn't brought my phone book, so I didn't have Cosimo's home phone number.

I was stymied, but I told the agents to give Romeo until the next day.

"Something must've held him up, eh?" I said.

At that point a light went on in my head. There was a way to reach Cosimo. I called my ex-girlfriend, Linda Cadwell, and asked her to go to Cosimo's home.

"Have him call me at this number," I said. "Have him call me as soon as possible."

Cosimo didn't call, but he gave Linda a message to relay to me when I called her back early the next morning.

"He said to tell you that the guy you were supposed to meet with last night was delayed by weather," she said. "He said he'll be there today, and he'll meet you at the same place and the same time."

As soon as she got off the phone, I called Murphy, who was in the same hotel. What I didn't realize was that he was in a room next to mine.

"He got held up in Toronto by fog," I said to Murphy. "He's coming into La Guardia today. I'm supposed to meet him tonight—same time, same place."

While I stewed in my room, Murphy was busy with Agent Mott and New York City detectives at La Guardia Airport, looking for Romeo. When they spotted him, he was moving from phone booth to phone booth, making calls.

When I saw Murphy later, he was upset. He said Mott had almost blown the surveillance by pulling the bureau's car to within fifty feet of Romeo as he stood by the curbside waiting for a cab to Stamford. Murphy said he had to insist that Mott get out of the car and open the trunk as if he were unloading luggage to avoid having Romeo spot them.

Things sometimes have a way of getting worse before they get better, and Murphy said that was what happened as they tried to tail Romeo. He said that Mott made a bad identification on the cab Romeo drove away in. The assisting surveillance cars lost him as he left the airport. They finally spotted him on Route 95, ten miles out of New York, heading toward Stamford. This time they kept the tail tight with other surveillance cars from the bureau and New York City police playing leapfrog so Romeo and his cabbie wouldn't notice.

It was early afternoon when my phone rang.

"This George?" the voice on the phone asked.

"Yeah, who's this?" I asked.

"This is Vince," he said. "We meet the same time, same place tonight."

"Okay," I said. "I'll be there."

After hanging up, I called Murphy again and told him that I'd gotten a call from a man who called himself Vince.

"I think it's the guy who gave Commisso the contract," I said. "He must have gotten my phone number from Cosimo."

"I've got to get you out of that room—now," Murphy said. "I don't want them to be able to watch you—set up a counter-surveillance—understand?"

Within minutes, Murphy was at my door and we left the area.

At 9:00 P.M. I entered the lobby of the Marriott Hotel in Stamford for the second time. There were agents everywhere, but they blended into the scenery. They were impossible to spot.

Vincenzo (Vincent) Melia didn't look all that impressive to me as he stood there with Romeo in the hotel lobby.

Romeo clearly treated Melia as though he was very

important, like a boss. Romeo was about twenty-four and
Melia was more than twice his age, fifty-two, I was told
later, but Romeo treated him like the mob treated Don
Corleone in *The Godfather*, with a great deal of respect.

"Please, Mr. Kirby," he said, "I'd like you to meet
Vince Melia. He's the man you're s'pos to meet."

I stood up and shook hands with Melia. He was
medium in height, with dark brown wavy hair, a thin,
clean-shaven face, and piercing brown eyes.

Melia was as important in Connecticut as Cosimo was
in Toronto. He was the boss of a family, and he didn't take
a backseat to many people. He was very close to Mike
Racco, the old man who had been the boss of bosses for
the Calabrian Honoured Society families in the United
States and Canada until he'd died in 1980.

Melia was an Italian citizen who had moved to Toronto
from Siderno and then to Stamford, where he operated a
construction business. No one, not the community, not his
neighbors, not the FBI, knew what he really was.

In the lobby of the Marriott, he was quiet, but
careful. The lobby wasn't a good place to talk, so we went
to a bar in the hotel, ordered some drinks, and sat down at
a table.

"Look, before I do anything," I said, "I want five
thousand dollars up front."

"Tomorrow, I'll have it for you tomorrow," he said.

"What about the gun?" I asked.

"You get that tomorrow too," he said.

"I'm going to need a picture so I know what she looks
like," I said. "Who is this broad anyhow?"

"Her name is Helen," he said. "A relative, he lives
with this woman. He's not to be harmed. Remember that.
I don't want him killed. He's family. The woman, she's
blond—a good-looking hairdresser."

He was somewhat nervous as he spoke. His eyes
shifted from table to table in the darkened bar, searching
for someone he might recognize.

We couldn't have been there more than ten minutes

when Melia leaned over to me and whispered, "That guy at the table over there—he looks like he's a cop."

"Nah," I said, glancing at the guy he had motioned to. "There's no cops in here."

Melia was nervous now. He was suspicious about everyone in the bar, and he wanted to leave.

"Let's go outside," he said. "I got someone I want you to meet."

We left the table and began to walk outside. I knew the FBI was watching. So was Murphy. But I didn't see any of them. Before I got outside, Romeo took me aside as Melia continued on ahead.

"Look," he said, "I don't want these guys to tell you what to do. You do what you gotta do. You do your own thing and we'll look after you." He spoke in clear English, with a trace of Italian. In court, he and his attorney said he couldn't speak English.

Outside, Romeo and I caught up with Melia, who walked me to the hotel parking lot and a Cadillac driven by another of their *paisans*.

"This is Jerry Russo," Melia said. "He's going to drive you to the house of the woman you are to take care of. He'll show you the house and her car. Then he'll take you to a hotel and a room we got for you. We also got a car for you."

"Don't want any of that," I said. "You keep the room and the car. I got my own equipment and no one knows where I stay. I do things my way. Incidentally, I'm not too happy about taking a ride with your chauffeur."

"Don't worry, don't worry," he said. "He's all right. But you can tell him to forget he ever saw you. He'll know what you mean."

He looked around, reached into his pocket, and handed me some keys. "Here," he said, "here's the keys to her house and her car." He fumbled in his pocket for something else. "Here's three hundred dollars for expenses and my phone number," he said. "Before you kill her, call me so we can be sure the relative's not there. Okay?"

I nodded. "Okay. And the five thousand dollars?"

"We meet here tomorrow. Two o'clock," he said. "You get everything then."

So I climbed into Russo's Caddy. I had noticed it as I walked into the hotel. I remember feeling a sense of satisfaction knowing that I had spotted it and made the connection. They—Melia, Romeo, and Russo—had all come in that Caddy early and checked me out as I arrived. Obviously, they'd spotted nothing, or the meeting and our conversation wouldn't have taken place.

While I drove off with Russo, Melia and Romeo climbed into Melia's yellow Ford and headed in another direction. I noticed a bureau tail car following them at a discreet distance.

Russo, about twenty-four, was a gofer. Melia was his boss, and he did what he was told. I guess women would think Russo was good looking. He had carefully cut, wavy dark hair, a manicured mustache, and sharp, expensive-looking clothes. All that on a thin, five-foot-seven frame. Soaking wet he couldn't have weighed more than 150 pounds.

We drove to the woman's home in Stamford. As we went by slowly, Russo pointed out which side of the house she lived in and which room she slept in. He pointed to her car, a Toyota as I recall. We continued past the house, a small bungalow, for about half a block and I asked him to stop. He pulled over to the sidewalk and I got out.

"Stay here," I said sharply. "I'm gonna take a quick look around. I'll be right back."

While Russo watched me, as did some unseen eyes of the FBI, I walked back toward the house and jotted down the license number of the car. As I turned to return, one of those supposedly unseen eyes came roaring up the street past me. I kept waving—keep going, don't stay around. Russo didn't spot anything luckily. The overprotective surveillance was understandable. The FBI was worried. Overall, they were super—concerned, professional, and tough.

The FBI had cautioned me before I met with Melia about staying out of the house and the yard. Murphy had told them the Commissos might be setting me up as well as the woman.

"Stay away from that house," one of the agents said. "Don't go in wherever it is. You could get blown away. This could be a setup, even with the cops. There could be a cop in there waiting to blow you away because they've been tipped you'll be breaking into the house." The message was clear enough. The Melias could have friends with the local coppers, and the agents didn't want any chances taken. Every step I took, every place I went, I was watched, and those I was with were photographed.

As Russo and I returned to the hotel, I carefully began pulling on some black driving gloves I had in my pocket.

"Word to the wise," I said menacingly to Russo. "You better forget who I am. And you better forget what I look like." I watched his face twitch slightly around the jawbone in the subdued light from the dashboard. Then for emphasis I added, "I don't want to have to make another trip down here."

When Russo dropped me off at the Marriott, I stood at the entrance for several minutes. I then hailed a cab and, after a few side trips downtown to be sure Russo hadn't the balls to track me, I headed back to Darien to meet with Murphy and the agents at the Holiday Inn and turn over Melia's phone number, the license number of the woman's car, her keys, and her address. The money I kept. Nobody said I shouldn't, so I kept it. I was tired of living off the nickels and dimes that Murphy had to scrape out of his pocket because the RCMP refused to provide support money.

I briefed the FBI and Murphy on what had happened and what I had to do the next day. Then I went to bed.

It was 2:00 P.M. Sunday when I got to the Marriott lobby. Melia was waiting.

"The girl will be back tonight," he said. "You'll have to kill her tomorrow—not today. Kill her tomorrow after ten in the morning. Somebody is with her up to ten. Wait till he leaves and kill her after that."

"What?" I said, registering surprise. "You don't want me to kill the guy she's with?"

"No, no, no, no. He's family," Melia said excitedly. "Don't kill him."

"Why do you want her hit?" I asked.

"She's caused trouble, a lot of trouble, and the guy she's going with is messing up," he answered.

He said nothing more but motioned for me to follow him out to the parking lot. We stood by Melia's car waiting for Russo to show up with the $5,000 and the gun.

"You know if you want to come back down here," Melia said, "I got other work for you to do—places to burn. I got lots of work here."

"Well, I'll have to think about that," I answered. "You'll have to talk to Cosimo about that."

"I know Remo many years—longer than Cosimo," he said. "I talk to them both."

"When do I get the other ten thousand dollars?" I said, as we waited.

"What other ten thousand dollars?" he said with a look of surprise. "You're supposed to get another five thousand dollars after you get this five thousand dollars."

"Hell, no," I snapped. "Cosimo said the job was worth fifteen to twenty thousand dollars. Now you're telling me ten thousand dollars!"

"It's ten thousand dollars," he said, his face darkening a bit with anger. "If you make sure she disappears and isn't found, I give you a bonus—an extra one thousand dollars. That's it!"

"Okay," I said. "I'll see what I can do. But the deal was for more."

Just as things started to get a little heated, Russo drove up in a silver Capri. He got into Melia's car. Out of the corner of my eye I could see Agent Schiman in a telephone booth maybe twenty-five to thirty feet away. There were agents hidden all over the place, snapping pictures of everything that was happening.

Russo handed me $4,000, and Melia reached in his pocket and pulled out an additional $1,000. Russo then pulled a bag from beneath his shirt that had been tucked under his belt. The gun was in the bag. I took the gun out and examined it.

"This isn't a fuckin' .38, it's a lousy .22," I said angrily.

"Well, that's all we got," Melia answered.

I took the clip out to make sure it was loaded, and I checked to see if there was a bullet in the chamber as well as in the clip. There was. It was a Sturm Ruger, nine-shot automatic. I noticed a long, thin silencer at the end of the barrel. I tried to remove it, but I couldn't. It was hand-made, and probably would work, but it wasn't the kind of silencer I felt comfortable with. Silencers usually screw into the barrel. They're usually custom-made for the weapon. A bad silencer can cause all kinds of problems. I made Melia know I wasn't happy with the weapon. I thought to myself, "Some Mafia bunch this is."

With the gun they handed me a picture of two women. One was a blond. Melia pointed to her. "That's the one I want killed," he said. "Remember, if she disappears, there's a bonus."

"Consider it done," I said.

With that we shook hands and I walked off, watching them as they drove away in Melia's Ford. When they were out of sight, I grabbed a cab for the Ramada Inn up the street, where I thought I was supposed to meet some agents and be picked up. I wasn't.

I stood there with the gun and the money for almost a half hour. I felt exposed, naked, in a dangerous spot. A local cop might check me out and find the gun. Finally, I hailed another cab and returned to the Holiday Inn in Darien. I sat in the lobby. Sooner or later, I figured, the agents and Murphy would find me there. The best thing to do was wait.

It was a little after 3:00 P.M. when a couple of agents spotted me in the lobby and escorted me to a room on the second floor. Murphy was there, so was Agent Schiman.

I drew the gun from my belt line and threw it on the bed. Schiman jumped up and grabbed it. I removed my jacket, dropped the $5,000, and threw it on the other side of the bed. Nobody touched it as I sat on the bed next to it. As far as I was concerned the money was mine and nobody was contesting that. I didn't say a word. I just scooped up the money and put it in my pants pocket and waited for them to debrief me.

Murphy was later reprimanded for not seizing the money. He couldn't. I'd warned him that if the RCMP wasn't going to pay my bills, then the Commissos were. Besides, I was helping save a woman's life, and Murphy's people weren't doing a damn thing to help me with my court problems.

After more than an hour of debriefing, the agents asked me to come with them to the woman's house. By now I knew she was a Greek hairdresser and the mother of a six-year-old girl. They wanted to set up a surveillance of the house in the morning and familiarize themselves with the neighborhood. Beyond that no one was really sure of what was going to be done the next day.

When Murphy and I returned to my room, he asked me to take out the money. "Let me record the serial numbers and take some sample bills," he said.

I agreed, and we spent more than an hour recording the numbers and carefully placing bill samples from four different stacks of the money in a special evidence envelope that Murphy had with him. He had $150 in sample bills, some of which I suppose had Melia's and Russo's fingerprints on them.

It wasn't until the next day that I knew what the FBI was going to do with the woman. They were going to keep her under surveillance, and when she and her boyfriend separated, they were going to snatch her.

"Can I come along on the surveillance?" I asked.

"Sure, why not?" Schiman said.

They put me in a van they had equipped with cameras, and I sat there with a couple of agents waiting and watching the house while other agents were parked in the area in other cars.

I guess it was a little after 10:00 A.M. when Helen Nafpliotis opened the door and walked to the car. I was looking at her through the Telephoto lens of the camera, and I snapped the first picture of her. She started the car, went back into the house, and came back out. This time the agent was doing the picture taking. I watched from a van window.

A minute or two later, a man about six foot, in his mid-forties, came out and climbed into her car. He was Nick Melia, the brother of Vince. I sat in the van as agents in other cars followed the couple at a discreet distance.

I was sitting outside the Holiday Inn in a car with two agents when the agents returned with Nafpliotis. They had waited until she dropped Nick Melia off in downtown Stamford. Melia at the time was appealing a state sentence in connection with a shooting in Stamford.

When the agents were convinced Melia had left the area, they flagged down the woman's car on the highway, flashed their identification, and told her it was urgent that she come with them to Darien. A bureau agent, meanwhile, took her car and hid it.

For the next three hours, the agents and Murphy questioned her while I sat in the car outside. I later read a statement that Murphy compiled of what she had to say.

She was born in Greece on July 26, 1947, and she had lived in the United States for about ten years. For all but six months of that time she had been living, on and off, with Melia, and out of that relationship came a six-year-old daughter, Christina. She also had three other children by a husband she'd split up with in 1977. He'd gone back to Greece and taken her kids with him without her knowing it.

She said that Melia had been arrested by the police for the shooting of Antonio Ianniello, a Stamford hairdresser that she had worked for for several years. The charges were dropped nolle prosequi, four years later.

For a while, she told Murphy and bureau agents, she had worked in Melia's shop, Continental Coiffures. That lasted until she was threatened, beaten and hospitalized for five days, she said. Charges against her attacker were dismissed in October 1981, when she failed to appear in court.

There were other incidents after that. The tires of her car were slashed. After they were replaced, new tires blew out as she was driving, causing her to lose control and almost roll her car just before Christmas of 1980. A year earlier, on November 3, 1979, her car had almost rolled over because of slashed tires that blew.

She said she finally couldn't take any more threats and flew off to Greece, where she stayed for five months. She said Melia's brother, Vincent, had told her it would be smart for her to leave.

She said she had tried, unsuccessfully, to break off her relationship with Melia several times, but each time he found her and made her return. She supported herself by working at a $300-a-week job and renting out two apartments in her house for $450 a month each. She had no other place to go.

"Where can I hide?" she asked the FBI. "Even if I go to God, Nick will find me."

She was really afraid of this Melia. He'd moved to Canada from Italy when he was nineteen. He'd come to Connecticut when he was in his twenties. She said she never saw him work. She knew he'd been accused of having stolen jewelry and of shooting Ianniello, but she didn't know anything about his "family" connections.

They had been to Atlantic City the weekend before I arrived and the weekend I had been provided with the money to kill her, they had been in Queens.

When the interview ended, Murphy, Schiman, and I had another meeting. They were going to provide protection for Nafpliotis, but they couldn't hide her forever. If the Commisso mob and the Melias found out she was still alive, I'd be a dead man.

"You're going to have to become a witness," Murphy said. "It's the only way we save her, and you."

I sat there for a while, thinking about it, looking for a way out. There wasn't any, and we had to return to Toronto. It was Monday, and as things stood I was supposed to go to jail Thursday. Without some sort of agreement, some deal with Murphy, with the Crown prosecutors, I was a dead man.

"Look, Murph," I said, "I'll be your witness. I'll help you get the evidence you want on other cases, but I can't do it without protection. If I talk to you about everything I know, if I help you, I want immunity from prosecution for past crimes. The Crown's got to support my family and me, relocate us, and give us something to live on when it's all over, when I'm through testifying."

"I can't promise that, Cec," he said. "I can't promise anything. I'll do all I can to help, but that's all I can promise."

"You get me what I want and I'll give you what you want," I said. "One thing more. I work with you, not somebody else."

Before we boarded our plane for Toronto at La Guardia, Murphy took a big gamble. He called Crown attorney Al Cooper and told him the whole story, and he held out the chance that they could wipe out the leadership of the Commisso crime family.

"We could do a lot of damage to organized crime in Toronto, Al," I heard him say. "Without him, we have nothing. With him we can do a lot. But not if they make him go to jail on Thursday."

Cooper, unlike Murphy's superiors, saw the dangers and the possibilities. He made no promises, but he agreed to meet with Murphy the next morning to see what could be arranged.

Even as they spoke, the FBI was busy in Stamford. They'd taken Helen Nafpliotis back to her house, let her gather her jewelry and a few belongings, and then staged a kidnapping that witnesses reported to police. They secretly sent her back to Greece, but it wasn't the last I was to hear of her. Even though I never saw her again, she and the FBI almost got me killed.

17

The Informer I

Corporal Mark Murphy's superiors at the RCMP were clearly not happy. By going to Crown prosecutor Al Cooper, Murphy had leapfrogged the chain of command that wanted me in jail, not running around gathering evidence against organized crime. Instead of being praised for saving a woman's life and doing a helluva job with me, Murphy was in deep trouble.

His bosses were furious that I had been permitted to keep the $5,300 Melia had given me. They were angry that I hadn't been forced to wear a body recorder. And they were critical of Murphy for going to Cooper. Trouble or no, Murphy met with Cooper as promised. They then went to see two prosecutors familiar with my B&E case— Steve Leggit, head Crown prosecutor in Toronto, and Frank Armstrong. Leggit and Armstrong were as inflexible as Murphy's bosses and biker squad officers Hall and Tavenor. It looked hopeless.

Some time after 6:00 P.M. on February 24, Cooper and Murphy were called to meet with the deputy attorney general of Ontario, Rod McLeod. At that meeting, Murphy told McLeod that in addition to putting the Commissos behind bars for conspiracy to murder the Connecticut woman, the Crown could also clear up most of the bombings that had taken place in the city of Toronto over the last seven years as well as extortions, arsons, and bombings in Guelph, Hamilton, and Montreal. All told there were more than twenty-three major criminal acts that could be solved and more than a dozen arrests effected.

McLeod wasn't as shortsighted as the others. He saw the potential and assured both Murphy and Cooper that I wouldn't go to jail on Thursday and that I would be made available to meet the Commissos and gather further evidence. The next day McLeod ordered Leggit to hold my case over. A deal was in the works.

"You're going to have to wear a body mike," Murphy said, as we talked about the promise McLeod had made. "You're going to have to wear a mike and get evidence to nail these guys."

I wasn't happy at all about the prospect. Becoming an informer for Murphy had been difficult, a gut-wrenching experience. It was against everything I had grown up to believe in. Up to that point I had justified it mentally by not fingering the crimes of friends—and I wasn't testifying against anyone. I could even excuse the Connecticut deal. I had helped save a woman's life and I had stiffed the Commissos and their mob for a change. Besides, I wasn't a witness.

"There's no way around it, Cec, you're going to have to testify—be a witness," Murphy said again.

I wanted to puke. It sucked—it really sucked. I was faced with doing what I was willing to kill others for doing. I tried to find a way out.

"Christ, I don't know, Mark," I said. "It'll never work. The Commissos, their friends—they're always putting arms around me, touching me, poking at me. They're sure to find any tape I'm wearing."

"They won't. I guarantee it," Murphy said. "Besides, I'll be close by."

"I don't know." I stalled.

"There's no other way," he said harshly. "Either you play the game or you go to jail. And you know what happens when they find out that the girl isn't dead, that the FBI grabbed her and you took their five thousand dollars."

"Sure. I'll be another unsolved homicide," I said. "I should never have come to you people. You got me between a rock and a hard place." I paced up and down, shaking my head. I was certain I was a dead man—I just wasn't in the box yet.

"What guarantees have I got?" I said.

"Only my word," Murphy said, "and these consent forms I want you to sign."

The consent forms were my ace in the hole, the protection for my backside that Murphy and I had talked about in Connecticut. They later became a center of controversy with the Crown prosecutors and with Murphy's brass, who disciplined him for living up to his word and using them to protect my interests.

Under the agreements, I had promised to wear a body mike and record conversations I had with the Commissos. Murphy had added a clause at the bottom and he attached these to the transcript of every recording I made. The clause, in effect, held that the Crown and police could not use the tapes or any conversations on the tapes without my consent, and if I consented, I would be protected against self-incrimination for any crimes discussed on the tapes or in testimony I later gave. Murphy had agreed to insert it to protect me if police or prosecutors welshed on their promises.

"Okay, Mark," I said. "But get that agreement drawn up and approved as fast as you can."

We both agreed that meetings with the Commissos should be arranged, as much as possible, away from the Casa Commisso. It was too difficult a place to surveil and record conversations at. The industrial nature of the area could cause interference in transmissions, and it would be difficult for Murphy and whoever was with him to get to me once I was inside.

I called Cosimo to arrange a meeting. He wanted it to take place at the Casa Commisso, but I convinced him to meet me at the Howard Johnson's.

I was nervous as they taped the body pack on me, and I was cautious. I wore extra clothing—a heavy sweater—to conceal the taping device and anything I thought might be bulging.

"Calm down," Murphy said. "He isn't going to spot anything. You'll do just fine."

I nodded, but I wasn't convinced. I worried about whether the body pack would break down. In future meetings, I would be equipped with a backup transmitter.

I felt clammy as I parked my car and walked toward the hotel. Droplets of cold sweat trickled down from my armpits, and I checked behind my jacket, under my belt, to see if I could reach the gun that I had slipped in there without Murphy seeing. Although I had not yet signed an agreement, I felt more secure with it. I wasn't supposed to carry a gun. What the hell.

At 1:15 P.M., Cosimo and I met. Parked nearby were Murphy and his immediate superior officer, Sergeant Norm Ross. They snapped pictures as Cosimo and I greeted each other.

Almost immediately Cosimo noticed the extra clothing. "Why you got so many clothes on?" he asked.

"I'm cold as hell," I said. "I been living up north and I'm just cold." I clapped my gloved hands together and stamped my feet. A sort of involuntary shiver went through my body.

He didn't poke me or put his hand on me or his arm around me as I expected, and I remember feeling relief. I wasn't sure how I'd react if he did.

"How're you?" Cosimo asked.

"You told me fifteen thousand," I snapped, catching him off guard, letting him know I was unhappy with what had happened in Connecticut. My purpose was to put him on the defensive—make him talk about the murder conspiracy—so Murphy and the Crown would have evidence to prosecute with. The body tape confirms the success of that strategy.

"Vince, he give you the money?" Cosimo asked.

"He paid me five—he didn't give me ten," I said.

"Five thousand?" Cosimo said.

"Yeah," I said.

"You do the job?" he asked. "When did you do it? Tuesday?"

"Hell no, Monday," I said.

"Monday night?" he asked.

"I don't want to get into details, okay?" I said. "Vince said to me—he said he'd pay me extra if she was a missing person. He's something else, that fellow. That's why I want the fifteen thousand."

Cosimo was surprised and somewhat puzzled. He didn't understand what had happened. My mind was working like a computer now. Set up an alibi, I thought. Protect yourself in case someone saw an FBI agent or Murphy with you. I was in high gear now, and my nerves were steady. I was in a game of cat and mouse, and I was enjoying it.

"I'll tell you why, okay?" I said. "I took another guy down there, okay? They didn't see him, okay? He didn't see them. I figured maybe I'd want an extra guy with me in case, you know, I get any static. We got the broad out, okay? She's gone. They'll never find her again. There's a lotta lakes around there. They got a big fuckin', you know, strait there, or sound—Long Island Sound."

"There's a lot of things to be done over there," Cosimo said, indicating that he had other jobs in mind, that Melia wanted me to handle other jobs for him. "Never mind this. You gonna get it. I'll make sure he gives it to you—the five—right away."

"I want it," I said. "I'm going to Vegas. Leaving at noon tomorrow."

"I'll try. Whatever I can get now for tomorrow, Cec," Cosimo said.

"Look, I told him [Vince Melia]. I said you want her missing, I said, I want an extra thousand. Six thousand, okay?"

Cosimo nodded his head. "Okay. Six thousand."

The discussion then turned to my court case, and I explained that everything had been postponed until April

10. Cosimo seemed to understand. He was appealing a conviction of his own. We agreed to meet again on March 10, at which time he said he'd pay me $5,000 more.

"We meet Marcha tenth," he said.

"All right, March tenth, here at twelve o'clock," I said. "I don't want to go near the bakery, okay?"

"I come—I come and see you at your house," he suggested.

"No, no, I'm never home," I said. "I tell you, I got this other broad, okay, up in Barrie. I don't want to be seen around too much, you know. When the court case is over with, okay, fine, but for now I'm keeping low. I don't want to go near the bakery anymore."

"All right," Cosimo answered.

"I worry about cops every time I go around there," I said, showing my concern. "I don't want the heat."

Cosimo didn't like the idea of returning to where we were now standing. He didn't have the control here. His friends and family weren't here. My friends were.

"Stop at my house," he said. "Nobody else comes to my house—you understand what I mean."

"Sure, I know that," I said, "but you never know—you might have the cops watching. I don't need the heat."

"All right," he said with resignation.

"March tenth—here at twelve o'clock," I said. "I want the fifteen, I want the six thousand."

"All right," he said again.

"And the rest later, a month later, okay?" I asked.

"Okay," he said with a shrug. "Have a nice time."

The recording session had gone well, but there was still no agreement. Murphy had outlined what I wanted at a special meeting of police brass representing RCMP, OPP, and Metropolitan Toronto Police. He also said that I would not work with anyone but Murphy while I was on the street, acting as their agent. I agreed to talk to others after an agreement was signed, but not before.

I was, by now, desperate for money. I owed more than $4,000 in legal fees, some $2,000 in credit-card charges, another $2,000 to my father, and I had a bank loan payment, alimony, and other bills to take care of. All that and no money coming in.

March 10 was on the horizon, and Cosimo was scheduled to pay me $5,000. Murphy said I had to turn that money in for evidence.

"Look, Mark," I said, "all I've gotten from your outfit up to now are two $100 expense payments. That don't pay the bills. You tell them they'd better pony up the money so I can pay the bills."

We met again on March 10.

"You got the money?" I asked.

Murphy shook his head. "Inspector McIlvenna said he'd have the five thousand in my hands before the meeting, but I haven't gotten anything. Look, Cec, you can't keep the money Commisso gives you. I'll have to seize it as evidence."

"The hell you say," I shouted. I was fuming and I let Murphy have both barrels. "You can tell the RCMP, McIlvenna, Sergeant John Simpson, and all the rest of them that they can go fuck themselves. The deal is off. I'll meet Commisso later tonight and get the money when you're not around."

Murphy pleaded with me to be reasonable, but for me there was nothing reasonable about the jam I was in, the bills I was facing, and the way his bosses were dancing me around. I knew they didn't have enough to make a case without another recording and without me.

Murphy got out of my car and walked back over to the car of Sergeant Ross. He told Ross what I had told him. Then he came back to my car and again tried to change my mind.

"Mark, I'm tired of getting fucked. I'm tired of their fuckin' promises that they never keep," I said angrily. "The only way I go through with that meeting for you is for you to promise, right now, that you don't take that money."

Murphy threw up his hands. He really didn't have much choice, and it was almost time for me to meet with

Cosimo. "All right, Cec," he said with a sigh, "you have my word. I won't seize the money."

The meeting went down as planned.

"You look sick, Cosimo," I said.

"Feel sick," he said.

I smiled, made light of his problem. "And me—all sunburned. I went to Florida instead."

Cosimo was mildly surprised.

"Yeah, I couldn't get to Vegas," I said.

"By yourself you went?" he asked.

"Nah, with a friend of mine," I said. "We went down to the Keys, the only place it was warm. It was just freezing everywhere else."

"It was freezin' there?" he said with surprise.

"Oh, it was cold near the top of Florida," I said, "so I went down the Keys, went fishing for a couple of days. I got sunburned out on the boat. I still don't feel well."

"I'm tired," Cosimo answered.

"You got the money?" I asked.

"Don't worry about it," Cosimo said. "I went and borrowed it for you."

"So how much is here?" I said.

"Five," he said.

I shook my head. "All right, you know, I told you [Melia] said he'd give me an extra thousand."

"Yeah, because you kill her, eh?" Cosimo asked. "The car—she disappear too? Her car?"

"Yeah, in a roundabout way," I said. "They'll never find it. She'll be a missing person sooner or later. That's it—it's better for everyone."

Cosimo was happy, and he promised to get the additional six thousand from Melia. I told him I had to pay my accomplice for helping me dump the woman and the car in Long Island Sound. Then he dropped the bombshell. He had a new contract for me. He wanted me to kill Peter (Pietro) Scarcella, one of crime boss Paul Volpe's associates. He wanted it done before he had to go to jail on the counterfeiting charges.

"When am I gonna see you?" he asked. "How can I get in touch with you?"

"It's hard," I said. "I'm with this broad. And she didn't even get a phone where we're at—out in the country."

"Still things to be done," Cosimo said.

What he wanted done was to hit Scarcella. He didn't identify him then, and he didn't say how much it would be worth to me. All that he would tell me a week later at his home.

Murphy, meanwhile, had to hold off the wolves. He went to Cooper, the prosecutor, and told him what had happened—that the RCMP hadn't come up with the money as promised and that he'd had to let me keep the money that Cosimo paid me because I would have shut down the investigation and taken the money without any photos or any tape.

Cooper took the problem to Howard Morton, the Crown attorney who had been assigned to handle the Commisso case. Morton wasn't that upset. "It doesn't really matter a row of beans if the money was seized or not," Murphy said he said. "The fact it was paid by the Commissos to Kirby is what really mattered."

By now my car, a Chevrolet, had been carefully bugged by Murphy's people. I had the body pack, and they had also rigged a transmitter inside a belt buckle. With all that equipment, it was sometimes difficult to get Cosimo into the car. Cosimo was suspicious of cars, of clothing, of telephone pagers, and strange buildings. He was afraid of being bugged by police. I always had to be creative, fast on my feet with my thinking cap screwed on right.

I remember on one occasion, Murphy wanted a clearer recording of our conversations, which often took place outside the Faces Discotheque and Howard Johnson's, where there would sometimes be the roar of overhead planes and nearby trucks.

One conversation Murphy had difficulty recording took place when Cosimo asked me to get him a gun.

"You mean one like this?" I said as I pulled out a .32 automatic from the small of my back.

"Yeah, something like that," he said, surprise registering on his face. "Why you carry the gun?"

"I got some problems," I explained, "so I carry a gun." Then I put it back.

From that point on Cosimo and his brothers knew I carried a gun. They knew I carried it either behind my back or in a pocket or behind my belt buckle in the front of my pants.

Knowing that, I think, had something to do with Cosimo not patting me down—checking to see if I was carrying anything unusual on me. I think he was always a little afraid of me because I had the balls to carry the gun and show him I was carrying it when we met.

The gun gave me a sense of security, but I wouldn't have been so secure if I'd known what the RCMP learned when I turned it in after all the meetings with the Commissos had ended. I had borrowed that gun from two rounders who were friends of the Commissos, but I had never had the chance to test it because I was always in the city working with Murphy and other investigators. When I finally turned it in, Murphy sent it to the RCMP laboratory to see if the weapon had been used before in a crime. He found that the gun had a faulty firing pin. If I had ever tried to use it to protect myself I'd have been hung out to dry. A cap pistol would have been more effective.

Losing most of my conversation with Cosimo about the gun and lacking clarity on some of the other tapes concerned Murphy. He was also worried about my safety and about the evidence they collected on the recordings.

To allay those fears, I showed up one day for a meeting with Murphy at the Skyline parking lot equipped in an unusual way. As Murphy stood by the car, I took off my shoe and my sock and pulled an elastic bandage from my jogging suit pocket. I wrapped the bandage around my ankle and looked up smiling.

"Guaranteed I get Cosimo in the car today," I said with a chuckle. Murphy was smiling from ear to ear as I drove off to meet Cosimo.

Cosimo spotted me as I pulled into the Faces parking lot and walked over.

"Get in," I said to him.

"Cec, you know I don't like to talk in the car," he said. "The cops, they could have bugged your car."

"No chance, Cosimo," I said. "The people I sent over to your place to do the debugging check the car out all the time. I never take chances. Besides, I can't walk. I can't get out of the car."

"What's the matter?" he asked.

I opened the door and pointed to the bandaged ankle and foot.

"Your foot—what's the matter with it?" he asked.

"I went jogging this morning," I said, "and I sprained— maybe broke—my ankle when I fell running down the street."

"Ah, that's a shame," Cosimo said, climbing into the car. The conversation that followed was clearly recorded without any feedback.

There were instances, though, when the bug—the transmitter that they'd hidden behind the dash—caused some problems. On the last day before the cops wrapped up the Commisso conspiracy investigation, I had to meet with Michele Commisso in the car. Michele wasn't as reluctant to get in the car as his brother was. He'd generally just jump in, no problem, and start talking. On this occasion, just minutes before he was due to meet with me, I turned on the radio. The transmitter started buzzing— giving off static right through the radio. I just told him that the radio wasn't working right, and he never suspected a thing.

There was one time, April 23, 1981, that Cosimo didn't even hesitate about getting into my car. I still remember the circumstances.

I was at Howard Johnson's waiting for him, when he

arrived in a taxi instead of his car. He paid the driver, walked over to my car with a slight limp, and climbed in.

"Where's your car?" I asked him. "Why are you riding in a taxi?"

"I was just in a car accident," he said as his hands seemed to flail at the air in frustration. "I hurt the leg—banged my leg against the dash."

After he paid me a thousand dollars our meeting ended and I drove him to the Cambridge Hotel parking lot and let him out.

As he started to get out of the car, I shouted to him, "Hey, start limping down the street. The cops are down there. You'll have witnesses, and you can put in for an insurance claim."

He turned and looked at me with sort of a smirk on his face. "Yeah, yeah, you're right, Cec," he said. "Good idea. The leg. It's swollen and I got the whiplash."

"Got another idea, Cosimo," I said. "Better than that. Put your fuckin' leg in front of the car and I'll run over it. Then you'll really collect."

Cosimo looked back, shaking a fist at me. "Fuck off, Cec," he said laughing. He slammed the door behind him, started to walk over to a car in the lot, then remembered and started limping again while the surveillance cameras snapped.

Murphy and those who helped him monitored and recorded the conversations in a specially equipped van. It was a three-quarter-ton, blue step vehicle with a big square box in the back and dual wheels on either side. It had glass windows on the back with a one-way mirror window. The coppers could look out, but nobody could look in while they were taking pictures.

The van was my security blanket, literally. It was a rolling recording and movie studio. It was loaded with sensitive electronic recording equipment—cameras of all types with special Telephoto lenses—and there were pictures all around of Cosimo and me together.

There were other vehicles that could pick up the conversations and record them, but the van was usually the one Murphy used, particularly when he was alone. There were at least five occasions that he had to cover me without any backup because of problems in his office.

I look back now at some of the things that happened— the bickering and shortages of equipment and personnel while I was out meeting these Calabrian mafiosi—and I marvel at the fact that I lived through it.

It was a little after noon of St. Patrick's Day when I drove up to Cosimo's house in North York. It was a nice home, a little on the conservative side, but comfortable. Cosimo was smart enough to know that if he lived too high off the hog—in too plush surroundings—he'd attract attention, and that's something he tried not to do. He tried, not too successfully, to keep a low profile with police.

I knocked on the door. There was no answer. I knocked again. Still no answer. I began to wonder if Cosimo had forgotten the meeting. I started to walk up the street toward Remo's house, talking as I went so that Murphy could record and understand what I was doing without becoming too concerned.

"Just going up the street here, to Remo's house for a second," I said as I walked. The recorder picked it up.

Within a minute or two I ran into Remo.

"How you doing?" I asked.

"Going," he said without elaborating.

"Where's Cosimo?" I asked. "He's supposed to be here at eleven thirty."

"He's home," Remo answered.

"I knocked on the door," I said. "There's no answer."

"He's home, for sure," said Remo. "I just called."

"Jesus, he must be deaf then," I said. "Must be sleeping, you know."

I returned to Cosimo's house and banged on the door. Just then his wife drove up with the kids.

"Is Cosimo sleeping?" I asked. She shook her head. "He must be deaf."

"Deaf?" she said.

"Deaf," I said. "I rang the doorbell, banged on the door about ten times."

She opened the door wide to let me in. I shouted inside. "You getting up, Cosimo?"

"Yeah, I'm ready," he answered.

As I started to walk inside, his wife cautioned me to take off my boots. Before I pulled them off, I turned to her and said, "I got my car running. If he's not going to be too long I'll just leave it running."

Cosimo entered the room then, and I showed him I was a little agitated about the delay. "I was out there a half hour waiting for you," I said. He appeared surprised. Before he could say anything else, I put the boots back on and started out the door. "I'll wait for you outside. I got the car parked out there and I don't want to get a ticket or anything, you know. Where we gonna go? Where do we have to go? north? south? Got enough gas?"

"South a little bit," he said.

"South of what? I only got a half tank of gas. Is that enough?" I asked.

"Yeah," he said.

I got into the car. While I waited, I talked into the transmitter, telling Murphy that we were going south on a particular road. I had to wait another twenty minutes before Cosimo finally climbed into the car.

We talked about Remo and three friends he had in a car. I got Cosimo to identify the car as a Pontiac and confirm that one of the men in the car was a big guy but he didn't say what they were doing. He did confirm my observation that I'd never seen them around before. He also promised to have the rest of the money from Melia by the end of the month. We hit a traffic jam and he gave me new directions.

As we drove there was a lot of small talk about my upcoming sentencing, which I said would be postponed again. When Cosimo asked if I'd seen Ken Goobie recently, the purpose of all the driving came into focus. It was to show me where Peter Scarcella hung out.

Scarcella was only thirty, but he had become one of

Paul Volpe's important associates. I don't recall ever meeting him or even seeing him until Cosimo brought him to my attention that day. Scarcella chauffeured Volpe to meetings; he frequently was seen at Volpe's home. He seemed to be one of the brightest young stars in the Volpe crime organization, even when he was charged with bribery of Metro Works employees at three incinerator sites in Toronto.

Now Cosimo wanted him hit and he was laying out the floor plan of his life-style, the places he lived and hung out, without explaining why he wanted it done.

I let Cosimo give the directions while I played the role of a tourist. He reeled off this street and that in an area where I grew up. He was directing me to an apartment that Scarcella used. I played dumb, repeating each street he named so the surveillance teams tailing us would keep up.

"Turn right, here," Cosimo said. "It's hard to get that guy."

"Hard to get him?" I asked.

"Over here, yes," he said.

"Why is it hard to get him there?" I asked.

"He lives with his family there," he answered.

"What is it, a house or an apartment?" I said.

"No. It's an apartment," he said.

"You got his name and everything?" I asked. Up to this point, he hadn't given me a name that I could record on the tape that day.

"Yeah, but first I wanna show you another two, three places where he usually goes," Cosimo said.

He showed me Scarcella's father's place and a location where he went to play cards two nights a week.

"He goes to poker games," he said.

"Poker games? What, around here?" I said.

"No, they move it every night," he said. "There is a restaurant he goes to almost every night."

"Around here?" I asked.

"No, no. On Dufferin and Castlefield—where Canadian Tire is," he said. "There's a restaurant on the corner. It's open twenty-four hours. He goes there every day."

He asked me how I was going to handle it—when I'd do it.

"I'll come back. I'll just keep watching this guy," I said. "There's no hurry for this, eh?"

"No, no," he answered quietly. "One other thing I want to give you, when it's time. I'll give you more, you know, particular details."

"Oh, I'll just watch," I told him. "I'll look around here, then I'll go to this restaurant. Does he drive his car by himself?"

"Most times, yes," Cosimo said. Then, as we drove from one location to another, he added that Scarcella parked his car outside his parents' apartment at Winston House.

"You got a license number?" I asked.

"Yes," he said. "Last three numbers are 747."

"Open this darn page," I said, "and write it in. Write his name down here so I can check it out myself, eh? Then the number where he lives with his mother and father."

I figured that if I got him to write down the information, it would be another nail of evidence to hammer in his coffin—an important nail.

"You got his first name?" I asked.

"It's Peter," Cosimo said.

"Peter?"

"S-A-R-C-E-L-L-A," he said, spelling it wrong at first and then correcting himself.

I tried to pry out of Cosimo why he wanted Scarcella eliminated. It came slowly, with great difficulty.

"He did something, the bastard," he said.

"What is he? A stool pigeon?" I asked.

"Look's that way," he said.

We got to the Branch Restaurant. It was the place Scarcella came every day to meet gamblers and a girlfriend who was a waitress. Then Cosimo dropped another nugget of information. Scarcella was going to be at the Commisso bakery the next day at 1:00 P.M.

"All right," I said, "I'll get a look at him. I won't come in, but I'll be around there, okay? I'll park across the street or something."

Cosimo nodded. "Just between twelve thirty and one o'clock."

"Between twelve thirty and one o'clock he's gonna meet you, eh?" I said. "And he'll be driving that car, eh?"

While Cosimo thought I'd be there watching, I wasn't. The members of the surveillance team were, and what they discovered was important. They spotted Scarcella at the Casa Commisso the day Cosimo and I met, and they tailed him that afternoon to the Four Seasons Sheraton Hotel in downtown Toronto, where he met with Paul Volpe and two other people. We didn't know it then but the Commissos were worried—worried about facing a gang war with Volpe and his people. They were busy plotting to strike first.

18

The Informer II

I was still working for Murphy, the Combined Forces Special Enforcement Unit (SEU), the RCMP, and the Crown prosecutor without any immunity, or any agreement, and I was getting nervous about it. All that was supposed to change with a meeting between me and members of a special steering committee representing the agencies involved in the Cosimo investigation. It was supposed to, but it didn't.

We met at the Holiday Inn in Toronto just two days after Cosimo had given me a contract to kill Scarcella. As we started to sit down, Inspector Wylie of the SEU told Murphy to leave while they talked to me.

As Murphy walked toward the door, I stood up. "If Murphy goes, I go," I snapped.

"Wait," Wylie said. He motioned to both of us to return to our seats. "Corporal Murphy can stay."

"Mr. Kirby, we'd like you to work with Sergeant Al Cooke of Metro and Sergeant John Simpson of SEU," Wylie said. "They're better equipped to handle this case."

I shook my head. I knew Cooke. He was all right. I had nothing against him. But he wasn't Murphy. I also knew Simpson. I didn't like him. Besides, I knew and trusted Murphy.

"It's Murphy or no one," I said. "I've said that from

the start, and that's the way it is. I trust him, period. If I don't work with him, I don't work."

I could see a lot of unhappy inspectors in the room. They were going to be even more unhappy before the meeting ended.

First, I rejected the agreement they had signed and asked me to sign. It met my conditions except the most important one—immunity from prosecution for all past crimes.

"Can't sign that," I said, "not till I get immunity. Without immunity I don't testify, and you can't use the tapes."

That really upset them. They had admissions on those tapes that represented solid evidence of two conspiracies to murder—and there was the promise of more to come. But they weren't worth a dime unless I testified and agreed to the use of the tapes. Stalemate.

"One other thing, gentlemen," I said. "I've got another payment of seven thousand dollars or so coming from the Commissos. I intend to keep it unless you people come up with money to pay my expenses and living costs."

They all agreed to pay my expenses, but the agreement was still unsigned when I left. I said I'd continue to work with Murphy as long as they took care of my expenses, but unless I had immunity, I was still a "confidential informant" of the RCMP, and I wouldn't have to testify. Murphy had given his word, and his bosses didn't like it.

For the next few days there were additional meetings, including one with Simpson, all designed to get me to work with other investigators. None of them succeeded. Then another meeting was arranged with Cosimo at his house. Events started to move rapidly, a lot faster and in a lot more directions than we'd expected.

Cosimo was awake and waiting for me when I arrived the morning of March 27. The last thing I expected him to talk about was what he considered a developing Mafia war, but that's what he ended up doing. As he talked, the transmitter in my belt buckle and the body pack near my hip recorded it all.

"Listen, I got a few things to talk to you about—about this Scarc [Scarcella]," I said. "Want to go outside? Let's go outside. Few problems I've had."

Cosimo wasn't in any hurry to go outside to the car. He was comfortable where he was as I talked, so I didn't press it. I didn't want him getting suspicious. I did, however, want to pick up the conversation where we'd left off the last time we met. The Mounties needed more on his plan to kill Scarcella. As a prod, I used information the Mounties had pulled together watching Scarcella from the moment he left his apartment to the time he went to the Casa Commisso.

"You know the day you told me he was going to be at the hall there?" I asked.

Cosimo nodded. "We were there."

"All right," I said. "I went over to the apartment there about nine o'clock and I sat there. I saw him come out. I got the license number of his car and everything, eh?"

"Yeah," Cosimo acknowledged.

"Now I followed him from there. I had a different car, a broad's car," I said. "I followed him right down to the Four Seasons Sheraton Hotel downtown."

"Yeah," Cosimo said, "and..."

"In the morning, okay?" I said. "I parked the car, I went in there, and you know who he's standing there talking to?"

"Who?" asked Cosimo, his interest raised.

"Paul Volpe," I said. "How come? What's he doing talking to Volpe?"

"He's close to him," Cosimo answered. "That's okay. Forget it for now."

"He's close?" I asked.

"You don't have to worry about anything," Cosimo said.

"But who wants him killed?" I asked, really puzzled by the events and his answers. "Is it Volpe who wants him killed, or you, or what?"

"No, no, no, I'm . . ."

I interrupted. "You know like I saw Volpe and I said, what the fuck's going on here?"

"I'm wondering. Maybe he wants to do it to me," answered Cosimo, obviously concerned. "Him and this fellow."

"It's you that wants this done, or Volpe?" I asked.

"It's me, not Volpe," he said.

"Volpe doesn't know nothing about this?" I said.

"No, no. Why?" he said.

"You know, I didn't want to stick around the lobby too long," I explained, "I've seen Volpe before. I don't know if he's seen me."

"You ever meet him before?" he asked.

"Oh, I've seen him before, with Chuck," I said.

"Where?" he asked.

"You know where Chuck's place is," I said. We were talking about Chuck Yanover, who was a member of the Volpe organization and was supposed to be out of town, in hiding.

"Recently?" he said nervously.

"No, about a year ago," I said.

"Nobody saw you?" he asked with concern.

"No," I said.

"You tell anybody about this thing?" he asked.

"No, nobody knows about it," I reassured him.

"Things—they're bad over here," he said, deep worry showing on his face. "I don't know why these guys . . . I don't know. They want to do me and my brother."

"They what?" I said with real surprise.

"They want to do me and my brother," he said. "Maybe I can't trust any one of them."

Cosimo was telling me that he and Remo were targets of possible mob hits and that Volpe and his organization were behind the plot. Scarcella was some kind of double agent, playing both sides for his own interests.

"Who, Volpe does?" I asked. "You think Volpe wants to kill you and your brother?"

"This guy," he said, meaning Scarcella.

"What, with this guy?" I asked to be sure I was getting his story straight.

"Yeah. It's the two of them," he said.

"What? This Scarcella's playing both sides?" I asked. "He's telling Volpe everything about you and him?"

Cosimo shook his head. "No, nothing about me and him. It's just that I don't know what's going to happen next year, you know. We just don't know."

"So what do you want to do?" I asked. "You want to kill Volpe in the future?"

"No. Not for now," he said, his voice trailing off.

"Not for now?" I asked.

"Like wait for this guy [Scarcella] for another week or so, okay?" he asked.

"Pass on him for a week?" I said.

"Yes," Cosimo answered.

"All right, a week," I said.

"'Cause I'm waiting for an answer," he said. "I wanna be sure it's him." Then he switched back to questions about Yanover, who he was obviously concerned about. "You talk to Chuck about these things?"

"About this?" I said.

"Yeah," he answered.

"No, he's on the run, Chuck," I said. "People are looking for him."

"For what?" asked Cosimo.

"He ripped somebody off," I said. "He sold somebody a kilo of coke or something. Ripped him. Bought himself a new Cadillac and he's gone. Yeah, he's too much. All right, so wait a week or so on this guy, eh?"

He nodded.

"Now what do you want?" I asked, to try and get more details out of him. "Do you want his body left laying around? Do you want him disposed of, or what?"

"Which way can you do it?" he asked.

"I can do it whatever way you want," I said.

"Gonna do it. You with me," Cosimo said, looking at me with a smile.

"That's right," I said. "I just did this last one [the girl in Connecticut] with no problem."

"You were with me," Cosimo said, staring at me, trying to read what I was thinking. "You be with me because there's lotsa things will go on with this fuckin' town. You see what I mean?"

The message was loud and clear to me. As far as Cosimo was concerned, a gang war was coming, and he wanted to be certain I was going to be there to help him.

"I don't know. I stay away from this shit now, you know," I answered.

"Yeah, you stay away, but be sure you are with me," he said sharply, "not with those other people."

"That's right, that's right," I said, "you know that."

The conversation changed suddenly. Cosimo wanted me to see a man he called "Lillo" at a furniture store.

"There's two guys workin' there," he explained. "One older and the young guy. The young one's the one. Just give him, you know, a couple of smacks."

But I still wanted more on tape about the Scarcella hit.

"You want him left laying in the street where everybody sees his head, sees him and says look, here's a stool pigeon that got a bullet in his head?" I asked.

Cosimo wasn't certain, but he was concerned that Scarcella would be suspicious, a difficult man to kill. "Some days, he's very suspicious," he said.

"I got a way of getting to him," I answered. "I got a dirty trick of my own I could get him with."

"You do?" he said with surprise.

"He's not going to be suspicious if I walk up to him and show him a badge and say, 'Here, you're under arrest. Come with me.' How can he be suspicious then?"

"That's right," Cosimo said with a broad smile on his face.

I reminded Cosimo that he still owed me $7,000 for the Connecticut job and that I was broke. He promised he would pay by the first week of April.

"You won't lose no money with me, you know that, Cec," he said.

"The point is you know I need it," I said. "I'm broke."

Still he was worried, worried about betrayal in his own camp, worried about being stabbed in the back by people he trusted, including me, particularly since I needed the money he owed me. I suspect that he wondered if I would sell him out for money. He didn't know it, but he'd already been sold out, for my life.

"You won't betray me, eh?" he asked. "You wouldn't go against me?"

"Never," I said.

"Thank you, Cec," he said.

"Never, Cosimo," I said again.

A feeling of exhilaration gripped me as I left. If the recording equipment had worked—and it had—the surveillance teams had some strong evidence from that meeting. I was certain Cosimo was convinced he could trust me, at least for the moment. I was equally certain that if I actually handled any of the hits he had planned—whether Scarcella or Volpe—I would be wasted eventually myself.

Cosimo was a very suspicious man. He had been very close to Scarcella. He was someone he trusted. Now he was ready to sink that knife into him once he was certain that whoever was whispering in his ear about Scarcella was whispering truth. Even if not, the seed had been planted, and it was festering like an open sore.

For the next few weeks, Cosimo stalled. He stalled on paying the money he and Melia owed me. He stalled on setting a date to hit Scarcella. On April 8, he came close to making a commitment on Scarcella.

Cosimo was nervous as we sat in my car talking. He noticed that my ankle was wrapped in bandages, and he seemed to accept my explanation that I'd injured it when I fell while jogging. Then he noticed a small telephone pager I was wearing on my belt. Immediately his suspicion reached an almost fever pitch. He appeared convinced it was a tape recorder until I told him I had gotten the pager so that he could reach me when he needed me. I gave him a number.

"Here it is," I said, "R, eight, nine, four, seven."

"Just call and give the message?" Cosimo asked.

"Right, and just leave a number," I answered. "Don't say a name there."

"By tomorrow night, they gonna page you, okay?" Cosimo asked. "If you can, grab more information on the guy—Peter."

Cosimo's voice dropped to a whisper as he mentioned Scarcella's name. He was still nervous about the car and the pager I was wearing. I repeated the last name, Scarcella, then I tried to ease his suspicions again.

"It's all right, this car," I said. "I check this car all the time, every week."

"Then next week, Michele gonna call you," he said. "And, without mentioning the name, he gonna say yes or no, okay? If it's yes, go ahead, okay?"

"If he says yes, go ahead," I said.

"Yes," Cosimo said without hesitation.

They needed another week to decide whether they had to kill Scarcella. Cosimo was planning a trip to Vancouver. He was establishing an alibi. I would be up to his brother Michele to pass on the hit order.

"All right," I said, "what about Volpe?"

"No, no, for now, forget about him," Cosimo answered excitedly.

"You're gonna have to get rid of him sooner or later, aren't you?" I asked.

Cosimo looked at me for a long minute before answering, shaking his head slowly. "You talk about anybody? About him?"

"No, I don't," I said sharply. "I don't talk to fuckin' nobody. I don't even talk to anybody, okay?"

"About anything?" he pressed.

"Nobody," I said.

"I'll tell you what they say," he said. "They spoke to me in jail. They say there's gonna be a war involved—a war over here in Toronto."

"Is that right?" I said with a look of surprise. Then I hit him with some information I'd gotten from a biker about his relationship with Ken Goobie.

"I could tell you things that people around this fuckin' city are shooting their mouth off about, okay?" I continued. "I just don't pay any attention to them—and Goobie's one of them. He's got a big mouth. You don't tell him nothing. Okay?"

"No, no, no," Cosimo said.

"All right," I said. "'Cause everything you tell him he repeats, you know?"

"That's right," Cosimo said in agreement.

"He [Goobie] told Gary [Barnes] about this thing down in New York."

I watched as Cosimo's eyes widened in surprise. He was obviously upset that anyone on the street would have any knowledge about the plot to kill Helen Nafpliotis.

"Yeah?" he said in shock.

"Yeah," I said, "I didn't tell him, so you had to tell him."

"Well, he didn't know you went," Cosimo said. "He didn't know that it was done."

"He said to Gary, he said, you wanna make twenty-five thousand?" I said watching Cosimo's reaction. "He says, there's a broad down in New York that they wanna get rid of."

Cosimo was flustered, upset. He had gone to Goobie and told Goobie he would pay him twenty-five thousand to kill the woman as added insurance if I failed to do the job. He was going to pay this bastard more than he offered me. Goobie had gone to Barnes to get him to help. The last thing Cosimo expected was that I would find out about it. Finally he admitted talking to Goobie. His suspicions that I might be talking were sidetracked now by a much deeper suspicion about Goobie, and I played on that.

"Well, he's told Gary," I said angrily. "So how many other people has he told?"

Cosimo was really on the defensive now. "I don't know. Because I talk to him, not to nobody else."

"You got a big mouth," I said. "I told you. Stay away from the fuckin' guy. He's no good."

"I don't see him anymore," he said.

"And don't trust him. I'm telling you," I warned.

"I don't trust nobody," Cosimo said. "Ah, Cec, I trust you. Things they gonna be for the betterment. Things are gonna be smooth in this town."

Suddenly his mood darkened and his eyes narrowed.

"We wanna know if we can trust you a hundred percent," he asked. "You with us?"

"Yeah, well, I have been all the time," I said.

His face brightened a little and there was a trace of a smile. "All the time, you for us, yes?" he said.

It wasn't until April 21 that I met with Michele at Howard Johnson's. He didn't have the money that was promised, but he had information that jolted me.

Michele had been to the States two weeks earlier to see Vince Melia and collect the money that was due me for killing Helen Nafpliotis. Melia had stalled, and the Commissos were having trouble raising the cash. Cosimo's legal fees were over $15,000, and they had other commitments. With all the problems, Michele said he'd have $2,000 for me in a few days, but I'd have to wait until Melia came to Toronto for a wedding later in the month to collect the rest.

"Vince, he gave me the runaround," Michele said. "He says there was some money missing in the apartment, some jewelry."

I was stunned, but it didn't show. I didn't know it, but the FBI had, in addition to staging a fake kidnapping at her home in Stamford, let Nafpliotis take all her money and jewelry with her. Melia and his crew had apparently searched the apartment for the jewelry and money, most of it things Nick Melia had given her and wanted back since she was dead anyway. When they didn't find it, they asked questions and tried to convince the Commissos I'd gotten enough with the jewelry and cash and the initial payment.

"Yeah, well, I made it look good," I said to Michele.

"You know what happened to him?" Michele said. "I've checked it and it's true. His brother [Nick Melia] is into some trouble down in Kentucky. And he's out on a hundred and fifty thousand dollars bail. He's waiting for his brother to beat the case and come up with the money."

"That could be another two years," I said angrily.

"No, in May," he said. "He's either in or out. But this week, he's [Vince] bringing some money, that's for sure."

When I threatened to turn up at a family wedding, which was to be held at the Casa Commisso banquet hall, and grab Melia and shake it out of him, Michele excitedly told me to stay away and guaranteed I'd be paid. Two days later, on April 23, Cosimo and I met. He handed me $1,000 and promised to pay me $500 a week from a business he was taking over so that I wouldn't be broke anymore.

"You know, we gonna put you in payroll," he said. "So much a week. Then when things are done, you gonna have a bonus for it. You see what I mean?"

I shook my head in agreement. "It's about time I got some extra, some sort of. . ." He cut me off before I finished saying "some sort of salary."

"Before, I couldn't do it," he said. "But now, I have something, ah, steady, inside." Then, without explanation he added, "Ah, Scarcella, forget about it for now."

"What?" I asked in surprise.

"Just don't worry about it for now," he said.

"For how long?" I asked.

"I don't know," he said. "A month, two months. We don't know yet. There's another guy I want to take care of."

"What?" I said.

"Another guy instead of him. [Remo] wants to do another guy," Cosimo said.

So you don't want to do him [Scarcella]," I said, making sure that his orders to kill another man were being recorded clearly. "You want to do another guy? Who, who the fuck's this other guy?"

"I'll show you," he said. "Next week you'll see."

"Make up your minds," I said with annoyance. "What is he? A close friend of Scarcella's?"

"Yes," he answered.

"Not Volpe?" I said, so it was clear to everyone listening in.

"I'll show him," he said. "Maybe you know the guy a little bit."

"What's his name?" I asked, trying to squeeze out more information without arousing his suspicions. "Maybe I do know him."

"I'll tell you, but you don't worry about the name," he said. "You see him, okay?"

"What is he, a gambler?" I asked. "Another gambler?"

"Ah, you know," he said with a shrug. "Next week. Next week you gonna have two thousand."

"Vince is coming in Saturday, eh?" I said. "I'd like to be there. I'd like to kick his fuckin' ass when he comes in Saturday."

"You don't have to worry about that," he said. "I'll do it myself."

On the night of April 27, ten mercenaries, including Toronto Ku Klux Klan leader Wolfgang W. Droege, arrived at a marina near Fort Pike State Park in New Orleans in a truck loaded with weapons. With them were three undercover agents of the U.S. Bureau of Alcohol, Tobacco, and Firearms (ATF). When they got out to unload the weapons, ammunition, and dynamite they were transporting, agents of the FBI, the U.S. Customs Service, and ATF were waiting to arrest them.

Just four days before that happened, I reported to Mark Murphy that the mercenaries were going to invade a 300-square-mile island called Dominica. I didn't know much about the island except what I had been told. It had been British, and it had been given its independence in November 1978. It was located between the French islands of Martinique and Guadeloupe and was about 400 miles southeast of San Juan, Puerto Rico.

All that and more had been told to me by Chuck Yanover, who I had seen at a discotheque while I was busy working for the RCMP on the Commissos.

Meeting with Yanover gave me an edge in my meetings with the Commissos, who were always afraid I would defect to Yanover's boss, Paul Volpe. Yanover was always a braggard and loved to talk about other people. As a rounder, he was in a position to hear about different rounders and hoods, including the Commissos. So I made a point of listening when he talked, because he could be a fountain of useful information when he wanted to. The last thing I expected him to talk about at one meeting was a plot to seize an island.

"Want a job, Cec?" he asked.

"Maybe," I said. "What have you got in mind?"

"How'd you like to go to the Caribbean with me, to an island called Dominica?" he asked. "We're going to take it over."

Yanover said that he had been hired by Wolfgang Droege and James Alexander McQuirter, national director of the KKK in Canada. Droege was about thirty-four, and McQuirter was twenty-three. The two planned to take over the island and set up their own government. Yanover planned to be made one of their top officials, set up a casino with the help of Volpe, and become very, very rich.

The island had all kinds of potential as far as Yanover was concerned. It could be used for gambling, as a jump-off point and storage warehouse for narcotics, a place to hide felons, and a sanctuary for mob money through offshore banks they would set up. There was just no limit to Chuckie's dreams of riches.

Yanover and one of his buddies, Michael Gerol, had gone to the island on what was supposed to be a vacation. They had photographed all the island's important locations, including its police station, its small military post, and the best approaches to the island from the sea. Yanover had turned over the information and photos to the two Klansmen so they could prepare for the invasion.

"Join us," Yanover said, "you'll make a fortune."

I shook my head. "Thanks, Chuck, but that's not for me. I got too many problems here to take care of."

I told everything I knew to Murphy, and he reported it to the SEU, the RCMP, and the OPP, all of whom launched an investigation. At the same time, I was told, they notified the FBI, who, with other agencies, had already infiltrated the "invasion force." If they hadn't stopped the plot when they did, a lot of people might have been killed.

Their plan, I learned later, was to team up on the island with some Rastafarians, called "Dreads" on Dominica, who grew pot, kidnapped and killed island residents, and threatened officials who stood in their way. That would have been some crazy team—Klansmen who hate blacks, and Rastas, who hate whites and extort and terrorize their own people to push drugs and what they call a religion.

Funny thing. On May 15, shortly after the Dominica story broke in the papers, Cosimo mentioned that the island had been offered to his crime group some time before.

"Looks like they're [the police] after Yanover," I remarked. "Those people in that Dominica plot, they got pinched. They're looking at about fifty years."

"You know that the first people they talked to was us," said Cosimo. "They came to us two years ago."

"What? About that?" I said dumbfounded. The last thing I expected him to say was that he and his brothers were somehow involved in Dominica. I was really stunned. "They approached you on it?"

"Sure. Before anybody else," he said with a smile.

"What, the people down there?" I asked, still startled by what he'd told me.

"The people down there—from Dominica," he said. "I was down there."

"You went down there?" I asked.

"Hey, it's nice—beautiful island, beautiful island," he repeated. "Well, first it was too much money. Then—at the time they approached me—the people in power were the right people."

I was fascinated by what he had to say, and for the most part all I did was listen, with little more comment than an occasional "Yeah."

"Then there was an election and they lost it," he continued.

"Then it changed," I suggested.

"You understand," he said with a smile.

"And now it's the same people from before?" I asked.

"Ah no, but now they changed, okay?" he said. "So that's why we dropped the idea. You know, we had people interested. Everybody was ready to go in. But then the people—they lost the election. These other people, they want nothing to do with it. The deal was twenty-five years we run a casino. Twenty-five years tax free."

"Is that right, eh?" I said. "Jesus. That would have been nice."

"What they wanted," he said, "was for us to build them a runway and an airport."

"An airport?" I asked.

He nodded his head vigorously. "Yeah, because they got no airport. There's no airport there at all."

"So you can't land a plane there," I said.

"Not a jet," he explained. "Just a small plane. So there was two million dollars' worth of work on the airport. They would give us the best side of land—five hundred acres farmland. For nothing. Just free. That way we'd be able to build on it."

"Yeah," I acknowledged.

"Okay—so much percent was to go to the prime minister there," he said. "That's all it was. Then this thing changed."

"Yeah, that's too bad," I said.

Cosimo was upset by the change, that was pretty obvious. The people he'd depended on were out, and there were new people trying to take over Dominica who had approached other people in Toronto. The new people wanted to overthrow the government and seize the island. Cosimo called that approach a waste of time.

"Dominica, it's beautiful, one of the best islands in the area and it's the most beautiful," he said. "There's just twenty-five thousand people on the whole island. It's one of the biggest islands. Bigger than Aruba. It's bigger than most of those islands up there."

He was really rambling on about the place, about the lost opportunity. Cosimo saw it as a gold mine for his group and a great place to spend his time.

"Like I said, that was no more than two, four, five years ago when we were approached," he recalled. "Then that thing in Vancouver happened [the counterfeiting bust] and then we laid around a little bit. A lotta things happened."

Cosimo was disappointed that his group hadn't been able to take over the island. But he was disgusted that Yanover had gotten involved and had blown the deal forever with the ridiculous invasion plot. The island paradise would never be a casino plum he could pluck.

Although the "invasion force" was arrested April 27, it wasn't until February 10, 1982, that McQuirter and Yanover were charged with trying to overthrow Dominica. Between those two arrests, Yanover had managed to get himself arrested for the Arviv Disco bombing and for a plot to assassinate the president of South Korea. He conned North Korean intelligence out of more than $600,000 with the help of Gerol, who played the role of a trained killer. Then he tried to con the RCMP and the American Central Intelligence Agency. He wanted to exchange pictures and tapes he had of the North Korean agents he was dealing with.

What Yanover had in mind was to have charges against him for the Arviv bombing and the Dominican plot dropped. He also wanted diamond-smuggling charges against his two bosses, Nate Klegerman and Volpe, dropped while he and Gerol were supposed to get immunity. Nobody was buying. Yanover eventually got two years running concurrent with his nine years for the Arviv bombing. Gerol got a year.

Nobody, so far as I was ever able to find out, got the

pictures, the tapes, and all the other evidence Yanover said he gathered against the North Koreans. And all those North Korean co-plotters of his never turned up to try to collect their $600,000 back, but I'll bet Chuckie wishes he'd never taken them for that. Deep down, he probably also wishes he'd cut a deal with the RCMP and the OPP. The truth is when Yanover gets out of jail he's going to find that Communist agencies like North Korean intelligence don't like being ripped off and embarrassed. They have long memories, and they intend to make him pay—with his life. Yanover may find that to survive he'll have to make a deal with the coppers. They are the only ones who will ever be able to help him.

19

The Last Contract

I felt more secure when I went to meet Cosimo on April 29 than I had in all the months I had worked for Murphy. For the first time I had a written agreement, signed the day they grabbed the Dominica "invaders," that guaranteed me immunity as a witness and protection and support for my family. I should have known then that all that glitters is not gold and things written on paper can always be altered. Promises made and sworn to are not always promises kept by men or their governments.

When I saw Cosimo at Howard Johnson's that day, I was concerned only with getting the evidence needed to wrap this thing up. I was tired and tense. Murphy was stretched to the limits of endurance—providing surveillance and protection for me and working long added hours checking out information I brought in. In his spare waking moments he was fighting with his brass, trying to get added physical and financial support for me. I have to say that I will always admire Murphy for his honesty, his integrity, and his guts. I'm alive today because of him.

Cosimo complained that he was still in pain from the injury he had received in the car accident. The leg still bothered him, and he was limping slightly. He looked terrible. His eyes were bloodshot, his round face looked drawn, and he was unusually nervous.

"I've got something I wanna talk to you about," he said. "Let's get outta the car for a second. I don't trust cars."

"All right," I answered. "Looks like you got a lot on your mind. Looks like you haven't been sleeping too good. You can tell when your eyes are all red."

His tone was sharp, and there was an edge of suspicion to his questions.

"Why do you want my brother [Remo] here?" he asked.

"Well look, you told me last week that you're going to put me on a payroll," I said, trying to explain why I had asked him to bring Remo to the meeting. Remo had not come, and Cosimo was annoyed about that request.

"Now I wanted to just confirm it with him in case something happens to you," I added.

"Nothing happens to us," he said. "What could happen to me?"

"Well, suppose you get picked up?" I asked. "Get another charge. Then I won't see you anymore."

"Don't you worry about that," he said. "You don't see me anymore, you think I'm gonna die?" He stopped and pointed to my hip. "What's that?"

I looked down and smiled. "The pager. It's off now. If I turn it on, it starts beeping." To put him at ease, I turned it on.

Cosimo switched to problems with his people in Connecticut. It was out in the open. Melia and his friends didn't believe that the Nafpliotis woman was dead.

"They still don't believe that it's okay because even her suitcase is missing," he said, with just a trace of suspicion reflecting from his narrowing eyes.

"Yeah, well, I took care of all that, okay?" I said.

"He [Melia] said that all the jewelry is missing," he said.

"Well, my partner took some jewelry and some stuff," I snapped, grateful that early on I had established with him that I had had to take some help with me.

I'd originally created the fictional helper in the event

someone from the Commisso crime group spotted me with Murphy or an agent in New York or Connecticut. Now that helper provided an alibi for taking the jewelry and cash that the FBI and the woman had cleared from her home without ever bothering to tell me or Murphy. Little mistakes like that can cost your life when you're dealing with people like the Calabrian Mafia.

The FBI hadn't given me or Murphy or the SEU a clue to what they had done with Nafpliotis. They never told us they'd taken her back to the house to get her jewelry and her clothes. They didn't tell us she was back in Greece, trying to sell her home and other property from there. I knew they'd staged a kidnapping, because that was reported in the papers. But the kidnapping required two men. If I hadn't created a fictional helper, the Commissos would have been certain things were phony, and I'd have been dead. As it was, the FBI endangered me and the undercover operation, not intentionally, but it still made me scramble and it raised unnecessary suspicions.

"This was his," Cosimo complained. The jewelry had all been bought by Nick Melia, and he figured he'd been screwed out of the money he spent on her.

Think fast, Kirby. Come up with a story he'll understand. My mind was in high gear, and my mouth was about to catch up.

"We took the stuff out to make it look like she more or less went on a vacation," I said.

Then Cosimo dropped another hot rock in my lap.

"Just a minute," he said. "You know the radio, the American radio, she says that she's living in Italy, in Greece, or in Toronto."

A little bell went off in my head. This could be trouble—real trouble—unless I played hard and fast with Cosimo, kept him off balance with my questions and answers. They say the best offense is a tough defense. I believe in that and I used it.

"Who said that?" I snapped heatedly.

The Last Contract

"The radio, but me, I'm not saying," Cosimo said defensively, afraid I was about to come after him.

"Radio? What radio?" I said. "Jesus Christ," I thought to myself. "Why the hell didn't the FBI tell us what was going on? The radio, yet. Jesus Christ what else?"

"Back there," he explained. "They didn't find the car yet. Where's the car? In the lake too?"

"Yeah," I said.

"That's where she died?"

"Yeah," I said again.

"Far away or nearby?" he asked.

"About thirty miles from there," I answered. "How fuckin' far do you want me to drive the car? Back to Canada?"

"No, no, no, no, that's good," he said nervously. "It's good, you know. Probably they just made those stories up. Give me twenty dollars."

"How much?" I asked.

"Give me twenty dollars because I'm broke," he said meekly now. "I'll give it back to you. Look, Cec, there's one thing, all of this—I think it's excuses because the guy is broke. So he's trying to, you know..."

"Look it, she's dead," I said.

"I know it," Cosimo said as sweat glistened on his brow.

"You got my guarantee on it, okay?" I said. "Do you want me to go show you where she's dead?"

He waved his hands in the air and then wiped his brow. "No, no, no."

"Well, why doesn't he fuckin' pay us?" I said. "My partner wanted to go back down there and see him, you know? What does he think? I got the broad shacked up here in Toronto or something?"

"Yes, that's what he says," Cosimo answered.

"Is that right, eh?" I said.

"Yeah," Cosimo said softly.

"Is he fuckin' nuts?" I growled. "Next time tell him to come with me. I told Michele the other day, I was gonna go out in that parking lot there and wait for him and give him a kick in the ass. You know, I still might."

Cosimo shook his head vigorously. "I know, but don't you worry about this money."

"If you can't trust me after this long..." I said.

"I trust you now," Cosimo said.

"I can see them being a little suspicious, okay?" I said. "But you know I'll go back down there. I'll show him where the fuckin' car is. He can go down there and swim. If she can hold her breath for fifteen minutes, she's the best swimmer I've ever seen in my life."

"Tell me one thing," Cosimo asked. "Was she dead when you..."

"Knocked her out," I answered, finishing his sentence. "I didn't use the gun. I threw the gun away somewhere else. I didn't know where this gun had been, all right? They hand me a fuckin' gun, and first of all it's supposed to be a .38 only it wasn't." I paused, looking at him, knowing he was on the defensive, convinced I had done the job despite what his friends from Connecticut had said. "They were making this up. You figure they were making this up so they won't have to pay you."

"That's what I think, but don't you worry about it for now, okay?"

I didn't. I knew he was convinced by what I'd said, and he was sore. He'd go back and collect now from Melia. It was time to turn the conversation to other important things, to Scarcella and to Volpe.

Cosimo was filled with surprises that afternoon. The plot to kill another man was off. There was no longer a need, as he had told me there was at a previous meeting, for him to take me to various locations and show me the victim's routine. Pure and simple, the hit was off and he had no name to give me. Then he dropped the other shoe. The plan to kill Scarcella was off too.

"You're in no rush to get rid of Scarcella?" I asked, surprised by his change of plans.

"No, no. We're gonna get him with us," he said,

shrugging his shoulders and gesturing with his hands in the air.

"You're going to what?" I asked. I was floored by the turn of events, but I tried not to show it.

"I think we're gonna get him on this side now," Cosimo said with a smile.

"You're going to have him on this side now?" I asked, to be sure those listening in understood. Scarcella the cheese company owner, the former union organizer for Volpe, his trusted companion, was now on the side of the Commissos. If only Volpe knew.

There was no such change of heart when Cosimo turned his attention toward Volpe.

"Kill him," he said heatedly. "You understand what I mean?"

"I do," I said. "I know where he's at. Yanover told me where he lives, okay? You know where he lives?"

Cosimo shook his head vigorously. "Nothing," he said. "I have nothing."

"I do," I said confidently. "You want me to get him, kill him tonight?"

"All right," he said.

I knew I needed more time to get things arranged, to talk to Murphy and other SEU investigators. So I changed tactics and stalled a bit.

"I'll go," I said. "I'll see what I can do, okay? I'll work on it in the next week or two. I'll guarantee you he'll be dead in the next two weeks."

"All right. Fine," he said with a smile.

"He's got dogs around his place," I explained. "You got to be careful. He's a very suspicious man, you know."

For more than twenty years, Volpe had been the mob power in Toronto. He had connections with the old Joe Bonanno mob in New York City and then he teamed up in the distribution of narcotics for the Stefano Magaddino family, according to testimony in the U.S. Senate in 1963. He'd gotten heavily involved in property in Atlantic City, according to the newspaper. He and Vincent Cotroni were close. He had built his own crime organization in Toronto, but, for some reason I knew nothing about at the time, he hated the Calabrian Honoured Society and they hated him. Now they were going to do something about their hatred.

Cosimo was worried about my seeing and talking to Yanover. He was particularly concerned that I might have tipped my hand on the Volpe hit by talking to Yanover about him. I denied it. In fact, I noted, Yanover had invited me out to see Volpe's heavily guarded, fenced-in estate in Nobleton.

"You asked Yanover about this guy?" he asked.

"Did I ask anybody about him?" I repeated. "No, no, no, I don't ask anybody. I can find out on my own."

"This Yanover. Couldn't he tell you?" Cosimo asked.

"He said, you want to go up to his [Volpe's] place?" I said. "I said, yeah, I wouldn't mind going up. He told me where he lives."

"Where's Yanover gone?" he asked.

"He's downtown," I said.

"But he was to have been on the run, they told me. He was on the run for something," he said.

Since I was the one who had originally told Cosimo about Yanover being on the run for a drug rip-off, I had to come up with a plausible story now for his not being in hiding.

"Oh, yeah," I recalled. "He's always fuckin' somebody. That's why I think he wanted me to go up and see Volpe or something. He told me almost exactly where he lives. His name's on a mailbox out there. He said, here's the address. Can you come up and meet me and meet him? But I never showed up."

"You still walk around with the gun on you?" Cosimo asked with concern.

"Yeah," I said with a half smile, knowing it worried him. We agreed to meet again on May 15 if I didn't go to jail May 5, when I told him I was scheduled to appear for sentencing on the B&E case after pleading guilty.

"I'll see you in here May fifteenth, two o'clock, all right? Read the papers," I said.

"Ah, don't you worry about it," Cosimo said. "You shouldn't be going in."

"I'm worried about you," I answered, "those accidents you're getting into."

Cosimo was smiling as we split, but I was worried. How was I going to show him that I had taken Volpe out without doing it? Did we have enough for a case, and if we didn't, what would I have to do? All those questions and more were to be answered by Murphy, but not without some problems from the people who gave him his orders.

Murphy was upset when we met later that day.

"What the hell are you doing carrying a gun?" Murphy shouted. "Are you crazy?"

"I feel safe with it," I snapped. "Besides, Cosimo knows. It keeps him honest."

"It's against the fuckin' law, Cec," he roared. "You could be in a whole lot of trouble and so could I because of a stupid thing like that. Jesus. Where the hell are your brains?"

I shrugged, reached under my belt, and pulled out the gun, handing it to him. "Okay, okay," I said apologetically, "but with the kind of support you're getting, what the hell do you expect me to do? You got one guy with you now, other times you're doing the fuckin' surveillance by yourself. Who's going to help me in time if things go wrong? Me—that's who. But here's the gun."

There had been references to the gun in prior conversations, but Murphy and the others listening in hadn't picked them up. It wasn't until months later that they transcribed all the tapes. They all assumed that we were referring to the telephone pager I carried when Cosimo asked me if I was carrying a gun or when I told him I was. That didn't cut ice with any of Murphy's superiors. They were convinced Murphy knew that I had a gun all along. Later it was one of the charges when they reprimanded him. I think the real truth was that none of them had the guts to do what he did on the street, and when all the glory for the busts came they wanted to grab it and leave Murphy out.

I felt naked without the gun, and I was going to feel even worse about it when I had to step into the pressure cooker again on May 15 and explain to Cosimo why I hadn't called to say I was ready to kill Volpe. I said what I needed was time to get a good rundown on Volpe and his way of life. I didn't know it until later, but there was no one better for getting that information than my friend Murphy.

For years, Volpe had been the Buffalo Cosa Nostra's man in Toronto. In 1981, because of the Commisso investigation, he became Murphy's confidential informant. His code number in the RCMP was 0-1943, and the people who were Murphy's bosses in the operation involving me didn't have the slightest inkling of that relationship.

Volpe took his orders from the Stefano Magaddino mob in Buffalo, and that mob also gave orders to the crime family in Hamilton that was run by Giacomo Luppino. Murphy told me that Jimmy Luppino, the son of Giacomo, used to visit Volpe every day in Toronto until the Commissos gave me the contract to kill him. Publicly, no one has ever said who gave the Commissos that contract. I had information from some mob friends that it was Vincent Cotroni. He was a former member of the Bonanno crime family, but more important he was from Reggio di Calabria, and his Calabrian ties and associations were strong. Many contracts for the Commissos, who were called Canada's Murder Inc., came from Cotroni.

It was a long time before I knew what kind of information Volpe gave Murphy, but Volpe trusted Murphy, and that was to become very, very important in the weeks ahead. Murphy later told me that he'd met Volpe when he started a project that turned into Operation Oblong, an RCMP investigation that in 1975 had severely damaged Volpe's gambling empire.

Volpe didn't become the valuable informant he could have because Murphy's RCMP bosses refused to let Murphy talk to him or accept information that Volpe was willing to give him. All that came to pass later in the year.

Everything was about to come to a head when I met with Cosimo at Howard Johnson's on May 15. All those months of undercover work were going to end, at least temporarily, although I had no evidence of that when I met with him in my car.

"This thing with Volpe," I said. "How much you gonna give me for that? I want to know. I don't want no payroll or five hundred bucks. I want it all in one lump. I want to know how much you're gonna give me and then how much you can give me after that."

Cosimo hesitated. He didn't want to set a figure, and in the back of my head I knew he didn't really plan on paying me. My payoff if I killed Volpe was going to be two in the head, burial in a shallow grave, or my body dumped in the Bayview Ghost.

"Ah, Cec, I don't like . . ." he started to say. I cut him off.

"I want out. I want to fuck off out of the country," I said. "I've been out in the rain for the last two nights watching the guy's place for chrissakes. I'm gonna end up with pneumonia."

Cosimo was edgy. He was always afraid of being bugged, yet he still talked.

"Cec, how is this car? Is it still okay?" he asked.

"This car is safe," I said. "I had it checked out two weeks ago by what's his name—you know, my friend there. We took it to a garage, and they went through the whole fuckin' car. You know, I got a dog up there. Nobody gets near this fuckin' car. Nobody! I don't leave it for too long, I tell you. All right now?"

Cosimo appeared satisfied. He stopped looking at everything in the car and began talking again.

"Listen, let's move this way," he said. "You see, I don't want to promise you any more to put up until I'm one hundred percent sure."

"All right," I said. "Your word's good with me. Your

credit's good with me, okay? You owe me five thousand dollars still, okay, from before."

"Yes," he acknowledged.

"All right, I just want enough money to get around in, and I want it after Volpe's killed. He'll be killed soon. I've been up there ten times. Do you know where this place is?"

"No, Cec," he said.

"It's out in the country, okay?" I said. "You can't park like here, like you do in the city. It's hard. I gotta park at least a mile away where I got a good spoke. I got a mile to go through the bush. I tell you, I've been fuckin' soaked the last three days."

"In the morning, Cec," he asked, "how's it look in the morning?"

"Ah, I must have got there too late," I said. "I usually get there at nighttime, eh? I want to see the place at night. He's got Foxhill on the mailbox, with TV towers and a tennis court back there. He drives a maroon Cadillac, and he's got a station wagon too."

"He drives one of those Audis, you know, the car," Cosimo added.

I shook my head. RCMP and SEU intelligence wasn't all it was cracked up to be. They didn't tell me about an Audi, probably because they didn't know about it. Think fast.

"Haven't seen it up there," I answered. "Unless he's got it somewhere else. He's not bringing it home. Maybe he's switching cars in between, you know? I've done that before."

"You know him?" he asked.

"I know him to see him. Christ yeah!" I said sharply. "Couldn't miss him. I saw him come home one night in the Cadillac and I didn't have anything with me at that time. I wasn't even expecting to. But I got a good idea, you know, of his hours, when he comes home. I have a very good idea and it's beautiful. Nobody'd fuckin' hear it out there."

"There's no people?" Cosimo asked.

The Last Contract

"There's no neighbors beside him," I said. "There's a house beside him, but it's up for sale and there's nobody in it. He won't be much of a problem. Just catching him at the right time is all I have to do."

"But you know him?" Cosimo said, making sure that there would be no mistakes.

"I know him," I said, showing my annoyance at his continued questioning on the point. "Tall, but sorta bald. Hair on the sides. He's had three-piece suits on sometimes. I saw him down at the Four Seasons with Scarcella. I've seen him around before. I saw him talking to Yanover one day, but I was off in the car, you know? He doesn't know me to see me."

"I wanna make sure, Cec," Cosimo said. "It's very important. You know what I mean, Cec. I wanna make no..."

"There won't be no mistakes in this, okay?" I said, finishing his sentence.

"All right," he answered.

"Definitely okay," I emphasized. "All right now, how much? You're not talking about some idiot on the fuckin' street or some dope hustler, you know?"

"Cec, I know," he said.

"This guy gets knocked off. How about twenty thousand?" I asked.

"I couldn't give you that. I couldn't give it all at once, not that much money," he answered.

"All right, twenty thousand over periods of time," I said.

"All right," he agreed.

"All right," I said. "Soon after, the next day after it's done, I'm going to come and see you."

Cosimo shook his head. "Four days after."

"Four days?" I said. "Okay. Make sure you have at least five thousand on you or somebody."

He nodded his approval. "Okay, Cec."

"Either you or your brothers or somebody—make sure you have five thousand," I emphasized.

"All right, all right," he said impatiently. "And then I'll pay you after two months."

"All right, no problem," I said. "I'm waiting now, you know. Like I've been patient about this other five thousand bucks for the thing in the States."

"I know, Cec," he said. "It's just the wrong time. We mortgaged ourself over our heads—four, five properties. Buy here, buy there—see what I mean? If we don't pay the mortgage, we lose the property."

"What? You got your house mortgaged too now?" I asked.

"No, no, no," he said. "I have property in Richmond Hill. It's four thousand dollars a month—property in Mississauga, it's a few thousand dollars a month, property in Burlington, it's four thousand a month, property in King City—it's all property."

"You own that much land?" I said, surprised by the amounts he said he was paying out.

"Yeah," he said. "I'm broke. I have no cash, okay, but we have lotsa property—we have maybe ten million dollars' worth of property."

I let out a low whistle. "Ten million?"

"Maybe. You see what I mean?" he asked.

I smiled. I had a solution to his cash flow. "Well, give me a lot," I said. "Give me some—give me a piece of property."

Cosimo shook his head. Most of the land was in large lots and couldn't be split up. One section alone was worth two million dollars. There was also a ten-acre section of land in King City, and I registered my interest in that.

"You know how much I paid for that, Cec?" he said with a smile.

"How much?" I said.

"Half a million dollars I paid for it," he said.

I was really surprised. Cosimo and his mob were heavy into real estate investments. They owned a large land section north of the luxury estates where a lot of rich people lived, King Cross. He said he planned to subdivide it in a year and then maybe, he added, he'd have some land for me. But I'd have to be patient.

He said that the land he wanted to subdivide cost more than $100,000 just to service. "That's what happened," he said. "We mortgaged ourselves right up to here [pointing to his throat]. We're talkin' maybe twenty-two thousand a month in mortgages. It's a lotta fuckin' money."

Before we split up, I had one additional question for him. Normally there are rules about how you hit a Mafia man. Wives and children are almost always left out—not harmed. That sometimes complicates the planning of a murder. It's got to be timed so that only the target is hit. I knew that Cosimo and his brothers wouldn't care. They didn't live by the rules and they didn't kill by the rules, but I wanted others to know it. I wanted their ruthlessness on the tape so that others would understand how they operated.

"What if his wife's with him?" I asked. "I'm getting impatient, you know?"

"I leave it to you," Cosimo said.

"I'll do the wife," I said coldly.

"It's not likely that they go out together," he replied.

The next twenty-four hours turned out to be critical. One of the big holes in the investigation was Remo Commisso. The SEU and Crown attorney Howard Morton were convinced that the evidence against Cosimo and Michele was sufficient for murder conspiracy charges, but the evidence against Remo was thin. He had said very little to me on tape. They had to get him out into the open. But how?

It was Lyle McCharles who came up with the idea. Why not stage a phony Volpe hit? Why not get Volpe to lend me his wallet and have me bring it to Remo while Cosimo was doing weekend jail time for the smuggling of aliens?

McCharles and Murphy floated the idea at a meeting of the SEU staff and Morton on April 30. Everybody laughed except Inspector Wilf Steferak, who had temporarily been assigned as officer in charge of the SEU. Murphy said he knew Volpe well enough to ask. Steferak said it was worth a try. The whole ball game was to go down on May 16. That morning Murphy called Volpe, who remembered him from past investigations. He told Volpe it was urgent that they meet.

Murphy and Sergeant Al Cooke of Metro Intelligence went to see Volpe at his home. They told him that there was a contract on his life and that there was one person involved who they lacked sufficient evidence to arrest. Would he help? Volpe said he would, provided he had Murphy's word that there would be no double cross. He got that, and Murphy got Volpe's wallet, complete with his driver's license, credit cards, and other identification.

Murphy and Cooke also got Volpe to agree to return to Toronto with his wife and to stay inside the RCMP headquarters on Jarvis Street for the entire day without talking to anyone. Murphy later told me he was surprised when Volpe agreed. Volpe had a condition, however. No one was to tell his wife, Lisa, why they were at headquarters. He would invent a story to explain it. Murphy and Cooke agreed, and they drove Volpe and his wife back to the RCMP.

Just after 11:00 A.M., I met Murphy at Bathurst and Steeles Plaza and he told me what had happened with Volpe. He handed me Volpe's wallet. By 11:15, I was at Remo's home. A woman answered the door. In the background I could hear a radio and a child's voice. I asked the woman if I could see Remo, identifying myself only as "George." Remo came out, and Michele was with him.

"I gotta talk to you," I told Remo. "Can I talk to you outside? I got something in the car I want to show you."

"You have something in the car?" he asked. "You want to take me to your car?"

"Yeah. Not in the house," I said. "There's something I got to show you."

Remo was suspicious. There was no way he was going to go to my car and talk. "Bring it to the house," he said. "We go downstairs some place to talk. I don't trust a car."

"I'll get it all right," I answered. "I know you don't trust cars. I don't trust houses."

"No, we go in the washroom," he said.

As I left his house to get the wallet I talked into the recorder to let those conducting the surveillance know what was going on. I knew my body pack and the belt buckle transmitter would get whatever he had to say on tape.

When I reentered the house I saw Michele with the kids and asked him if he was baby-sitting. He shook his head. Weekends, he said, he stayed at the house to play with the kids. "Atsa nice mafioso," I thought to myself.

Remo was standing nearby and motioned for me to follow. We went downstairs, through his recreation room to a washroom. He put his finger to his mouth. Then he turned the cold water tap on just in case there were bugs in the house. He signaled that we could talk.

"Volpe, he's dead," I said.

Remo looked surprised, almost at a loss for words. "How come?"

"I just killed him, an hour ago," I said matter-of-factly.

"What happened?" Remo asked.

"Well, Cosimo told me you and him wanted it," I said. "Want to go outside? Wanna talk in here?"

"George, you should never come here," he said. Remo was very upset, apparently fearful that police might be watching and that I'd lead them to his house.

"Well, look it," I said. "He's dead, so's his wife, too, okay?"

His face was clouded, and he was getting more and more upset. "You should never come here."

"Well, listen," I continued, "I need some money. I'm broke. I told Cosimo yesterday when I saw him. I said, I'm broke. I need some money and I wanna get the fuck out of the country now. Okay? I want some money today."

"Tell me when I'm gonna get it to you, George," Remo said.

"Well, a thousand or something just to get me out of

here," I said. I pulled out Volpe's wallet. "I took this right out of his back pocket."

"You should have thrown it away," he said excitedly as he looked it over and checked the identification.

"Well, listen, you people have doubted me in the past," I reminded him.

"All right," he said, "don't worry. We'll take care of you. You know we respect you like a brother. Don't worry about it."

"Yeah, but look at before," I said. "You've told me. Cosimo still owes me five thousand."

"You know you'll get the money from him," he answered.

"All right, but now there's two people dead," I said.

"I don't even want to talk about these things," he said shaking his head.

"All right. I got this thing on him partly just to prove to you," I said.

"That's all right," he answered, returning it to me. "Throw it away. Don't leave it."

"No, I'll get rid of it," I promised him. "I'll drop it down the sewer, far away from here."

"Where you wanna meet?" he asked. "Maybe tomorrow up here, or Monday?"

"I need some money now, I wanna leave today," I said urgently. "I'll meet you down at the hall."

"Where'm I gonna get the fuckin' money today?" he asked.

"A thousand bucks," I said.

"All right, but it's not good to come by the hall," he said.

"Then where?" I asked. "Get Michele to meet me down at Howard Johnson's again, okay? At five o'clock. A thousand dollars."

"Okay," he said.

"I'll be taking off for a week or two," I said. "I want the rest of the money. I told Cosimo yesterday twenty thousand bucks, eh? I want at least five thousand."

"I know nothing about this," he said. "I didn't know that he told you to do it."

"But he told me a long time ago, you and him wanted this done," I said.

"Me?" he exclaimed. "I never said that. Oh come on, George."

"That's what he told me," I replied.

"Did you ever talk to me about this thing?" he asked.

"No, but he, hey," I said, "you didn't know this?"

"No," he said, shaking his head. "What's the difference? So what? All right. Michele will meet you at five."

"All right," I said, "I got to be back in two weeks. What about this other guy, this Scarcella?"

"Forget about him," Remo said. "We don't want to do nothing no more. No problem."

So I went, taking the wallet with me, back to the car and then to the location where all the cops were recording the conversations. A security detail that had been assigned two weeks earlier to protect me was waiting to escort me out of the area.

I handed the wallet to Corporal Danielle Bouchard, who was supervising the case. One of the supervising sergeants piped up, "That cinches it. You're finished."

"Are you sure?" I asked. "Don't you want me to meet Michele at Howard Johnson's and get the money off of him?"

"No, no," he said smiling, "we don't need it. We're finished. We've got them all."

I shrugged and walked off with my security guards. I remember saying to them, "You know what? I think they're going to want me to meet him."

We went to a bar, had a couple of drinks and about three or four beers, and then went back up to the room. Murphy was on the phone, and he was upset.

"Cec, you don't have to do this," he said.

"I know what you're going to fuckin' ask," I said. "You want me to go back there with Michele."

He laughed nervously. "You're right, Cec. You gotta go back and pick up that payment."

They had followed Michele after I left Remo's house and seen him go to the home of Domenic Racco, the son of the old Calabrian Mafia boss and the man everyone was saying was going to succeed his father. At the house Michele got the money to pay me with.

The RCMP intelligence had information that Michele, and two other men who Volpe was in partnership with in some real estate, had gone to Buffalo to get a green light for the Volpe murder a couple of weeks earlier. The information came from Volpe. He said his two partners had been stopped at the border, but that Michele had slipped through and seen some people in the Buffalo Magaddino mob.

Volpe might have been right, but two weeks earlier a good friend of mine in the mob had told me that Racco had gone to Montreal to meet with Vincent Cotroni. My friend said it was Cotroni who gave the order to kill Volpe, and Racco had given the contract to the Commissos. Racco wanted the Commissos to have someone else do the job, but Cosimo had hired me, so they went to him for the money to pay me until they could figure out how to get rid of me later.

When Murphy arrived at the Holiday Inn where I was staying with my security detail, I got into the bugged car with him. We drove like we were at the Indianapolis 500 to get to the meeting on time. We must have been doing 90 MPH or more.

When we got there I had to piss, in the worst way, but I didn't have time. They had body-packed me. I had to pull in my stomach for the body pack, and I damn near pissed in my pants.

With all the problems, I got to Howard Johnson's and parked in front of the Faces Discotheque about five minutes before Michele arrived in his Oldsmobile. Murphy and his surveillance van were perfectly situated to get pictures and record. There was another special team of sharpshooters nearby ready to gun down anyone who tried to hit me.

I waited maybe ten minutes and Michele pulled up. There were four in the car, including three cousins of his. Michele got out of his car and walked to mine and handed me what he thought was $1,000. He didn't count right. It was $1,100.

"Who's with you?" I asked.

"My kid cousins—Claudio, Remo, and Johnny," he said. "We got to go to a wedding in Niagara Falls."

"Yeah, well, I'm going to Miami in about another hour," I said.

"Take care of yourself," Michele said.

I nodded. "How much is there?" I asked.

"One," he said.

"A thousand? Good," I answered.

"Take care of yourself," Michele said.

"I will for sure," I answered as I watched him leave.

When Murphy and the special marksman team spotted Michele's car with four inside, everyone got their rifles ready. If someone had gotten out of the car with Michele, the marksmen were all prepared to waste them on the spot.

I remember saying to Murphy, "But they were just kids on the way to a wedding."

"You're right, Cec, but at that moment we didn't know that, and we damned sure weren't going to take chances with your life," he said.

In the hours ahead Michele would be stopped for speeding and arrested on the murder conspiracy. Remo was arrested at the home of his girlfriend. Cosimo was charged in jail. It was a clean sweep.

20

Bye, Bye, Paulie

Two weeks before the arrest of the Commissos, I was placed under the protection of the RCMP. I had bodyguards with me day and night. I was getting a $250-a-week allowance for my hotel room and my meals. It was like living in a prison only worse. In prison, what you can't see, you don't miss and you forget about. The way I had to live, I could see all the goodies of life but I couldn't touch. There was very little wine, women, and song—the high road that the news media and lawyers said I was strolling down—to enjoy. There were four walls, the faces of my protectors, some card games, and an occasional drive in a Chrysler leased for me by the government. Those drives were never alone. There were always a couple of bodyguards along.

The leased car arrangement, which strangely drew a lot of criticism from the media later on, was a necessity. I needed wheels, I needed to feel a breath of fresh air on my face, to get out of my room if I was to retain my sanity. Unless you've lived in an undercover situation, you can't know what it's like.

A car, like a motorcycle, was like an extension of myself. I had never been without one or the other. It was part of my way of life, the way I moved from place to place, saw people, did things, and, yes, committed crimes.

Bye, Bye, Paulie

When the investigation of the Commissos began, the Mounties and the SEU had to use my car. If I'd suddenly changed to a new car, Cosimo and Remo would have immediately become suspicious. So they bugged my car, they photographed it, wherever I went to meetings that car was with me. Only it wasn't really my car. It was my dad's.

Once the Commissos were arrested, the car had to be stripped of its equipment and returned to my dad. I couldn't use it again. It would be the first thing the Commissos and their associates would look for—Cecil Kirby and his Chevrolet. The alternative was the leased car, and that was only for a short time. Eventually, it became impractical for protective purposes. I was too hot a property to be allowed out in the open, even with bodyguards at my side. Not only was I in danger, but they were also in danger should some crazy Calabrian decide to take me out.

Picture the circumstances. What I'd done was about to wreck the crime careers of some of Canada's most powerful criminal leaders for at least a decade. They were naturally furious—mad enough to kill, mad enough to make it worth anywhere from $100,000 to $250,000 for someone to kill me. Of course, if anyone had succeeded, the chances of their living to collect that contract money were about one in a billion. Dead men can't tell tales, they can't be arrested and later forced to testify in courts.

With all that money on my head, the mission of the SEU and the Crown was to keep me alive, at any cost, and round-the-clock protection was a must. It wasn't always successful, but it was a must. When it wasn't successful, it was my fault, not that of those assigned to protect me.

For a street criminal, life in confinement is impossible. I was a socializer. I loved to hit bars and clubs where my rounder friends were. Now I couldn't, or I wasn't supposed to.

It would be safe to say that I wasn't exactly a model protected witness. It would also be safe to say that the art of handling protected witnesses in Canada hadn't been perfected. It still hasn't. The model they were using was the witness protection program of the U.S. Marshals, and that is one of the most criticized programs in the States. That criticism comes not so much from the press but from witnesses and other law enforcement agencies.

To protect me, the SEU assigned three-man details— one officer each from the RCMP, the Ontario Provincial Police, and Metro Toronto Police—to each shift. I didn't go to the bathroom without their checking out the room first. If we weren't in a hotel room—and many of our meals were eaten there—I was on the road with SEU investigators, showing them where I'd planted bombs, where I had dynamite and blasting caps buried, the location of biker hangouts and other crime centers.

In early June stories were breaking in the United States and Canada about the plot to murder Helen Nafpliotis and the Volpe murder plot. The stories centered around attempts by the Canadian government to extradite Vincent Melia and Gerardo Russo to stand trial for conspiracy to commit murder.

One of the FBI agents, John Schiman, testified in federal court in Bridgeport, Connecticut, that the FBI had staged Nafpliotis's abduction to make it appear that she'd been kidnapped and murdered. He said he'd worked with me as I gathered evidence on the case and collected money for the planned murder.

"He was suave," Schiman testified. "He knew what he was doing. He was the best source I have ever seen. He knew how to handle underworld figures." As I read the story I remember thinking, "Yeah, but how do you handle living like this?"

It was so confining that a month after I was placed under protection I slipped out of my hotel room one night and went to the Beverly Hills Hotel for a couple of beers with an old friend. I was gone most of that night. I stayed at the home of a friend who worked for a catering company. Murphy, everyone, came down on me like a ton of bricks for my stupidity.

June 12 was another day of jangling nerves, a day I

wanted to kick and yell about being surrounded constantly by dozens of noticeably nervous plainclothesmen. It was the day I had to appear in county court with Linda Cadwell, my ex-girlfriend, and Alan Stewart to plead guilty to charges of breaking into a home in metropolitan Toronto in 1979.

The court looked like an armed camp. Everyone was checked. The security people had me so tightly guarded it would have taken a team of commandos to reach me.

The charges against me stemmed from a planned theft from a gun collector Stewart had told me about. Stewart said he had a key to the place, that the collector was going to be gone and it would be a simple matter for us to get into the house and steal the guns. He estimated there were forty to sixty handguns there, guns I could sell to the Commissos and others. The collection was gone when we broke in. It turned out Stewart didn't have the key, and all we found were five antique guns that couldn't fire bullets.

Sergeant Lyle McCharles of the OPP testified that my life was in danger. "I've received reliable information," he testified, "that a one-hundred-thousand-dollar contract has been placed on Kirby's life." Crown Attorney Howard Morton told Justice Lloyd Graburn that my work as a police operative had resulted "in laying fourteen very serious criminal charges. My submission of sentence is he ought not to receive a jail term. It's not a submission the Crown takes lightly." As I listened, I found myself wondering what Morton would be saying if Murphy hadn't made them come up with the agreement that we all had signed.

Graburn passed sentence on June 14. Noting my previous convictions for assault, drugs, and theft, he placed me on probation for two years with the "special condition" that I testify in court when subpoenaed by the Crown. Linda and Stewart got suspended sentences of twelve and eighteen months. At the same time the Commissos were being held in Ontario Supreme Court without bail on conspiracy to murder charges involving Volpe, Scarcella, and Nafpliotis.

My having walked away from my security detail earlier and arguments I'd had with some of the investigators upset and embarrassed some people in the detail, who decided to put me in a squeeze play without telling the Crown prosecutors or Murphy. One of them, who is now a friend of mine, told other investigators that "we have to get a hammer to Kirby's head to make him testify."

The hammer they tried to use was Linda, who had been my girlfriend since 1978 and who was being provided protection and secret living quarters. Her whereabouts was a secret to those who wanted to use Linda to get at me.

I asked Murphy, as I often did, to call Linda so that I could talk to her to make sure she was all right. He placed the call and then put me on the phone. When she told me about the visit by the two investigators, I went wild.

I turned on Murphy like a cornered tiger and began shouting. "So that's the way you fuckers keep your word," I shouted. "You're trying to put me in jail, you bastards!"

"What the hell are you talking about?" he roared.

"I'm talking about two of this fuckin' outfit's flunkies going to Linda and trying to get her to testify against me, that's what," I shouted. "After all I've done, after all the risks I've taken, some people are still looking to shaft me. Hey, go to hell. Take this whole fuckin' thing and shove it. I'm getting out. I'll take my chances on the street alone."

I thought Murphy was going to go into orbit then and there. For two hours or more he tried to cool me down. I wanted to go out and get the two guys who Linda said had talked to her. Luckily, Murphy talked me out of that, but I told the detail that I was going to see Linda whether they came with me or not. They came and stayed in another room while Linda and I had a helluva argument. I finally belted her in the mouth.

Later the newspapers made it appear that I was in a jealous rage. One reporter tried to have the security guards and the attorney general publicly roasted for not arresting me for violation of probation for hitting Linda.

Linda never pressed charges. I admit I hit her. I lost

my temper, knocked out one of her teeth, and cracked another. My troubles with Linda were to continue later.

My nerves were razor thin, and I was walking on the edge. There were nights when I went to bed hoping I wouldn't wake up. There were other nights when I seriously thought about killing myself or getting myself killed by going after some of those I knew wanted to do me.

Depression is a constant companion when you're an informer and a witness. You don't think too highly of yourself. You've cut yourself off from the people you know to enter a different world with people who don't respect you, don't like you, even hate your guts. I had nothing in common with any of those on my security detail or in the prosecutor's office. I was a means to an end for them, and they were my ticket to survival.

After the Cadwell incident, the strings that were binding me were loosened somewhat, and I managed to get along better with many of the men on the security details, who were really decent guys doing a tough job.

Murphy, meanwhile, never let up on providing me with the best security possible—not just through physical protection, but through street intelligence. One of his sources was Paul Volpe.

On July 29, Murphy met with Volpe secretly, and the old man provided him with information on those behind the contract to kill him. It was his belief, and he had ways of getting information, that some former partners of his in real estate both here and in Atlantic City were behind the hit order. The motive was greed, pure and simple—more than two million dollars collected in a sale and millions more that Volpe was laundering through land transactions. The former partners wanted it all, or so Volpe thought.

Volpe was also convinced that with a little pressure from the coppers, one of the former partners would roll over and begin talking. If he talked, he could bring down a lot of high-level people in organized crime. To this day, no one that I know of ever went to talk to that guy, and nothing was ever done to develop Volpe as an informer. In fact, Volpe was never given official RCMP informer status, although he was given the "O" number designation.

Volpe also predicted there would be no trial on the murder conspiracies. "The Commissos and their friends are going to plead guilty," he told Murphy. "They don't want this to go to trial."

Murphy said that Volpe was grateful to me for helping save his life. He wanted to show his good faith. He told Murphy he had heard that there were a lot of bikers in Canada, particularly Toronto, who were hot to kill me. He promised Murphy to do what he could to cool off the bikers through his underworld contacts. Murphy said he kept his promise, and many of the bikers that were actively hunting me turned their attention to other things.

Like clockwork, the three Commisso brothers and Romeo plea-bargained with Crown attorneys. Rather than face trials for conspiracy to murder, the four pleaded guilty in return for a guarantee of less than maximum jail terms. The Crown went for the deal because it would eliminate costly trials that they could not be certain would be decided in their favor.

Remo and Cosimo got eight years each, but they were going to face considerably more time in jail on charges relating to other crimes they'd hired me for. The charges in those cases would be based both on their admissions in the covert tapes I recorded and on recordings I made with others who admitted they had paid the Commissos to hire me to bomb and torch buildings for them.

Romeo and Michele Commisso got just two and a half years because they were more message carriers than actual plotters.

A couple of months passed before Volpe touched my life again. This time I was technically no longer under Murphy's protective wing but under that of the SEU and Corporal Ted Bean of the OPP. Nevertheless, the message from Volpe went to Murphy, and it probably saved my life and those of my security detail, including Corporal Bean.

On October 6 Volpe, believing Murphy was still

protecting me, called to tell him that the detail protecting me had been spotted by some members of Satan's Choice.

"They spotted your friend Kirby and his three security guards in Aurora," Volpe told Murphy. "They're going to kill him and the guards."

Murphy was between a rock and a hard place when he got that call. He couldn't tell anyone that his tipster was Volpe, but the people on the security detail would want to know where the information came from to judge how valid it was. Murphy told me in confidence that the bikers had found out where I was staying and that they were going to kill all of us.

"We've got to figure a way to move you and the detail," he said. "And we have to do it without telling anybody that we know who tipped us."

I had no patience for the politics of the moment, and I didn't have to worry about the chain of command the way Murphy did. I called one of the detail supervising sergeants and told him. "The wrong people know I'm here," I said.

He didn't believe me, and he refused to order the detail to move me. "It's just another street rumor," he said. "More bullshit. You stay put."

That ticked me off. I didn't waste any time. I did the only thing I could at that moment to save our necks. I walked to the security detail's room, picked up the telephone, and called my dad.

"Dad," I said loud enough for everyone to hear me, "I just want you to know where I'm at before something happens. I'm here in Aurora, at the hotel."

The security agents stood there dumbfounded. "Jesus Christ," one of them yelled, "you've just blown our security."

"Good," I said. "I'll just take a taxi and get the hell outta here." And that was exactly what I did. It was the only way for me to get out of the area and to get the detail moved before something happened. I had to figure a way out without blowing Volpe as the source. So I took off. I returned to the security detail about a week later. They were having fits, and Inspector McIlvenna wanted to have me thrown in jail as a material witness until he was told that he didn't have that right unless I failed to answer a subpoena or to appear in court.

Murphy told his bosses about the Volpe warning and that Volpe had also offered to turn over, no strings attached, information and evidence on a Korean international terrorist organization in Toronto. They didn't want to hear about it. They told Murphy he could not accept any information from Volpe and ordered him to cut off all further communication with him.

Talk about shortsighted people. They had a golden opportunity right then to develop Volpe as the most important informer in Canadian organized crime investigations. Volpe knew his days were numbered, and he was reaching out, like I had, to make a deal. He could have buried a lot of people.

Instead, nothing was done and Volpe was later killed before he could tell what he knew. I guess Murphy's bosses were afraid Volpe would use the RCMP and they'd get criticized for dealing with someone like that, but the law in the States has dealt with bigger guys than that to get testimony in major Mafia cases.

"They blew a helluva opportunity," Murphy later said. "With a little work Volpe could have been the most important informer in mob history." The government's attitude, particularly that of the RCMP, was that Volpe was trying to use the RCMP to escape some charges he was facing. The truth is Volpe probably was looking for a way out. He knew his days were numbered, just like I did. By turning him down, the knuckleheads who make these decisions blew the biggest source of information on organized crime in Canada. He could have provided them with a warehouse full of information on the States, on international mob plots and on casinos from Haiti and Cuba to Atlantic City and Las Vegas. It's amazing to me how shortsighted and jealous people get in law enforcement. That's why the mobs are always ahead.

Maybe a week after Volpe saved my life with his tip, I decided to see him. I told Murphy what I wanted to do.

"Have you lost your mind?" he asked.

"I don't think so," I said. "I want to see him. I want to thank him for what he did."

"You could be killed," he said. "You could get your head blown off."

"I'll take that chance," I said.

Without another word, I left the place where I was in hiding from the bikers, the mob, and my own security detail, and drove off in my car to Foxhill, the Nobleton home of Paul Volpe.

It was impressive. Behind the giant iron gates at the entrance was an almost palatial home, like that of some English lord. A castlelike turret with a circular, domed room was the centerpiece of the giant two-story home. The house had once belonged to a retired judge from Toronto. I forget what Volpe paid for it, but it was worth hundreds of thousands of dollars then and maybe a million or more now. In the back was a big pool and two tennis courts. A little further back were overhead floodlights and some guard dogs led by a particularly annoying pet of Volpe's, a mongrel—part shepherd, part who-knows-what, named Caesar, who bit my leg three times while Volpe chuckled, barely scolding the dog.

When I arrived, Volpe's wife answered the door. I showed her my identification and asked to see Volpe. He wasn't home, she said, but he would be back by 5:00 P.M. I promised to come again.

I returned as promised. Volpe was there waiting. We met, for the first time, at the door. I showed him my driver's license and assured him that I was by myself and unarmed.

"Come on in," he said with a friendly smile. He was a tall man, maybe a little over six foot, bald, with sad eyes. He wasn't muscular or as strong as I was, but he wasn't in bad shape either. He could probably have handled himself pretty well if he'd had to, even at his age, which was about fifty-four then. He pointed ahead of me and said, "Come on downstairs where we can talk."

As I followed his directions, we walked through his

living room into a kitchen with a long counter and a table off to the side. Off the kitchen was a staircase leading to the recreation room.

As I walked down the stairs, Volpe's damned mongrel bit me on the back of the leg, almost sending me sprawling into the rec room. I wanted to kick that bloody mutt in the teeth, but I held my mouth and my foot as Volpe called the dog off and mildly scolded him.

I was taken aback by the view of the rear yard through the huge glass windows and doors. Over to the side of the rec room was a small bar with a cappuccino machine on it.

"Can I get you a cappuccino?" Volpe asked. I shook my head. "How about some food? A steak maybe?" he said with a smile, pointing to his nephew, Anthony, who I'd seen up in the kitchen cooking.

"No thank you," I said, "I'm not hungry."

Without another word I opened my briefcase so he could see it was clean, with no tapes or bugs.

"Look, Paul, I got no tape," I said. "I just came here to thank you for helping me the other day." I opened my jacket so he could see there was nothing hidden there either.

He nodded with a broad smile on his face. "Okay, Cecil," he said, "I believe you."

He was warm and friendly. He smoked heavily, drawing long pulls into his lungs and watching the thin blue smoke curl out into the air in front of him as he exhaled. I felt like choking every time he took a puff like that.

He was attentive to what I had to say. I had a feeling of real sincerity when he talked, and his eyes were soft, sometimes a little animated, but never cold as we sat there. He had a rather gravelly voice. There wasn't the slightest hint of an Italian accent when he spoke, and I guess there shouldn't have been since he was born in Canada.

"Do the cops know you're here?" he asked.

I shook my head. "Nope, just Murphy," I answered. "He's the only one who knew I was coming to see you."

"Okay," he said. "I want your word that you're not going to give me up. I don't need that kind of trouble."

"You've got my word," I said. "Nobody's gonna know we met or talked." And nobody did until after he was killed. Everybody had something bad to say about the poor bastard after he was killed. I can only say good things about the man I met that day. He was a man and he talked straight—no bullshit.

"I want to thank you for saving my life," I said. "You saved the lives of some cops as well, but they don't know it. Probably never will."

We started talking about the case a bit and about the characters involved.

"I can't understand why they [the Commissos] would want to kill me," he said. "You know what jail they are in?"

"Kingston," I said.

He grinned, those sad eyes sort of twinkly as he spoke. "Got a lot of friends in there." He continued smiling, and said nothing else about the Commissos— nothing like I'm gonna get them or they're going to have an accident.

"You know, when I found out you were here I had you checked out with Chuck [Yanover]," he said. "He really has high regard for you. He says you're a very capable person."

"The truth is I don't like Yanover," I said looking him squarely in the eyes. "I don't trust him, and if I were you I wouldn't trust him. He set up one of his friends with my ex-girlfriend."

Volpe waved his hands, brushing aside the discussion. "It's foolish to have hard feelings over women," he said. "They aren't that important."

Volpe turned the subject toward my future. "Why don't you walk away from it [testifying and being a police operative]?" he said. "If you want I can get you a job down in my casino in the islands. You can stay there for a couple of years—work there for me and come back and I guarantee nobody I deal with is gonna fuckin' bother you. Of course, I can't guarantee the bikers. I have no influence with them."

Volpe didn't say what casino he was talking about or exactly where it was and I didn't ask. It was supposed to be in the Bahamas, but he didn't identify it. I knew he and his brother had operated a casino in Haiti at one time and some in other parts of the Caribbean and the Mediterranean as well. I just thanked him and said I'd think about it.

I did ask him if there was some way he could lend me a couple of thousand dollars. "I'll pay it back as soon as I can," I said. "You can go to the bank with that."

"I'll have to talk to my lawyer about it, Cec," he said. "Come back in about a week or so, about eight in the morning."

I gave him a number where he could leave a message for me without worrying about the cops. Then I thanked him and promised to see him the following week.

When I returned, we once again went to his rec room and for a second time that lousy dog of his nipped my ankle. I felt like kicking the fucker through the glass window, but I restrained myself as Volpe whacked him lightly on the fanny and sent him off to another side of the room, where he lay staring at me. I could see in that dog's eyes I was dead meat if I ever made a move toward Volpe, not that I had any intentions of doing anything like that. For some reason that damned dog hated me from the start and I hated the dog.

"I haven't been able to talk to my lawyer about that loan yet," he said, "but I will. I'll have an answer for you next week for sure. Incidentally, I told Peter Scarcella about your being at the house. I'm expecting him here later today."

Now I didn't feel too great hearing that. Scarcella, I was convinced, had sold out to the Commissos to save his own skin. They had said as much in taped conversations with me. I thought to myself, that's not the kind of guy you should trust, Volpe, not at all. I sure as hell didn't trust him, and I didn't want to be around Volpe's house if Scarcella knew I was there.

Just then the telephone rang. It was Scarcella. When Volpe was through talking to him, he turned to me and said, "I told Peter that I had an old friend of his here visiting with me. I told him I wanted him to meet you. It's a shame. Peter said he couldn't come. He has a touch of the flu." There was a strange smirk on his face when he said that.

I wanted to say something but I bit my tongue. Instead I said good-bye and promised to see him again the following week.

Our third meeting took place outside his garage. That fuckin' Caesar was by his side again as I got out of the car, and again he went for my leg. Volpe called him off. "Caesar, I'm afraid, doesn't like you," Volpe said with a chuckle.

I didn't think it was too funny but I didn't say anything about it. "Talk to your lawyer yet?" I asked.

Volpe nodded. "I'm afraid he's advised me not to give you any money while you're working for the police," he said. "It could cause a lot of problems. I'm sorry, Cec, but I don't want the cops on my back and they would be if they knew I was lending you money."

"I understand," I said. "Don't worry about it. Nobody's gonna know we talked. I appreciate what you've done and what you tried to do."

It was months later, March 1982, that I heard that there was a contract to kill Volpe. Murphy had been tipped, and he had asked his bosses for permission to warn Volpe and see if he could convince him to roll over and become an informer. The RCMP turned thumbs down on his request. He was told that he was not to speak to Volpe or have any further contact with him.

On November 14, 1983, I flew into Toronto International to meet with some security people about a case that was pending. The airport was swarming with cops. At 2:40 P.M. that day they had found Volpe's body stuffed in the trunk of his wife's BMW at the Terminal 2 parking garage. He'd been shot in the back of the head.

Who did Volpe in? I can't be positive, but I had good information that Vincent Cotroni had ordered the hit after he'd sent his brother Frank to Toronto to meet with a lot of Volpe's friends and enemies.

Frank Cotroni was facing heroin-smuggling charges in Connecticut, interestingly enough, in September, just two short months before Volpe bought it. I was told he met with Johnny (Pops) Papalia and an old Sicilian Mafia boss who was wanted by the Italian government on narcotics charges. A good source told me that a Montreal assassin and friend of Cotroni's was at that meeting. He was supposed to be in Toronto around the time Volpe's body was found. He was arrested on homicide charges in another case and, I was told, was questioned about the Volpe hit. He refused to talk to the cops about it because the Cotronis had been so close to him, like family.

They decided Volpe had to go. It was embarrassing to the Mafia. Here he'd been set up for a hit in 1981, and two years later he was still walking around, telling people what to do, running gambling in Toronto, making millions in real estate in New Jersey and Ontario, collecting from casinos around the world, and running big loan-shark rackets. It's probably true that he was living in fear behind the floodlights at his home, certain that someone would carry out the contract that had started when the Commissos tried to have me do the job. But he was still in business, still a boss.

On December 10, less than a month after Volpe was knocked off, four guys gunned down Domenic Racco, the son of the old Calabrian don. Now that couldn't have been done without approval from some Mafia bosses, but none of the four who were arrested and convicted in the case ever said who was behind it, and the Commissos were behind bars. Being in jail, of course, never stopped a boss from running his business, and the Commissos were no exception.

One of the last people to see Volpe was his good

friend Scarcella, who told the coppers that he'd had coffee with Volpe the morning of November 13, the last day Volpe was seen alive. Volpe had told his wife that he was going to meet someone at the airport. That's where they found him. For anyone to get a crime leader like Volpe required some planning and the help of someone he trusted. I've always thought I knew who that trusted Volpe friend was. What I am certain of is that with the killing of Volpe and Racco, the Commisso crime group became the most powerful of all the Calabrian groups in the United States and Canada.

21

Run, Stoolie, Run

When I broke away from my security detail in October I was frustrated, bored, and upset. I'd be a liar if I said I wasn't worried when I learned that the bikers knew where I was staying with the security men. I was concerned about my life and the lives of the men protecting me. I knew bikers. I knew them better than any security supervisor at the SEU. I knew them better than the RCMP. When Volpe told Murphy that the bikers were coming to the hotel in Aurora to kill all of us, I knew that that was just what Satan's Choice would do. They'd have no hesitation about blowing me away and anyone who was with me.

Since I couldn't tell the detail who tipped me, blowing the location was the only choice I felt I had left. I wanted no one killed, least of all myself.

I want to make it clear that the men who provided me with protection during the years that I was a witness were really super guys. They were all different—guys that came and went—and I barely got to know them the way I would have liked to. Not all of them were lovable or even likable, and a few of them didn't like the idea of protecting a criminal like myself, but 99 percent of them were super guys with a lot of guts. You have to have guts to be on a detail like that.

Run, Stoolie, Run

I think most of them tried their damnedest to make life a little easier for me. They lived in a room next to me and tension was always present, as was the danger. Every move had to be thought out. Wherever we went, whether it was to a court proceeding or to an interview, the men of the security detail preceded me and stood in front of me. If assassins had been waiting and started shooting, many of my protectors, most of them family men, would have fallen first attempting to save my life.

There were some light moments. When I wanted to go jogging, one or more of them would jog with me while others followed in special unmarked vehicles. The joggers had a hard time keeping up with me, and I'd often kid them about what lousy shape they were in when they ended the jog, huffing and puffing like old men.

We played cards together and pool, anything to provide a relief from the boredom of waiting, always waiting. One of the team members, a young guy named Byron, was a pool shark. He beat the hell out of anyone he played—me, the detail, anyone who challenged him. He literally made the pool cue talk.

At times we left the city to go to a place for a quiet drink. One location I remember vividly and enjoyed the most was a small island about 300 miles north of Toronto. We spent two weeks there just to relieve the tension and relax. It was a fantastic place to fish, to exercise, and to just plain talk.

As a team, the details were always heavily armed, alert, and damned well trained in the use of all types of firearms. They checked out each place we went thoroughly before they would let me go near it. They would also spend hours talking with me, picking my brain about people who might be looking for me, who might want to kill me. What did they look like? What kind of weapons would they use? Who were their friends? Where were their hangouts? The questions seemed endless, yet they were all designed to protect me and the detail from a surprise assault by assassins.

They had photographs of Ken Goobie, Armand

Sanguigni, a dozen or more bikers, Calabrian mafiosi, rounders, every type of criminal who was a serious threat to my life.

I was convinced during that period, between 1981 and 1983, that my most serious threat was from bikers, not the Calabrians. There were so many damned bikers all over Canada and in the United States that you never knew when you'd run into them. In August 1981 I was taken to Florida for three weeks for security reasons and to ease the tension. While we were there, I remember worrying the most about running into bikers—Outlaws, Hell's Angels, Pagans—who had connections with biker gangs in Canada. I was certain that pictures of me had been distributed to other gangs by Satan's Choice and the Vagabonds.

I often told detail members that outlaw bikers were more likely to make a stupid open hit than Mafia members, who were more conservative, more careful. The bikers were reckless. They didn't and still don't care who else might be killed in trying to get at me.

Some might think that going to bars or hotels or jogging was dangerous. It could be, except the element of surprise was to our advantage, and every location was checked out before we used it.

A lot of agents protected me—people like Murphy, Byron, Ted Bean, and Lyle McCharles—and their lives were in danger from bikers too. I know that Murphy was threatened. He had to take precautions not only for himself but for his family. He had to live on the edge for a long, long time. So did some others.

Bikers are persistent, if nothing else. I remember one ex-member of the Saint Catharines Outlaws, a guy named Jimmy, that I had real trouble with before I became a witness. He and another guy they called Gypsy had threatened to blow my head off. I caught up with Jimmy in a gym one day and beat the hell out of him. He couldn't open his eyes for a week. In fact, he had to use a seeing-eye dog to get around.

The trouble was over Linda. She and I had split up

for a while. We had an on-again, off-again love affair that was often violent. Anyhow, they tried to make a move on her. I told them to keep away from her. One night they figured the best way to get rid of me was to lay in ambush outside her house with shotguns for me to come to the door. I didn't show up, but not because I was tipped. It was only luck that they didn't nail me. When I did hear about it, I was very concerned.

First I went to the Saint Catharines Outlaws and told them that I wanted these two guys. I made it clear I was going to get them. They didn't care. Both Jimmy and Gypsy had broken with the gang and were on their own.

Gypsy was about six foot two, weighed about 220 pounds, and towered over me. I had a little trouble with him at first in the gym when he tried to wrestle with me. He didn't want to fight. But I broke loose and I gave him a helluva beating. He was bloodied, and I got my pleasure beating his face in. I told him if I ever heard him mouthing off about me or making a move on Linda again, I was going to come back and kick his head in.

Linda was a problem for the security detail, mainly because of me. Being shut up with three men or in a room by myself drove me up a wall. There were times I felt I had to see her, despite our fights. She was living at a secret location arranged and paid for by the RCMP. When I wanted to see her or she wanted to see me, they'd work it out for us to be together. After she'd leave, we would always pick up and move to a new location. They didn't trust her, and for good reason, although I didn't agree with them for a long time. I had to be hit with a hammer quite a few times before I realized I couldn't trust her.

That relationship came to a head October 28, when Linda tried to set me up. I was still on my own, away from the security detail, when I learned that a warrant had been sworn out for my arrest for possession of a .308 rifle. I had gone to stay with my brother in Nottawasaga Township. My plan was to go up north and do some moose hunting with a rifle I had. I decided to test the gun at my brother's and fired three shells at a tree. Next thing I knew, some coppers came to find out what the shooting was about and my brother, Mark, said I had spent the night on the roof of my mother's house with a loaded rifle firing rounds into a tree to test the weapon.

Technically, I was on probation. When the coppers came and my brother came up with that tale, I had to get rid of the gun fast, and I did. Then I turned myself in when I heard there was a warrant for my arrest. I was charged with having a weapon dangerous to the public peace—a charge that was dismissed on January 28, 1983, in court.

Some members of the press played the hell out of the case. They used that and my troubles with Linda to try to have me jailed by having my probation revoked.

Then one night Linda called and said she was at a local Toronto bar, and asked me to go to her apartment to make sure her daughter was all right. She said that the baby-sitter was there watching her.

I told her I'd take a taxi and be there before she was. I went up to her apartment, knocked on the door, and got no answer. I tried the handle and the door was open. There was a note on the floor, so I walked in. I don't know who the note was from, but it read: "Your daughter is next door." So I sat there and waited.

It wasn't long before I saw a Chrysler pull up instead of a cab, and out stepped Ronald Ambrose, a friend of Linda and her former husband. They came upstairs and rang the buzzer. I wasn't about to answer it. They left. About a half hour later, Linda came up the stairs. She entered the room and for a moment didn't notice me standing there. Finally she saw me. "Where's Lisa?" she said.

"Next door," I snapped.

She left the room to get the kid and put her to bed. When she returned the phone rang. It was Ambrose. She answered and all I could hear her say was, "Yeah, come on over." Then she turned to me with a sneer on her face and said, "You know who's coming here? You better take off, he might have a gun."

Ambrose lived in an apartment across the street, and I could see him come running across and through the front door of her apartment house with a rifle. He started ringing the buzzer. I yelled at him, "Look, I saw you coming across with the gun."

He yelled back, "Open the fuckin' door."

I didn't answer. I went to the phone, called the police, identified myself, and told them there was a man with a rifle standing in the hallway waiting to shoot me.

The cops got there fast, let me tell you. I was going to go out, but I decided I'd wait until I saw the cops. I looked out the peephole and there they were wrestling this guy out in the hall. I opened the door, and suddenly the cops were throwing cuffs on me, telling me I was under arrest. They didn't say what for, but I went along, figuring it was to get everybody under control.

The cops swarmed over the apartment, searching it. Linda was going nuts. She saw Ambrose in the hall being held by three cops. She wound up and hit one of the cops. Then she shouted, "Yeah, an' he [pointing at me] raped me."

I looked at her and started to laugh. "You better come up with something better than that," I said. "You should have said that when they came in the door instead of dreaming it up now." She wanted me so bad she could taste it. She was willing to do anything, say anything to get me.

One cop had the rifle. He stood there beside me, pulled the bolt open, and the bullet popped out. I looked at him and said, "That fuckin' bastard was gonna shoot me." The cop, who had been looking down the barrel of that gun when Ambrose pointed at him, was upset. So were the other cops. They took the cuffs off me.

Ambrose was only twenty-four and a punk. But I'd have been out of my mind to go out to meet him without a gun. He was crazy enough to gun me down in the hallway for sure. His brother had been convicted in Nova Scotia for killing two RCMP officers—he made them dig their graves first, then shot them.

They charged Ambrose with pointing a loaded rifle at a policeman, and in April 1982 I was forced to testify in the case by his attorney, Michael Caroline. Ambrose's defense was that he acted because he thought Linda was in danger and he believed I was a man above the law because of what the media said about me. Caroline, who later became my lawyer, asked me in court what would I do "if a man like yourself, Cecil Kirby, came at you with a gun." I answered, "I would have gone out and bought a bigger gun." Ambrose still got convicted and sentenced to six months in jail.

In November the Ontario attorney general, Roy McMurtry, asked the press to keep a lid on stories about me. The reason was that I had been asked by the Crown and the SEU to carry a body mike to gather additional evidence against businessmen who had hired me through the Commissos to commit arsons, bomb buildings, or extort money. The plan was to nail down more charges against the Commissos and against those who had gone to the Commissos to hire me.

The idea of hitting the streets again, gathering evidence, jolted me out of my depression. My adrenaline was flowing, and the excitement of the hunt gripped me. I once again was working with a team of top investigators, including Corporal Danielle Bouchard of the OPP and SEU, who was going to pose as my girlfriend, but Murphy wasn't allowed to participate. He'd been transferred and admonished. He was eventually disciplined for standing by his promises to me in the face of orders to sink me by some of his superiors.

Most of those we approached and taped knew me only as "George." They did not put "George" together with Cecil Kirby, and since the Commissos were in jail, they were unable to call them to see if I was still acting on their behalf.

Make no mistake, what we were doing—the investigators, myself, the security people—was dangerous. A slip of the tongue, a chance meeting with the wrong person could have cost me and them our lives. There was always the chance that one of them might have found out that George was Cecil or have made a successful effort to talk to Cosimo or Remo in jail about "George." If they had I would have been dead.

For a while it worked fine. I recorded admissions by a number of businessmen, including Armando DiCapua, Bruno Spizzichino, and Rocco Mastrangelo, who had paid Cosimo to have me blow up their sporting goods store in Guelph. I recorded admissions by Istvan Szocs, a real estate salesman who went to Cosimo in 1978 to get help in collecting $15,000 that he said Cornwall developer Hugh Fitzpatrick owed him from a 1973 land deal. Szocs paid me $200 to break Fitzpatrick's arms and legs and threaten his family. I never got to Fitzpatrick, but I spent two weeks trying. Szocs claimed he never collected the $15,000.

There were other cases, and there could have been more except that a reporter, for reasons I've never been able to figure, broke stories about the immunity and support agreement I had with the Crown and charges from Linda and her attorney that I had beaten her while my security guards stood quietly by in another room.

The stories had an even more serious effect. They terminated the undercover investigation I was working on, endangering not only my life but those of Bouchard and other investigators on the case. On February 8, 1982, we tried to tape admissions from another Commisso associate. All we got were denials and claims of total innocence. I got the strong feeling that this guy knew who I was. My role as an undercover agent was over.

A reporter had created an atmosphere that made it impossible for me to continue my work for the Crown. Metro Police Staff Inspector Don Banks said that the stories carried "distortions of facts" that made my underworld connections "wary and on their guard. He was still making connections until the publicity made it impossible to continue." Banks headed the intelligence squad and had worked closely with the investigators from the time I started working on the Commissos.

McMurtry was furious, and he went public to attack the press stories. He said that "irresponsible reporting" had undermined my effectiveness. He pointed out that until I had confessed under immunity, law enforcement in Canada had had no evidence against me for the crimes I talked to them about. He defended the new agreement the Crown had with me that provided me and those in my family with $1,950 in support plus my living quarters and travel expenses. But he refused to disclose the terms of the agreement, and I was and have been prohibited from disclosing them. If I disclose more than I've been required to in court, all bets are off—the Crown can walk away from me.

RCMP Chief Superintendent Donald Heaton, who was also upset by the newspaper disclosures, said that police had known about the criminals I'd worked on for twenty years. He said that despite millions of dollars spent on investigations, no one had ever put them in jail. "For the first time ever we had someone [Kirby] on the inside . . . and they [organized crime figures] were going to jail."

It was over—the street work, the recordings, the moments of exhilaration and anxiety. All that remained now were the trials ahead and the boredom.

If I had it to do over, I probably would never have become a witness. I certainly wouldn't recommend that other criminals follow my path. The reason is simple. Aside from the danger, the boredom, and the frustration that a witness faces, there are the threats to his family, the spiraling costs, a life constantly on the run without any stability, and the broken promises of the government.

When I first signed an agreement on April 7, 1981, the government promised me immunity from prosecution for past crimes. It also was to provide physical protection for me and for my family during the criminal proceedings, including all the trials. The agreement was revised on November 12, 1981. While it increased my expense allowances from about $700 a month to $1,960 plus $550 for rentals, it was still inadequate.

Reporters and the public read figures like that and say, hey, I could live on $32,000 a year plus very nicely, thank you. Sure you could, if you didn't have to live in hotel rooms, if you weren't required to move almost every week, if you didn't have to eat in restaurants most of the time, or to fly or drive hundreds and thousands of miles in the course of a month. When you live the life of a nomad—not by choice but by necessity—it's costly. I can't remember a week when I haven't been broke or the end of a month when all I had was more than five dollars.

It's a hell of an existence. There have been a couple of updated agreements, each one narrowing the promises made by earlier agreements, each one making it tougher and tougher to live.

There have been a lot of broken promises along the way. I've publicly challenged McMurtry for breaking his word. His answer was to deny me the help I wanted and then, in 1984, to get bodyguards for his personal protection because he thought I was going to hurt him. That had to be the dumbest thing I ever heard of. I might have been mad, but I'm not stupid enough to go after the Ontario attorney general.

The most important thing I wanted—more than the money I had requested—was a sense of security. I'm supposed to have a documented new identity. What good is an identity if there is nothing in the history of that identity to show you existed before 1981? Without a history, without something to show you went to school, someone to verify that you were employed someplace, it's almost impossible to establish credit or to get a job. Who's going to hire a man with no history? Dozens of times I've applied for jobs and the employer was ready to hire me until I was unable to come up with that history that says you exist, you are, you've worked and lived somewhere and gone to school.

So it's do an odd job here, an odd job there—nothing

with security, nothing with a future, nothing where you can earn a solid salary.

You can't establish roots that way. You can't move into a community and try to buy a home if you have no background, no money to put down on a house, no steady job to pay the mortgage and the taxes and all the other bills that a man has to pay.

There should be some job training, something that would prepare me to work in something I hadn't done before. I can't drive trucks cross-country with bikers and the Mafia hunting me. The job training promises turned out to be empty. The government hasn't made the slightest attempt to train me to earn a living.

I don't want to live from government check to government check. Too often they let you hang waiting—that check comes a week, two weeks, a month late. You call, you protest, your attorney does the same, and everyone ignores you. They don't need you anymore. They've got their big convictions, now they don't want to know you or live up to their word.

When I began taping the Commissos, not only did the RCMP never supply a car, there were times I was afraid that when Murphy and I had to go to locations for meetings I wouldn't have enough money for gas. They didn't give Murphy money, and I didn't get it. They just insisted that I continue using the car the Commissos were familiar with, my father's Chevrolet. It was only three years old then, with very little mileage on it. Once the Commisso investigations ended, the car was stripped of its electronic listening devices and returned to my father. There was no attempt to replace it, to pay for the maintenance, or to paint the car a different color.

That caused him problems. One evening two guys with full beards smashed into the rear of his Chevy and tried to force him off the road. They were bikers who had recognized the car and were trying to get at me through him. The car had to be sold later at a loss. In December 1982 my father's truck was shot up at my brother's cottage in Wasaga Beach. The bullet went through the tailgate and a steel box into the cabin of the truck, where it hit a steel jack behind the seat. It then cut through the seat and slammed through the glove compartment before finally stopping at the engine fire wall. Police found it was an armor-piercing, .303 rifle slug. An hour before that another bullet went through my uncle's house, two or three miles away. It went through the front door and whistled over his head while he was sleeping in bed. The papers reported it, the police investigated, but nothing happened—nobody was ever arrested.

You would have thought that after the shooting, police would have driven up and down the street a couple of times at night or sat out in front of the homes of my father and my uncle for maybe a half hour. No such luck. Nobody provided protection or even offered to.

In March 1982 my brother, Mark, was arrested for selling a small quantity of marijuana to an undercover detective. Mark shouldn't have been fooling with drugs, but he was all screwed up at the time. He had to fight his way in and out of bars as every biker tried to take him on. I appealed to the judge in the case, County Court Judge Donald Thompson, not to send my kid brother to jail. I told him it could cost the kid his life, that prisoners associated with the bikers or the Mafia could kill him in prison. Judge Thompson didn't listen. He said it was up to jail authorities to make sure my brother was safe. Then he sent Mark to jail for ninety days. That Mark survived without harm was a matter of luck. It wasn't because the Crown or the courts took any special precautions for him.

While I was testifying against the Commissos and others, the government did not provide protection for my mother or father, and both were subjected to threatening calls constantly. Almost every weekend, my mother would get calls from some biker's broad or some biker threatening her. They were messages to me, really. They were telling me, here's trouble for you, informer. And there's more to come. Here's how easy it is to get at your family if we want you. It was hell on both of them. It still is.

Since May 1981, it's been hell on my family, particularly my father. From the beginning, when my name hit print, he received threatening phone calls. The RCMP put a tap on his line to find out who was making the threats, but they got nowhere. Their answer to the problem was to tell him to sell his house, to move. When he did move, he lost $20,000 on the sale and the RCMP provided him with only $500 for moving costs. All told, he's had to move nearly a dozen times, and the government's provided just that one payment of $500. It costs that much to move all your belongings to a new location just once.

In addition to the threats, there have been endless attempts by bikers and the Commissos to frame me, to discredit me as a witness by attempting to show I was a liar or had committed crimes after signing my agreement. Anthony Speciale is a typical example.

I first met Speciale through Ken Goobie and Andy the Rounder. At the time he was on the run for shooting someone. Until I told police about the incident, they weren't aware that Speciale was involved in the shooting.

Speciale was pretty wild. He'd rather shoot you than fight you, and he always had a .38 snub-nosed revolver on him for protection or murder. I remember one night we all got stopped in a radar trap in Toronto. The cop was walking over to our car when Speciale, who was sitting in the back, reached for his gun.

"Jesus Christ, Tony," I said, "leave that fuckin' gun right there and don't say a word. Just let the cop give us the ticket and we'll leave."

He had a real cruel smile on his face, half sneer, half smile, and there was a kind of faraway glint in his eyes. He was ready to blow that cop away until I said something.

Speciale had a long record. He had gone to jail for assault, for car theft, for B&E, for robbery and wounding, but in 1978 he hit the heights—he got life imprisonment for killing three people, including a rounder named Stan Norman. Norman begged for his life, but Speciale just shot him through the head. Then he shot Norman's girl, Diane. She was shot twice and lay there, hearing him reload the gun to shoot her again. Somehow she survived to tell her story.

Now, I had been with Speciale that day just before the killings started. He was with me waiting for a guy, a courier, who we were supposed to rob. We waited a few hours, the target never came out, and we left the area. I dropped Speciale off at some girl's place in Mississauga. The next day I saw the Sunday paper, and splashed across the front page was the story of Speciale and the shootings.

While he was in jail for the murders he came in contact with Cosimo Commisso. In March 1984, while he was serving time in the same jail with Cosimo, Speciale tried to implicate me in the Norman murder. He charged I was with him when he killed Norman. Luckily, I was able to prove I wasn't but it was clearly an attempt by Cosimo to destroy me as a witness.

Cosimo had tried that before, in September 1982, when he got Nicolino Pallotta and Richard Cucman to claim that I had ripped them off, taken $140,000 in jewelry they'd robbed from the Dolly Jewelers in 1981, fenced it, and kept the money for myself. It was a lie, of course. I'd tipped Murphy off about the jewelry and the fact that they'd handled the robbery.

Then there was Satan's Choice biker Joe Ertel of Kitchener. Ertel had a long record of convictions for robbery, assault, trafficking in drugs, and possession of stolen property. With a record like that and a hatred for cops, he still hated me more and charged that I had murdered another biker named Duke Coons. I was questioned by Crown prosecutors in the case and told them I knew nothing about the homicide. I took a lie detector test and passed it.

Today, I'm still on the run, still looking for a hole I can crawl into and survive in. Canada's a big country, but it may not be big enough. Wherever I've gone, I haven't been able to stay long because I was unable to get a job, unable to obtain credit and show a history of employment.

For several years the government was concerned. I was important to them in 1981 and through the trials that led to the conviction of more than fourteen criminals—people who burned down hotels, people who wanted to extort money, so-called respectable people who wanted other people's legs and arms broken.

I was important because they needed me to crack the Calabrian Mafia and put away their leaders, people like the Commisso brothers, and Vincent Melia, who's now free after serving only three years of a nine-year jail term for paying to have Helen Nafpliotis killed. I was important because they wanted my intelligence information, my tips—tips that led to major drug busts, to the arrests of gamblers and jewel thieves, to biker crimes and Mafia plans for murder.

But now all that's over. Prosecutors can't make headlines and further their political careers on sensational disclosures from Cecil Kirby. They can't win press notice by dueling with prominent defense lawyers who try unsuccessfully to discredit me as a witness. They are content with their press notices and, for some, new and lucrative jobs outside government that resulted from their "handling" of Cecil Kirby. So what happens to Cecil Kirby is no longer of concern to them. If members of the Outlaws find where Kirby's living, as they did in 1985, don't bother telling him. He's finished testifying, and it's not our responsibility to keep him alive forever.

In truth, the only ones that care are a few dedicated cops—members and former members of the SEU—who, after doing their jobs, were returned to their units with the RCMP, the Ontario Provincial Police or Metro Toronto. They've tried to help in many ways, but what they've done, they've done on their own out of a sense of responsibility and decency.

I don't mind one bit saying that I'm bitter. I'm no angel, never pretended to be. I was a hardened criminal. But I've tried to follow a new path, keep within the law, and the bureaucrats that run this nation don't make it easy. If I survive, it won't be because they helped or kept their word. It'll be because I kept my wits and my instincts keen.

In the end, they and the public will be the losers. For while I've kept my word and done all I was asked to do, there won't be any other Cecil Kirbys willing to come forward. And without witnesses who trust the government as I once did, organized crime—whether it be outlaw bikers, the Mafia, or Chinese triads—will flourish, picking the pockets of American and Canadian citizens alike.

Epilogue

From Orlando, Florida, to Toronto, Ontario, Americans and Canadians alike are under siege. They are hostage to a new and increasingly dangerous organized crime intent on intimidation, extortion, drug trafficking, murder, and the infiltration of the consumer marketplace. Their aim—to accumulate wealth.

Motorcycle gangs larger in membership than the Cosa Nostra; Asian gangs with hundreds of thousands of members internationally, from Hong Kong to the Netherlands; the Calabrian Honoured Society that insidiously blends into the melting pot of North American society and Australia as well; Colombians who export death in the form of tons of cocaine; Russian émigrés who murder, steal, cheat, and sell doctored oil while evading hundreds of millions in fuel taxes; Israeli Mafia hoodlums who traffic in narcotics and dupe insurance companies out of millions; dozens of new and dangerous ethnic gangs that prey on their own people before branching out to victimize society in general; and the Cosa Nostra, the criminal enterprise that spans two nations and infiltrates every fabric of society— all are corrupting, murdering, and plundering society's resources.

It is a frightening array of criminal organizations that the law enforcement community and governments must face down and fight with an increasingly limited supply of weaponry and an even more limited number of experienced, qualified investigators.

Wiretaps, bugs, informers—all are vital to the battle. So are laws such as the Racketeer Influenced Corrupt Organization statute, so successfully employed in recent years against the Cosa Nostra and other organized crime groups by federal authorities in the United States. Canada lacks such a law, but its law officers seek one.

The most vital and effective tool of all is the witness against organized crime. He has to be cultivated and nurtured. He has to be carefully used and, more important, his role as a criminal must be weighed against the value of the evidence he can provide.

Witnesses can be forced to testify, sometimes with the threat of jail or other dire consequences, but generally, in organized crime cases, they testify only when the government agrees to a deal. That deal frequently embodies immunity for past crimes, a promise of job opportunity and training after testifying, subsistence for the witness and his family while he's testifying, and a new identity.

Since the U.S. Congress authorized the creation of the Witness Protection Program, more than 6,000 witnesses have passed through that program after testifying for federal and state authorities. Under the control of the U.S. Marshals, the program has been often maligned, sometimes with justification, for failing to live up to the promises given to witnesses and to provide proper protection, identity documentation, and job opportunities.

Canada had a golden opportunity to learn from the mistakes of the U.S. program and provide a more stable future for its witnesses. It has failed miserably with Cecil Kirby.

Like him or not, Kirby made a deal with his government to gather evidence against the kingpins of organized crime in Ontario. He was successful beyond the wildest dreams of those who cultivated him. He was, unlike so many witnesses, a man of his word. He lived up to the promises he gave to testify. In fact, he went a giant step further, carrying a body mike after charges had been filed against a number of Calabrian crime leaders to gather more evidence against more criminals.

Without question, the Canadian government saved millions of dollars by using Kirby. He provided them with a wealth of intelligence on outlaw bikers and the Calabrian Mafia and led agents into the world of the rounders—all criminal societies with codes of silence that law enforcement had been previously unable to penetrate.

Kirby is owed a debt—a debt payable by promises made to him when he embarked on his dangerous adventure. While his subsistence has continued, the promises of job training and a solid, documented new identity have not been kept. Worse, Kirby has been left to his own devices, to survive on his instincts without the necessary protection, counseling, and guidance in relocation, reidentification, and job placement.

Incredibly, Kirby worked for government agencies for some months without immunity, without an agreement in writing, without subsistence or expenses. He lived by his wits. He was forced to use the funds collected from criminal conspiracies to pay his bills and feed his family. He was required to use his father's car, and quite often his father paid for the gas used to help the government gather its evidence.

By any standard of law enforcement undercover operations, the pennypinching practices of the agencies involved were amateurish and patently dangerous. Kirby should have been properly funded and, as a result, never permitted to keep the proceeds of a criminal investigation, as in the case of the conspiracy to murder Helen Nafpliotis.

Unless a vigorous and carefully constructed witness program is developed in Canada, law enforcement officers and prosecutors will soon find that witnesses such as Kirby will not become willing weapons against organized crime. Sources of information and intelligence will dry up, and the word will spread in the underworld that the law and those who administer it do not keep their promises. Without trust, there can be no effective fight against organized crime in Canada or the United States. In a world where new organized crime groups are breeding like rats on the waterfront, that could have a profound and immensely costly effect on all of us.

Appendix I

Convictions as a Result of Kirby Testimony

COSIMO COMMISSO
1981 Conspiracy to murder, three counts (Helen Nafpliotis, Pietro Scarcella, Paul Volpe): eight years each count, concurrent. Beating (assault): two years, concurrent.

1984 (March) Conspiracy to bomb (Guelph sporting goods store) and possession of stolen cigarettes: sixteen months, consecutive to time already being served.

1984 (April) Inciting to murder, bomb, arson, assault, and extortion (sixteen counts): eight years, consecutive to the thirteen years already being served.

ROCCO REMO COMMISSO
1981 Conspiracy to murder, two counts (Scarcella, Volpe): eight years each count, consecutive.

1984 (March) Possession of stolen cigarettes: six months, consecutive to the eight years already being served.

1984 (April) Assault, extortion, bombings, arson, and inciting to commit murder, seven counts: six years, consecutive to the eight years and six months already being served.

MICHELE COMMISSO
1981 Conspiracy to murder, three counts (Nafpliotis,

Scarcella, Volpe): two and a half years each count, consecutive.

1984 (April) Planned arson: sentence suspended, two years' probation.

ANTONIO ROMEO
1981 Conspiracy to murder (Nafpliotis): two and a half years.

GERARDO (JERRY) RUSSO
1981 Conspiracy to murder (Nafpliotis): two years, ten months.

VINCENZO MELIA
1982 Conspiracy to murder (Nafpliotis): nine years.

COSIMO MERCURI
1982 Second-degree murder and arson (Dominion Hotel, Acton): life imprisonment, no consideration for parole for ten years.

MICHAEL McCRYSTAL
1982 Manslaughter (Dominion Hotel, Acton): two years less a day.

ARMANDO DI CAPUA
1983 Arson conspiracy (Guelph sporting goods store): two years.

ROCCO MASTRANGELO
1984 Arson conspiracy (Guelph sporting goods store): one year.

BRUNO SPIZZICHINO
1984 Arson conspiracy (Guelph sporting goods store): two years.

NICHOLAS PALLOTTA
1982 Robbery (Dolly Jewelers): three years.

Appendix I

RICHARD CUCMAN
1982 Robbery (Dolly Jewelers): two years.

ISTVAN (STEVE) SZOCS
1983 Attempted extortion: six months.

RICHARD CORBETT
1983 Possession of stolen cigarettes: three months.

ARMAND SANGUIGNI
1983 Possession of stolen cigarettes: three months.

In addition to the above, Kirby supplied information that led to the arrest and conviction of twenty more people, including disco owner Harold Arviv for the bombing of Arviv's disco; disco manager Yvo Sajet for filing a false report with the police in the robbery of the cash boxes from the Hippopotamus disco; and Charles (Chuck) Yanover for his part in the plot to overthrow the government of Dominica, possession of forty-two pounds of hashish (three people arrested), conspiracy to smuggle gold out of British Guiana (one person arrested), five robberies, two shootings, and information on six unsolved homicides.

Appendix II

Honoured Society

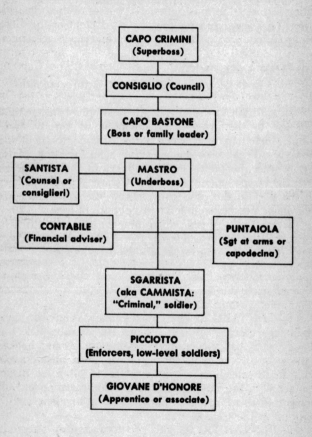

CAPO CRIMINI
(Superboss)

CONSIGLIO (Council)

CAPO BASTONE
(Boss or family leader)

SANTISTA
(Counsel or
consiglieri)

MASTRO
(Underboss)

CONTABILE
(Financial adviser)

PUNTAIOLA
(Sgt at arms or
capodecina)

SGARRISTA
(aka CAMMISTA:
"Criminal," soldier)

PICCIOTTO
(Enforcers, low-level soldiers)

GIOVANE D'HONORE
(Apprentice or associate)

Appendix II

1. **CAPO CRIMINI:** The highest-ranking boss in the Honoured Society or Calabrian Mafia. The equivalent of a "boss of bosses," but the title rarely exists. Last known boss of bosses was the late Don Antonio Macri of Siderno.

2. **CONSIGLIO:** The sitting council or ruling body, which includes the most influential bosses of the organization. The *consiglio* is roughly the equivalent of the Cosa Nostra Commission, with between nine and eleven members.

3. **CAPO BASTONE:** A boss. This is an archaic term that has been supplanted by the shortened title of *Capo* or *Head*. This includes all bosses in each area. There are fifty-four bosses in Calabria and three suspected bosses in Canada, including the late Mike Racco, and Cosimo Commisso. A *capo bastone* is the equivalent of a Cosa Nostra crime boss, such as Anthony Salerno of the Genovese family or Antonio (Ducks) Corallo of the Lucchese family.

4. **MASTRO:** Second in command of a Calabrian family. The *mastro* is similar in stature and responsibilities to the underboss of a Cosa Nostra family. He is the *capo bastone*'s right-hand man.

5. **SANTISTA:** The family adviser, the equivalent of the Cosa Nostra's *consiglieri*. The *santista* gives counsel if asked to by the *capo bastone* or the *mastro*. He is usually an older man with experience who enjoys the respect of family members at both high and low levels. The name is derived from the Greek word that means "to act as an honorable person."

6. **CONTABILE:** The family's financial adviser, generally an attorney or accountant. He usually picks up money, gets bail for incarcerated members, and invests money for the *capo bastone*. He can be a businessman with legitimate business fronts. He is often in direct contact with the boss and directs communication on important financial matters. There is no equivalent of this position in the Cosa Nostra.

7. **PUNTAIOLA:** Roughly the equivalent in stature of a Cosa Nostra *capodecina* or crime captain. The name literally means "a stick with a nail at the end used to move animals," a prod.

8. SGARRISTA E. CAMMISTA (CAMORRISTA): The equivalent of a higher-than-average soldier in the Cosa Nostra. He approaches businesses for extortion and gives orders to associates and *picciottos* who work under him. He is a visible operator of the family.

9. PICCIOTTO: The worker, the out-front hustler and enforcer who plants bombs or beats loan-shark victims. He is the muscle of the Honoured Society and would be most associated with criminal activities. His equivalent in the Cosa Nostra is the soldier, the "made guy," the "wise guy."

10. GIOVANE D'HONORE: A person who wants to become a member of the Honoured Society. In the Cosa Nostra he would be known as the trusted associate vying for initiation as a member. He is required to do favors for the organization to prove his loyalty, have the right background and the right friends, and be sponsored by someone in the Honoured Society. Once accepted he is initiated, as are new members of the Cosa Nostra, in a ritualistic ceremony in which he swears loyalty to the organization and *omertà* (silence) on pain of death.

Index

315

Index

Index

Index

Index

Index

ABOUT THE AUTHORS

CECIL KIRBY is living under an assumed name in Canada.

THOMAS C. RENNER has authored two best-sellers, the internationally acclaimed *My Life in the Mafia* with Vincent Teresa, and *Mafia Princess*, with Antoinette Giancana.

Renner is a veteran of thirty-two years on the Pulitzer Prize-winning *Newsday*. He has won recognition as an organized crime expert and was recently one of five reporters cited by the president of the United States for significant contributions in exposing organized crime. He was the first reporter in America to be assigned to investigate and write solely about organized crime and was a key member of the "Arizona Project," a prize-winning investigation of corruption and crime in the southwest. Renner was awarded the coveted Louis M. Lyons Award for Conscience and Integrity in Journalism in 1983 by the Neiman Fellows of Harvard University. He is the recipient of numerous awards for excellence, integrity and community service.

BANTAM BOOKS
GRAND SLAM SWEEPSTAKES
Win a new Chevrolet Spectrum . . .
It's easy . . . It's fun . . . Here's how to enter:

OFFICIAL ENTRY FORM

Three Bantam book titles on sale this month are hidden in this word puzzle. Identify the books by circling each of these titles in the puzzle. Titles may appear within the puzzle horizontally, vertically, or diagonally . . .

Bantam's titles for July are:

THE UNLOVED

'TIL THE REAL THING COMES ALONG

MAFIA ENFORCER*

In each of the books listed above there is another entry blank and puzzle . . . another chance to win!
Be on the lookout for these Bantam paperback books coming in August: OMAMORI, FANTASTIC VOYAGE II: DESTINATION BRAIN, RICH AND RECKLESS. In each of them, you'll find a new puzzle, entry blank and GRAND SLAM Sweepstakes rules . . . and yet another chance to win another brand-new Chevrolet automobile!

MAIL TO: GRAND SLAM SWEEPSTAKES
                Post Office Box 18
                New York, New York 10046

Please Print

NAME _____

ADDRESS _____

CITY _____ STATE _____ ZIP _____
*U.S. ONLY

OFFICIAL RULES

NO PURCHASE NECESSARY.

To enter identify this month's Bantam Book titles by placing a circle around each word forming each title. There are three titles shown above to be found in this month's puzzle. Mail your entry to: Grand Slam Sweepstakes, P.O. Box 18, New York, N.Y. 10046

This is a monthly sweepstakes starting February 1, 1988 and ending January 31, 1989. During this sweepstakes period, one automobile winner will be selected each month from all entries that have correctly solved the puzzle. To participate in a particular month's drawing, your entry must be received by the last day of that month. The Grand Slam prize drawing will be held on February 14, 1989 from all entries received during all twelve months of the sweepstakes.

To obtain a free entry blank/puzzle/rules, send a self-addressed stamped envelope to: Winning Titles, P.O. Box 650, Sayreville, N.J. 08872. Residents of Vermont and Washington need not include return postage.

PRIZES: Each month for twelve months a Chevrolet automobile will be awarded with an approximate retail value of $12,000 each.

The Grand Slam Prize Winner will receive 2 Chevrolet automobiles plus $10,000 cash (ARV $34,000).

Winners will be selected under the supervision of Marden-Kane Inc., an independent judging organization. By entering this sweepstakes each entrant accepts and agrees to be bound by these rules and the decisions of the judges which shall be final and binding. Winners may be required to sign an affidavit of eligibility and release which must be returned within 14 days of receipt. All prizes will be awarded. No substitution or transfer of prizes permitted. Winners will be notified by mail. Odds of winning depend on the total number of eligible entries received.

Sweepstakes open to residents of the U.S. and Canada except employees of Bantam Books, its affiliates, subsidiaries, advertising agencies and Marden-Kane, Inc. Void in the Province of Quebec and wherever else prohibited or restricted by law. Not responsible for lost or misdirected mail or printing errors. Taxes and licensing fees are the sole responsibility of the winners. All cars are standard equipped. Canadian winners will be required to answer a skill testing question.

For a list of winners, send a self-addressed, stamped envelope to: Bantam Winners, P.O. Box 711, Sayreville, N.J. 08872.

Special Offer
Buy a Bantam Book
for only 50¢.

Now you can have Bantam's catalog filled with hundreds of titles plus take advantage of our unique and exciting bonus book offer. A special offer which gives you the opportunity to purchase a Bantam book for only 50¢. Here's how!

By ordering any five books at the regular price per order, you can also choose any other single book listed (up to a $5.95 value) for just 50¢. Some restrictions do apply, but for further details why not send for Bantam's catalog of titles today!

Just send us your name and address and we will send you a catalog!
